THE CIVIL WAR IN WORCESTERSHIRE

Civil War cavalry on patrol in Worcestershire. The county held an important strategic position during the Civil War. The armies of both sides travelled back and forth across the countryside and there were a number of Royalist garrisons. Patrols of cavalry such as these would therefore have been a frequent sight on the roads and in the countryside as they foraged for supplies and tried to raise taxes. (Copyright: Paul Lewis Isemonger.)

THE CIVIL WAR IN WORCESTERSHIRE

MALCOLM ATKIN

ALAN SUTTON PUBLISHING LIMITED

HEREFORD AND WORCESTER LIBRARIES AND ARTS

First published in the United Kingdom in 1995
Alan Sutton Publishing Ltd
Phoenix Mill · Far Thrupp · Stroud · Gloucestershire
in association with Hereford and Worcester Libraries and Arts

British Library Cataloguing in Publication Data. A catalogue record for this book is available from the British Library.

ISBN 0-7509-1050-X

Cover illustration: Re-enactment of Civil War cavalry (© Paul Lewis Isemonger), with a background map of the Battle of Worcester, 1651 (Worcester City Library, with permission).

Typeset in 11/13 pt Garamond.
Typesetting and origination by
Alan Sutton Publishing Limited.
Printed in Great Britain by
Hartnolls, Bodmin, Cornwall.

CONTENTS

PREFACE

One cannot live in Worcestershire for very long without becoming aware of the central position of Worcester as the alpha and omega of the Civil War years, from the first major skirmish between the opposing forces to the final bloody horror of the 1651 battle. But now, just as then, most popular discussion of the subject seems based on rumour and the personal prejudices and assumptions of the speaker.

This fascinating book tries to go beyond the romance of the period and show something of what the war actually meant to the community of Worcestershire. Malcolm Atkin breathes life into the ghostly armies of their generals and of the village communities still striving to earn a living whilst war raged all around them. As you turn the pages you know here is truth, or as near to truth as you will get when you look for rhyme or reason in the wars of man. The painstaking research that has gone into this work has brought the seventeenth century to life; it has revealed aspects of the conflict in Worcester and the surrounding county that have previously been little understood and it is therefore a book for the historian of the period as well as for the general reader.

The first time I met Malcolm Atkin as our new County Archaeology Officer he was bending over a mock excavation (actually a large sand pit!) with a group of spellbound seven-year-olds who were discovering for the first time that the ground beneath their feet was full of fascinating clues to the past, and realizing that history can be every bit as exciting as looking into the future. That enthusiasm for his subject and determination to bring the past to life comes across very clearly throughout this book.

It is an added pleasure to record that the proceeds from this book will go to the Archaeology Service in order to help fund more research into our history, and bring the joy of learning about our past to people of all ages. I hope that you enjoy reading about it as much as I have.

Councillor Diane Rayner
Chairman: Libraries, Recreation and Environment Committee
Hereford and Worcester County Council
July 1995

INTRODUCTION

Say you have been at Worcester, where England's sorrows began, and where they are happily ended.

(Hugh Peters, Parliamentary chaplain, Powick Bridge, 1651)[1]

It is difficult now to think, as we look around the peaceful countryside of modern Worcestershire, that 350 years ago the fate of England was being fought out in the fields, lanes and streets of the county. Few places, village or town, were spared some involvement, although the only memorial is often simply a record of the burial of an unknown soldier in the parish register, or possible place names such as 'Scots Graves' at Broome, Ordnance Hill at Ripple or widespread folklore connected with Charles II's escape from Worcester in 1651 as at Bromsgrove.

The English Civil War lasted 9 years, divided into three main episodes: 1642–6, 1648 and 1650–1. There is a tendency to view this period in a colourful and romantic light, but for the people involved it was no less horrific than civil wars of more modern times. Recent estimates put the national death toll at around 185,000 men and women but the local casualty figure is more difficult to estimate.[2] Although there were few major battles (the most notable being the Battle of Ripple in 1643, Evesham in 1645 and the Battle of Worcester in 1651, where 3,000 Scots died in the space of a few hours) frequent skirmishes were recorded. Indeed, the county saw action during the whole course of the war. No less traumatic was the grinding effect of repeated plundering and the disruption caused by the relentless progress of hungry armies of both sides as they roamed across the countryside heading for Oxford, Chester, Hereford or wherever the focus of action happened to be at that time. Or, indeed, the relentless demands for money that sucked vast amounts out of the local economy, or the conscription of local working men into the armies. Up to one-quarter of the male population may have been brought into the struggle.

In the seventeenth century, Worcestershire stretched from Dudley in the north almost to Stow-on-the-Wold in the Cotswolds. It was essentially an agricultural county, although it had important industries that could be turned to war production (Chapter 1). The county was an important military thoroughfare, and the constant movement of large bodies of men through an increasingly impoverished countryside had as disastrous an effect on the local communities as the actual combat. Action concentrated at the route centres: the bridging points on the rivers Severn, Avon and Teme at Worcester, Bewdley and Upton-upon-Severn,

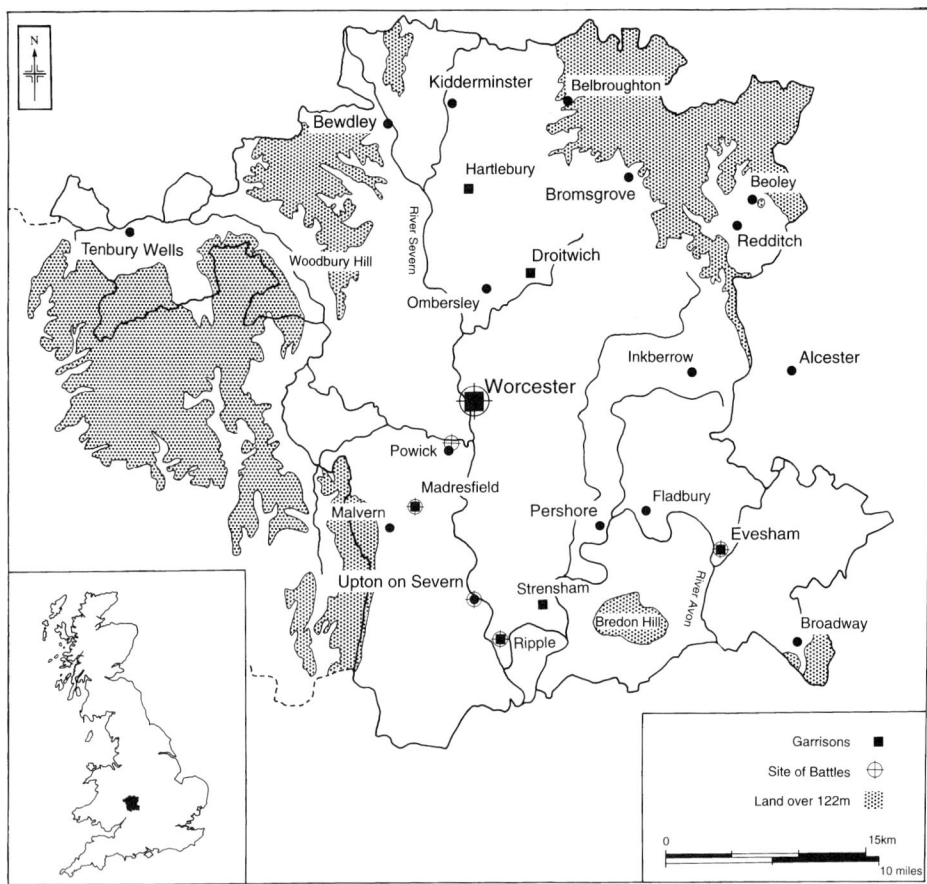

Map of Worcestershire, showing principal places referred to in the text.

Evesham and Powick, and the road junction at Kidderminster. Worcester and Evesham suffered particularly badly. Worcester was occupied in 1642, besieged in 1643, threatened in 1644 and 1645, besieged again in 1646. The final battle of the Civil War was fought here in 1651. Evesham became the key to many a campaign. Army after army passed across the bridge which controlled the route from Wales to the king's capital at Oxford. Bridges were a particular casualty; that at Upton-upon-Severn was part-demolished and then repaired in 1643, 1644 and 1651.

The events of the period have now passed into popular mythology. Worcester is famous as the 'faithful city', a slogan coined at the siege of 1646. But a great deal of the legend was cultivated after the Restoration out of political expediency in order to gain favour (unsuccessfully) with the new monarch. A more accurate assessment would be of a rather moderate county. The conservatism of its inhabitants naturally aroused Royalist and Anglican sympathies in support of a constitutional government but this was not necessarily strong enough to arouse any great desire to fight for them.[3] By the end of the First Civil War in 1646 the population was distinctly anti-military at both an official and a popular level. Contrary to popular belief, Worcestershire troops took a notable part *against* the Royalist forces besieged in the city in the final battle of the Third Civil War in 1651. The Royalists, relying on a foreign army of Scots, were seen as disturbing the peace that the exhausted country sought. But, at any time, the activists of either side were in a minority.

Indeed, the whole history of the Civil War as it has been passed down to us by contemporaries is a fascinating study in the use of propaganda. In 1642, the presses of London produced over 2,000 different pamphlets and tracts. The official documents – account and minute books, parish registers, etc. – provide only limited details of particular aspects of the period, concentrating on financial arrangements. For Worcestershire, they are a remarkably thin source as compared with other counties. But the history of the war is enlivened and enriched by the personal accounts of local men such as Henry Townshend of Elmley Lovett, Richard Baxter of Kidderminster and Nicholas Lechmere of Hanley Castle or of campaigning soldiers such as Nehemiah Wharton, Richard Symonds and Sir William Brereton. But none of these writers was an unbiased source. Pamphlets and news-sheets are more obvious forms of propaganda but ones that can give a good flavour of the emotions of the time. Many of these are preserved in the important collection of *Thomason Tracts* in the British Library or the smaller *Palphey Collection* in Worcester Record Office. The conflict in sources is amply illustrated by the differing accounts of the skirmish at Powick Bridge in 1642.[4] The letters of Nehemiah Wharton show how quickly rumours of atrocities could spread (Appendix 1). Any casualty figures have to be regarded cautiously. Accounts glorifying the actions of their own sides or damning their opponents must also not be taken too literally, although those accounts complaining about their own sides are of more interest. One of the most detailed sources is the diary of Henry Townshend. Although a Royalist, he is open in his criticism of the account of the war in Worcester, both of the competence of the soldiers and the commitment of the civilians. At first appearance, this may seem a good indicator of an objective writer; but he was part of a civilian faction of the Royalist Commission that was periodically engaged in bitter dispute with the military.[5] Similarly, tales of atrocities are best believed when reported by one's own side, as with the execution of Irish prisoners taken at Beoley, near Redditch, in 1643.[6]

Unfortunately much of the local Royalist propaganda was later taken at face value, especially in periods such as the late eighteenth century, when the romance of the period was being cultivated to deflect renewed republican tendencies, fanned by the French Revolution.

Archaeology should offer a more objective source in support of the documentary evidence, although study of this period in the region is still in its infancy and there are remarkably few finds at present recorded from the county. Archaeology is a study of the physical evidence of the past, in this context particularly the remains of

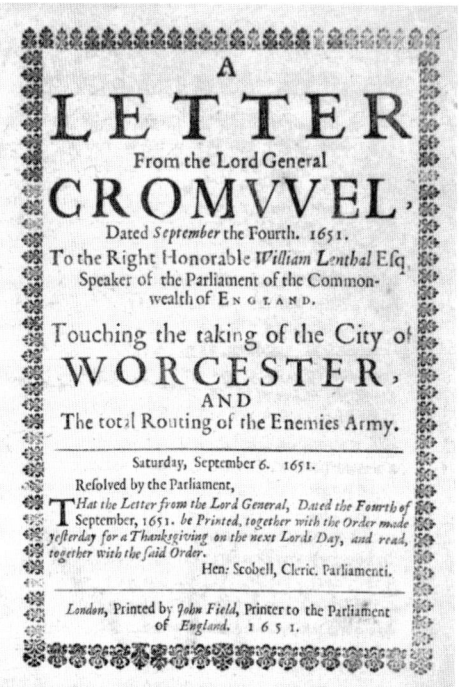

A

LETTER

From the Lord General

CROMVVEL,

Dated *September* the Fourth. 1651.

To the Right Honorable *William Lenthal* Efq;
Speaker of the Parliament of the Commonwealth of E N G L A N D.

Touching the taking of the City of

WORCESTER,

AND

The total Routing of the Enemies Army.

Saturday, September 6. 1651.

Refolved by the Parliament,

THat the Letter from the Lord General, Dated the Fourth of
September, 1651. be Printed, together with the Order made
yefterday for a Thanksgiving on the next Lords Day, and read,
together with the faid Order.

Hen: Scobell, Cleric. Parliamenti.

London, Printed by *John Field*, Printer to the Parliament
of *England*. 1 6 5 1.

Cover of the publication of one of Oliver Cromwell's letters in 1651. The wide range of letters and personal accounts that were published at the time as propaganda help provide a personal aspect to the war. (Hereford and Worcester Record Office, with permission.)

defences and siegeworks, and of fragments of military equipment. Such physical evidence can therefore complement the administrative and campaign details obtained from the documents. The scale of Civil War defences can be impressive – not least when one considers that the ditches, ranging from 4 to 10 m wide, were all dug out using hand tools. Excavated evidence of such defences in the county has so far only been revealed in Worcester (Chapter 5) and Droitwich, but they are still visible at Evesham and the fort at Strensham. Archaeology can also provide evidence for everyday life, over which the particular history of the times ebbed and flowed. But the nature of the dating evidence is not precise enough to be able to identify any short-term interruptions of supply during the war – such as the pottery industry of the Malvern area – while other indicators of trade and wealth do not survive in the ground. In the main, the archaeological material found within the defences does not represent the period of the conflict but rather the period after their abandonment, when the ditches were used as convenient rubbish tips. As yet, there is little physical evidence for the movement of the large armies of men (and women) from other regions, and indeed countries, that zigzagged back and forth across the county during the war. One possibility for future study is a detailed examination of the seventeenth-century clay tobacco pipes found in the region. Clay pipes developed clear regional styles and although it appears that the pipes were quickly discarded, a study might be able to identify some material that was brought into an area by roving armies.

Unfortunately, modern development has already reduced the potential for recording Civil War sites in a number of areas, before mechanisms were put in place to ensure an adequate record was made of the archaeology of all periods, not just from medieval or earlier times. Outside Bromsgrove are Battlefield Farm and Battlefield Brook. There are local stories of 'armour' being found beside the brook, and the area is believed to have been the site of a Civil War skirmish. But there is no definite proof of that now and much of the site was probably destroyed for the construction of a motorway. A great deal of material from battlefield sites has been found in recent years by metal detectorists, but few of these have been accurately recorded and little of the information on such finds has found its way on to the official Sites and Monuments Record for the county. On the whole, remarkably little Civil War material from the county is preserved in the public collections of the local museums. Opportunities for scientific examination of these sites, perhaps before they are destroyed for ever, may well have been lost.

In general, the war has left little physical trace – the trampled crops were eventually re-sown and houses rebuilt – and is perhaps most evident now in the repairs to Pershore and Powick Bridges. What other damage there was tended to be quickly expunged after the war. Most of the defences were designed as temporary structures with permanent defences only at Worcester. Those at Evesham and garrison forts such as Hartlebury, Strensham and Dodderhill at Droitwich had to be constructed during the war. Some, such as those at Bewdley, relied on rapidly-constructed surface defences (e.g. chains across roads and turnpikes) and strengthened gates. Bewdley still had its medieval gatehouses across the main streets and on the bridge but there is no evidence that there was ever a system of wall and ditch around the town.[7] Siegeworks would usually be quite insubstantial; cannon would be defended by stone-filled baskets (gabions) rather than by built emplacements and by narrow slit trenches (saps). Particular efforts were made by the local inhabitants to destroy these as soon as possible after an engagement to prevent them being re-used.

Even place-name evidence needs to be treated with some caution. It is possible that 'Scots Graves' is a corruption of 'Scotchman's Grove' with 'Scotchman' being used as a common term for a peddler. Their true explanation must await future testing in the field. But one of the particular interests of the period is the way in which such a wide variety of sources can be used to reconstruct the past.

Strategic location

The key to Worcestershire's importance in the war lay in its position as a strategic route centre. It lay astride the king's supply route from Wales to his wartime capital of Oxford and the route from Bristol and the sea to Lancashire. Worcester itself was a veritable hub of routes in all directions, its strategic location marked in the past by a Roman settlement and a medieval castle. The natural topography of the county was dominated in strategic terms by the rivers – making the bridging points of Bewdley, Upton and Worcester on the Severn; Twyford, Evesham and Pershore on the Avon; and Powick on the Teme of especial value.

The county was also of economic importance as a supply centre for both agricultural and manufacturing products. The county supplied both men and materials for the war effort. Shot came from Stourbridge, cannon from Dudley, steel from north Worcestershire, gunpowder from Worcester and timber from the forests. Even the well-established Malvern pottery industry may have been brought into war production in making ceramic hand grenades, although none has yet been positively identified in this fabric.[8] The county became one of the main centres of

One of the most effective types of troops used in the Civil War were the dragoons. These were mounted infantry who rode into battle but then dismounted to fight as musketeers. In Worcestershire they played a notable role as advance guards, particularly in seizing bridges. (Copyright: Paul Lewis Isemonger.)

arms production for the Royalists who were denied the arsenal at London. There were also the day to day necessities: salt from Droitwich, caps from Bewdley, clothing from Worcester and Kidderminster, shoes from Evesham. Equally important were flocks of sheep, herds of cows and the crops of grain, peas and beans that supplied the armies of both sides as they periodically invaded the county. The production of perry and tobacco in the Vale of Evesham also, no doubt, provided some comfort to the troops.

The war in the county largely consisted of manoeuvring forces from one garrison to another as each seemed to come under threat, in order to block routes and retain resources. Unlike neighbouring Gloucestershire, the county did not have the large number of fortified mansions so that 'every corner of the county is pestered with garrisons'.[9] Nevertheless, Hartlebury, Strensham, Hawkesley, Madresfield, Stourton and Frankley provided important targets for the raiding parties of both sides. The garrisons of each could only support themselves by plundering the neighbourhood so that loyalty to one cause or another soon wore thin for the local population. The movement of armies through the county also led to skirmishing and, perhaps more importantly for the inhabitants, heavy charges in the cost of maintaining such forces (of both sides) either through 'free-quarter' or simply from plundering. A particular cause of conflict came from the activities of parliamentary strongholds on the county's boundaries – Colonel Massey in Gloucester, 'Tinker' Fox from Edgbaston or Thomas Archer from Alcester (although the latter was not a permanent garrison), who raided the county to maintain their own security and also to win fresh supplies.

The following chapters will outline the military campaigns as they developed in the county. This is the story of the activists in the conflict. The book will also try to illustrate the effect of the war on the more passive population. Whether 'faithful' or not, the enduring impression is one of a desperate battle for a survival of normal life in one of the most bitter periods of English history.

CHAPTER ONE

LIFE IN SEVENTEENTH-CENTURY WORCESTERSHIRE

Worcestershire is a pleasant, fruitfull, and rich countrey, aboundinge in corne, woods, pastures, hills, and valleys, every hedge and heigh way beset with fruits, but especially with peares, whereof they make that pleasant drinke called perry . . .

(Nehemiah Wharton, Worcester, 30 September 1642)

This was the picture of Worcestershire painted by the London journeyman, Nehemiah Wharton, then a sergeant in the Earl of Essex's army as it marched through the county on the first campaign of the war (Appendix 1).[1] It is an idyllic scene, and to appreciate fully the impact of the Civil War on the county it is necessary to try to understand what normal life had been like prior to the traumatic events of 1642.

Worcestershire was then, as now, essentially a rural county served by a network of small market towns, villages and hamlets, but it also had a significant industrial base. This element should not be underestimated. Farmers, carters, consumers and manufacturers all formed part of a closely knit economic system, through which the armies of the Civil War passed like a swarm of ravenous locusts. A great deal of the county had probably changed little since the medieval period. This timelessness is perhaps reflected in the natural conservatism of the region, as seen in some of the attitudes displayed during the conflict. But change was afoot. Men such as Andrew Yarranton, later the author of *England's Improvement by Sea and Land* (and a Parliamentary officer in the Third Civil War), were probably already thinking about improvements in agriculture and industrial innovation.[2] Yarranton promoted the use of clover (which fixes nitrogen in the soil) to increase land fertility as part of crop rotation. With hindsight, we can also see this period as the last phase of the open field system. Enclosure had already been progressing gradually across the county, especially in the north and west, and in the Severn Valley, changing the look of the countryside. There was a small and scattered population of around 57,000 in the county, with the main distribution in the south and east.[3] Before the war, Worcester was the twelfth largest city in England, with a population of around 7,000 people. Then came Bewdley, Bromsgrove and Kidderminster with

Eighteenth-century engraving of a prospect of Worcester (1764), showing the city from St John's. Note the former bridge, the castle, and the city wall in front of the cathedral. Note also the hills rising behind the city, making it vulnerable to attack from the east. The Rivers Severn and Avon were key arteries of trade in the county. Those places such as Worcester, Bewdley, Upton-upon-Severn, Evesham and Pershore that were bridging points became particular targets in the fighting. (Worcester City Museum, with permission.)

populations of over 2,000, followed by Droitwich, Evesham, Pershore, Tenbury and Stourbridge. The present towns of Malvern and Upton-upon-Severn were then only villages, with populations of less than 500.

The county forms a shallow basin, with the Malvern Hills rising on the west, the Cotswolds on the east and the Clent Hills and Wyre Forest to the north. Within these bounds, the topography of the fertile plain is dominated by the great river systems of the Severn, Avon, Stour and Teme. These were both important arteries of trade and supply and also barriers, providing key points at the river crossings as at Tenbury, Bewdley, Pershore, Evesham, Upton-upon-Severn and Worcester itself. All of these places came to play critical roles in the story of the Civil War in the county. The River Severn was one of the key trade routes of the country, carrying both long-distance and inter-port trade between the Bristol estuary and Pool Quay (near Welshpool) in Wales, with Bewdley acting as the necessary transfer point into smaller vessels. The river carried raw materials, such as iron ore, lead and timber, and a wide range of manufactured goods, including calf skins, cheese, salt, cotton, linen, tobacco and groceries. The importance of the river was enhanced by its 'free status'. It was, theoretically at least, not subject to tolls – although this right was regularly tested during the seventeenth century by the ports of Gloucester and

Worcester. These cities tried to impose tolls on any vessel passing under their bridges. The River Avon was made navigable in 1637 by William Sandys of Fladbury, who built locks at Tewkesbury, Strensham, Nafford and Evesham. This development was opposed by Worcester as being prejudicial to the city's trade. The opposition was led by Sir William Russell of Strensham, and the consequent antagonism between him and Sandys continued into the Civil War, although both were Royalists. The war brought great disruption to this river trade. Some vessels were seized on the Severn; on the Avon the navigation itself seems to have fallen into disrepair.

As in many parts of the country, the roads were in a dreadful state even before the tramp of thousands of army feet and the passage of convoys of heavy wagons and artillery trains. Nehemiah Wharton complained in 1642 of marching into Worcester on roads 'so base that we went up to the ancles in thick clay'. Their maintenance was a regular headache for the authorities and, in 1633, twenty-four parishes were indicted for their roads being in need of repair.[4] Many roads were merely woodland tracks. The parson of Alvechurch complained of getting repeatedly stuck in the mud of the roads, and, because travel was difficult, having to sell his tithes at below-market price. In 1634, John Blourton of Worcester obstructed the highway by building a sheep-fold on it. In 1662, just after the Restoration, there were complaints regarding the state of the road north out of Worcester at Claines. 'Mucke' had been dumped there, and archaeological recording near by has shown the road to have been unpaved, rutted and eroded.[5] Bridges regularly collapsed through lack of maintenance. In 1635 the Dean and Chapter of Worcester (as lords of the manor) were indicted to the Quarter Sessions for neglecting the bridge at Shipston-on-Stour. The dangerous state of some bridges may partly explain the sudden collapses of Pershore and Evesham Bridges during supposedly controlled demolition work during the war.

Agriculture and industry

Over 130 trades were listed for the county in the Quarter Sessions records up to 1643.[6] These were mainly connected with agriculture, but with strong interests in the metal-working, clothing and salt industries. The accounts of the deprivations of the war have left a good impression of the agricultural economy of the county, based principally on wheat production, as part of a rotation system with barley and peas or beans. Rye was also grown on the cleared uplands of the north and west, although much of this remained wooded and pastoral. This was all part of a mixed farming system, with cattle and sheep grazing on the open fields after harvest. The Vale of Evesham had, of course, its own speciality in fruit production and market gardening, making the perry that Nehemiah Wharton praised as being better than could be found in London. The war years have been regarded as generally producing good harvests, but unfortunately, harvest time coincided with the main marching and fighting season, with the armies scavenging the local farms for the corn, peas, sheep, cows and fruit.[7] The area became a granary for the armies that marched this way and that. Of equal value were the teams of oxen and horses that normally pulled the ploughs and carted the produce to the network of markets and fairs in the small towns. Farming was, of course, much more labour intensive than it is today, and conscription must have hit local communities very hard. In all, 27 per cent of the Recognances in the Quarter Sessions (1591–1643) were engaged in agriculture.[8] Townsfolk and village craftspeople also retained an interest in agriculture. One of the properties excavated on the former Powick Lane North in the centre of Worcester is documented as containing a pigsty in 1637.[9] The ability of a town to feed itself was to be of great importance in prolonging the sieges of the Civil War.

The towns were important as markets for agricultural produce. Worcester was particularly significant in lying at the junction of the western pastoral area, the corn-growing south and the fruit-growing of the Vale of Evesham. The towns also supported widespread industries based on the agricultural hinterland. The clothing industry was in some decline in the 1640s, which was in itself a contributory factor in the rising tensions in the country. But this industry, increasingly decentralized, was well represented throughout towns and villages of Worcestershire. There was weaving of wall-hangings and bed furniture in Kidderminster, of clothing in Worcester, of woollen caps in Bewdley. There was silk weaving in Worcester, Evesham and Pershore. Evidence of tenteryards (to dry cloth from the fulling industry) was found on excavations at Blackfriars in 1985, which were destroyed to construct the Civil War defences of Worcester.[10] Tanning was also widespread in the eastern part of the county, including Worcester, Pershore and Evesham. One seventeenth-century tannery was excavated during 1992 at the rear of 37 High Street, Pershore; it was contained within two brick-built basements. One was divided into four large brick-walled tanning pits and there was also a series of clay-lined tanning pits.[11] There was leather-working in Worcester, Bewdley and Feckenham Forest, with saddlery and harness-making in Pershore and Evesham. Gloving was particularly important in Evesham, Pershore and the south of the county. Evesham also made shoes and was forced to supply the king's army with 1,000 pairs in 1644.

The north of the county was rapidly developing its own industrial character. The streams and forests of north Worcestershire fed a number of iron-working forges whose normal production of nails, scythes and farm tools was quickly turned to pikes, musket barrels and shot. There was already a tradition of making weaponry in the area. The Cottrell family of Bromsgrove were cutlers operating in the 1620s. Their stock included pikes, swords, muskets, bandoliers and 'coslets' (armour).[12] Dudley, Bromsgrove and Stourbridge were the main centres of the iron-working industry. Dudley was particularly noted for its nail production, although this was widely distributed down to Bromsgrove and Belbroughton. The industry had been revolutionized in the region by Richard Foley's introduction to Stourbridge of the slitting mill in 1628, which cut the iron into rods for easier manufacture into nails. One third of the names in the seventeenth-century Quarter Sessions relating to Belbroughton were engaged in the metal-working industry, particularly scythe-

Reconstruction of a seventeenth-century smithy. The important iron-working industry in north Worcestershire was quickly turned to war production. The area became one of the most important centres of arms production for the Royalist armies during the war. (Copyright: Paul Lewis Isemonger.)

making and -grinding. Many of these craftsmen had other incomes as well. One scythe-maker, Roger Waldron, was also a maltster whose wife bought malt on the highway to serve unlicensed alehouses. He was also a constable and was accused of pocketing fines!

Droitwich was a town founded on one industry – salt. Salt had been extracted from the brine springs there since at least the Iron Age.[13] In the Saxon period it was described as 'a wonder of Britain' and the need for salt for preserving meat was just as important in the seventeenth century. Salt 'droveways' fanned out on all sides from the town as packhorses carried the produce far and wide. The importance of the industry to all did not mean that it was spared during the war. At one point, the threat of destruction was used as a bargaining counter to try to protect Parliamentary-held Nantwich in Cheshire. Nevertheless, the medieval timber-lined brine pit survived in use until the eighteenth century, an indicator of the traditional nature of this industry.

A long-established pottery industry was based in Hanley Castle and down towards Upton-upon-Severn by the seventeenth century. This appears to have made the county virtually self-supporting (although its importance had declined with the increasing use of metal vessels). The bulk of pottery found on sites of this date are

Excavation of a post-medieval salt-boiling furnace from Droitwich. This vitally important industry was disrupted in 1643 when Parliamentary soldiers stole the lead implements to make into shot.

either coarse-ware cooking pots, bowls and jars, or brown/black-glazed drinking vessels made in the Malverns and elsewhere in the county, or imported from Staffordshire and the present West Midlands (Wednesbury). Imports from further afield are therefore comparatively rare, although some were reaching the county from the continent, probably via the river trade on the Severn.[14] The manufacture of clay tobacco pipes is only documented in Worcester from 1676, when Francis Barker is recorded as being in St Nicholas's parish, but the industry was probably in existence earlier.[15] St Nicholas's parish was established as the centre of the industry by the end of the seventeenth century. Unfortunately, many of the pipes of the mid-seventeenth century are unmarked, which makes identification of source difficult. Nevertheless, only a relatively small proportion of pipes found in the county are definitely from the large centre of manufacture of Broseley (Shropshire), which suggests that there was a strong local industry (including sources from Herefordshire) that was well able to compete.[16] There were also local workshops operating in the Dudley area at the time, and considerable numbers of clay pipes of the period have been found within Dudley Castle. These were presumably those used by the besieged garrison and form one of the best identifiable Civil War assemblages from the region.[17] A rare benefit of the war may have been to encourage the development of these local industries against the competition of Broseley.

One little-known local industry in east Worcestershire was tobacco-growing – an

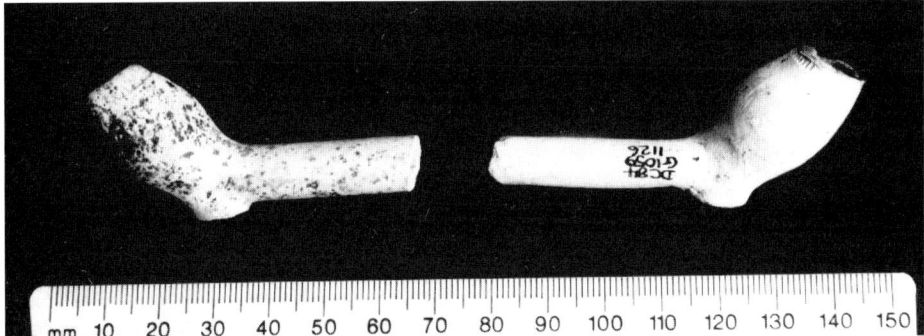

Civil War period clay tobacco pipes found within Dudley Castle. Tobacco-growing was an important Worcestershire industry in the seventeenth century, although faced with continual opposition from the government (who wished to protect the Virginia tobacco plantations). This may have been a factor in the opposition of the Evesham area to the Royalists. (Dudley Metropolitan Borough Council, with permission.)

outlier of the Gloucestershire industry centred on Cheltenham and Winchcombe. Fourteen plantations in Worcestershire were known as early as 1627. The industry was continually under attack from the government which was trying to protect its income from the Virginia plantations. This initially encouraged the growers to support the Parliamentary cause, but the Commonwealth took the same line. In 1659 court cases were brought against plantation owners in Kempsey, Upton Snodsbury, Pensham and Eckington for growing and curing tobacco. Each had 400 poles (10,117 m²) under cultivation, and each was fined £400 (£1 per pole).[18] The North American variety that was grown in Worcestershire was slightly hallucinogenic, which may have explained the vehemence with which it was defended. The industry survived until the end of the seventeenth century.

Social conditions and housing

The county was relatively well-off, but it still had a serious problem with poverty, especially in the towns. Dealing with this was a major element of seventeenth-century administration. There were those who were chronically poor, unable to support themselves even in a good economic climate – people such as the sick, old and widows – and those low-paid landless workers who were vulnerable when crops failed or product demand collapsed. The latter class may have included Kidderminster journeymen, fearful of competition from lower-paid workers, and also wandering vagrants.[19] The latter were treated very harshly in order to move them on. Such men provided a ready source of recruitment, at least initially, for the armies that were to mobilize across the country.

Serious crime was relatively rare, mainly sheep and cattle rustling with occasional assaults. The range of trivial matters brought before the Quarter Sessions suggest that gossip was one of the chief amusements of the day. Life was hard, enlivened by entertainments such as John Browne's waits (musicians) in Worcester. There were sharp disagreements as to the propriety of innocent, and not so innocent, pleasure. In 1633 the vicar of Cropthorne brought a case against six parishioners for playing football. They were committed to trial 'to abide such order as shall be enjoined to them concerning the usage of the unlawful game of football contrary with the statutes of the land' and would have been liable for a fine of 40*s*.[20] Even the clergy could be accused. In Alvechurch in 1642, the newly appointed vicar – a Royal appointee – was accused by parishioners of being a frequenter of alehouses, spending time there on Sundays and with 'idle and riotous company'. He was accused of quarrelling, fighting and 'is greatly famed of incontinence with his neighbours wives': 'incontinence' being the seventeenth-century term for adultery. The vicar was also accused of being 'accompanied with a dangerous and armed papist'.[21] The puritan sympathies of the parishioners were clear. Such activities had been curtailed elsewhere by a successful rising tide of puritanism in official circles. By-laws at Kidderminster in 1640 tried to stamp out 'unlawful games' and 'tippling' on Sundays and festivals. Taverns and alehouses were searched during Sunday services to seek out 'householders and men of worth' who should have been at church and offenders were reported to the Bishop. The noted lecturer Richard Baxter railed against the annual carnival, where the costumed inhabitants were taking the opportunity to make fun of him. He despised their plays, Sunday sports, cock-fighting and maypoles. This did not endear him to the lower classes in Kidderminster who were thereby encouraged to take the Royalist side against the puritan master-weavers and their dreary lecturer.

Conditions were unsanitary by modern standards. Latrine pits might be constructed within the houses, or in the back yards. In towns, they were frequently shared between neighbouring properties. (A privy in the Trinity, Worcester, served twenty-four almshouses.) These arrangements were supplemented by the use of pottery chamber pots. Rubbish disposal was rudimentary, largely consisting of stone- or timber-lined pits dug in back yards, or piled into heaps, for periodic collection for spreading on the fields as manure. In 1634, six persons in St Peter's and St Martin's parishes, Worcester, were indicted for obstructing the highway by placing 'muck hills' thereon.[22] But the filth did actually have a value in an age that depended on natural fertilizers or used dung as a building material. The inventory of Nicholas Bennet (d. 1643), a scythe-maker of Belbroughton, lists amongst his assets 'Item Dunge about the house . . . £1 0*s* 0*d*'. Urine might also be collected for use in the fulling, dyeing and tanning processes. There were other unpleasantries. In 1637 Anthony Brooke of Broadway was indicted for keeping pigs' blood in his butcher's shop to the nuisance of the local residents.[23] As a consequence, the dangers of disease of one form or another were always with the people, especially in the towns. There were regular outbreaks of plague in Worcestershire during the seventeenth century – in 1609, 1610, 1617, 1625, 1630, 1637 (when around 10 per cent of Worcester's population may have died), and another during the war in 1644–5.[24]

From the late sixteenth century there had been notable improvements in living standards. A new waterworks was built for Worcester in 1635, replacing an earlier experiment of 1619–23, and which provided piped water to individual houses. Until the later seventeenth century, most houses were essentially of timber construction, stone was used for footings and some brick for details such as fireplaces. Roofs were supposed to be tiled to lessen the fire risk (Worcester had a well-established brick- and tile-making industry). The surviving houses, typically timber-framed with overhanging jetties on to the street frontage, tend to be those of the better quality. Archaeology is only just beginning the process of uncovering the houses of the otherwise anonymous urban poor. Many families would have lived in a single room, cheek by jowl with much wealthier neighbours in both the town and the extensive suburbs. Unfortunately, one of the characteristics of the Civil War was the readiness with which whole areas of housing could be sacrificed to clear ground around the defences, and Worcester was no exception.

There was a wide variety of house types in the towns, from the very large to single-roomed houses measuring only 3 m × 3 m. The most common type of house probably had a two-roomed plan with a living room/kitchen and bedroom. All would appear draughty and damp to modern eyes. But, from the later sixteenth century, there had been an increasing trend towards greater room specialization, notably the appearance of distinct bedrooms and a wider range of movable goods. This process was offset by the tendency to subdivide existing properties under pressure from an increasing population. Excavations on Deansway in Worcester revealed evidence of the subdivision of houses from the late sixteenth century as landlords took advantage of the shortage of housing. This led to a shift in social structure in some parts of the town as once fine houses were broken up into one- or two-room units. In turn, this produced increasing contrasts between cramped housing and large, open spaces within the town. Landlords may have found it cheaper to modify existing housing to meet the demand rather than build anew on undeveloped plots. Nevertheless, and even during the war itself, there is evidence of builders taking up leases on vacant ground in order to speculate with new building.[25]

Analysis of surviving inventories of properties illustrates the wide range of life-styles within the class wealthy enough to have had possessions recorded at their death. This is clearly seen in the analysis by David Lloyd of a group of Restoration period inventories from Bewdley, Ribbesford and Wribbenhall; 40 per cent of them had values at less than £20. In all, over 75 per cent had values less than £100.[26] Having scraped together what luxuries were possible, many suffered the trauma of a plundering army demanding quarter and goods in lieu of pay. The richest had estates of over £2,000. In Bewdley, the pauper Samuel Clare (d. 1674) was assessed at only £5 11s; he had basic furniture, three flock beds, but only three pairs of sheets and just four pewter dishes. The dyer William Holmes (d. 1662) was assessed at just under £20; he had five beds with 14 pairs of sheets and a range of pewter and brass ware. Alderman William Clare (d. 1668), a baker, was assessed at £233 3s 2d and had feather beds and £3 10s worth of silver ware. But this is all as nothing compared to the grocer, Alderman Thomas Wooton (d. 1667) who was assessed at an incredible £6,227 8s 6d. He had silver and gold plate, and even a parrot!

Reconstruction of a scene within a seventeenth-century kitchen. The contents proved an irresistible attraction to plundering soldiers of both sides throughout the Civil War. (Copyright: Paul Lewis Isemonger.)

A similar picture emerges from a group of inventories dating to the 1640s from Worcester which give a flavour of the goods that were at risk from marauding soldiers. The estate of Francis Denice (d. 1645), possibly a weaver, was valued at £14 12s 8d (including £12 owed to him). He had only one bed, one sheet (and four others described as 'old'), and one each of a pewter pot, brass pot and a small kettle. Jerome Bullocke (d. 1640) was a Worcester clothier whose estate was valued at £24 15s plus £137 10s in debts owed to him. As well as his loom (valued at £1 6s 8d) and 12 lb of flax worth 8s, he had a good range of brass and pewter ware, and his other possessions included two beds with eight pairs of sheets and five blankets. John Byrde (d. 1640) was a tailor in St Swithin's; his goods were valued at £84 1s 2d and give a vivid picture of the range of kitchen equipment in what was described as 'the Hall'. There is the grate with its fire dogs and fire shovel, a pair of bellows to maintain the fire, bars and hooks to suspend the cooking pots over the open fire, as well as a spit and a chafing dish (used to keep food warm). Vessels of iron, brass and pewter are all specified and other items – a pie plate, flat dishes, flagon and quart pot – may (but not necessarily) have included earthenware. Seven pairs of sheets are listed, as well as blankets and bed hangings. Special mention is made of his Bible and a testament. Joane Breynton (d. 1640), from All Saints, lived in a house with chamber on the street frontage, closet,

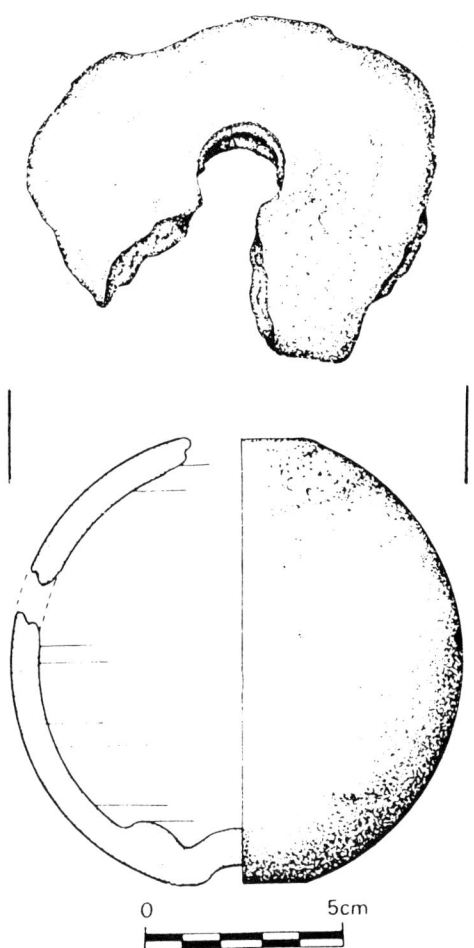

Ceramic hand-grenade, found within Civil War destruction layers at Dudley Castle (excavated in 1984). It is 11.5 cm in diameter and made in a pinkish-buff earthenware. The grenade was probably made in a mould. There would originally have been a wooden fuse filled with gunpowder rammed into the hole at the top. (Dudley Metropolitan Borough Council, with permission.)

hall and chamber over, and kitchen. Her goods were valued at £259 6s 8d. She possessed £30 of clothes, 25 pairs of sheets, 24 table cloths, blankets, napkins, curtains, carpets, books, tables, chairs, stools, pewter ware and brass ware, 10 chamber pots, commode and a warming pan.

Pottery – that basic form of archaeological evidence – is rarely mentioned in such inventories or other documents. It was evidently considered of little value at the time. Thus, chamber pots are rarely mentioned in inventories but are a frequent find on archaeological sites. However, the greater variety of pottery vessels in the archaeological record also points to increased sophistication in this period, through new cooking habits and tastes, with easier access to imported sugar and spices. This was all made possible through improvements in cooking methods brought about by more efficient brick-built fireplaces incorporating ranges and ovens.

There is other evidence of a greater sophistication in people's lives at this time. Many were literate, eagerly devouring the political pamphlets being printed in huge numbers in London. There were strong contacts with the capital. Many of the Worcester and Kidderminster merchants maintained warehouses in London, and the county was a major thoroughfare both from east to west and north to south. So the inhabitants were probably well attuned to the debates and conflicts emerging across the land.

This was a society very much unprepared for war. Of the towns in the county, only Worcester had significant defences and these were in a dilapidated state by 1642 (Chapter 5). Large suburbs had also grown up outside the line of those defences and proved a great liability during the war. There was no standing army before the Civil

War. Defence was in the nominal hands of the 'Trained Bands' of around 800–900 men in Worcestershire. These were intended to be a middle-class force, with gentry officers to protect as much against internal riot as invasion. But it was an unpopular service and it proved difficult to recruit men of the expected calibre. Training was confined to an annual muster and other occasional training days. For many, it was only an excuse to escape the routine of normal life, and discipline was a severe problem. In 1640, men of the Worcestershire Trained Bands destroyed the Worcester gallows – possibly erected (mistakenly) as a warning to them to behave during their muster.[27] John Corbet, in neighbouring Gloucestershire, was expressing a commonly held view when he described the Trained Bands thus: 'the main support of the realm and its bulwark against unexpected invasion, [they] were effeminate in courage and incapable of discipline, because their whole course of life was alienated from warlike employment'.[28] Some foreboding of what war might bring had come with the Scottish war of 1640, when 600 Worcestershire men had been pressed into service from south Worcestershire and the county had been required to house and feed part of the assembling army. This experience may well have coloured the unenthusiastic response of many to the rising danger of war on a much larger scale.

Late sixteenth- and seventeenth-century pottery found in a latrine pit at 29 Sidbury, Worcester. The group includes vessels imported from Spain as well as more local material from Malvern Chase. (Worcester City Museum, with permission.)

CHAPTER TWO

TAKING SIDES

I think there were very few parishes where at one time or another Blood had not been shed.

(Richard Baxter)[1]

The factors that led up to the outbreak of war and the choices that people made in supporting one side or another were a complex mixture of general economics, religious belief, mistrust and more local grievances and loyalties. All combined to produce a quarrelsome atmosphere of rising rancour. It was a difficult time for many as they wrestled with their consciences, splitting class and family, and in some eyes threatening an imbalance in society itself. A full discussion of the causes of the Civil War is outside the scope of this book, which concentrates on illustrations of the main themes as they developed in Worcestershire. What emerges is a more complex pattern of loyalties than suggested in the common popular assumption of Worcester as the 'faithful' city or of Worcestershire as a 'Royalist' county. Instead, there is a picture of a moderately conservative community, that was ultimately dominated by events out of its control.

It is all too easy to assume that the loyalty of the area equated with the words and actions of the small number of activists – principally among the gentry and upper classes. It is, however, true that the majority of the latter in the county supported the Royalist cause to varying degrees. Most of the major Worcestershire landowners seem to have taken little direct part in the actual fighting, although they gave financial support and served the Royalist administration on the Commission of Array and later

King Charles I (1600–49), engraving after Van Dyck, 1649. He brought many of the problems of the conflict upon himself, but war was an anathema to him. 'It is a hard and disputable choice for a king that loves his people and desires their love either to kill his own subjects or be killed by them,' *Eikon Basilike*. (Worcester City Library, with permission.)

on the Committee of Safety. The main Royalist activists were Sir William Russell of Strensham (Governor of Worcester, who raised his own regiment and spent a considerable fortune in the Royalist cause), Sir Thomas Lyttleton of Frankley (commander of the county Trained Bands in 1642, and later Governor of Bewdley) and Samuel Sandys of Ombersley (Governor of Evesham and later of Worcester). All of them raised their own regiments during the war, probably initially relying heavily on the loyalty and obligation of their tenants. The Sandys family was particularly noteworthy. Samuel was the wartime Governor of Evesham and later of Worcester. His brother, Martin Sandys, commanded the Worcester militia. Their uncle William, from Fladbury, also served temporarily as Governor of Worcester and then commanded the garrison at Hartlebury. Samuel Sandys died in 1685. His epitaph includes the lines:

> None greater courage shewed to serve the crown
> And church when haughty rebells cry'd them down.
> To both he faithful was; life and estate
> 'Tis known he priz'd not at so great a rate,
> As to spare either for the public good;
> So little valu'd he his dearest blood.

Sir Arthur Haselrig, one of the five MPs whom the king tried to arrest in January 1642, precipitating the crisis of war, was dismissive of the majority of society in the country. He considered that for as long as possible, the ordinary folk let the long-standing arguments of king and Parliament as to who should effectively rule the country pass over them – 'They care not what government they live under so as they may plough and go to market'.[2] The Royalist Clarendon shared the same opinion after the Restoration: 'the number of those who desired to sit still was greater than of those who desired to engage in either party'. This patronizing attitude was probably only partly correct. The country was increasingly literate and used to political debate, especially from the 'middling sort', enjoying a modicum of electoral power. Other men, such as John Corbet in neighbouring Gloucestershire, feared that the encouragement of popular feeling in the war could threaten the established order.[3] The mob might support either side. In London, the apprentices took the side of Parliament. In Kidderminster the poor journeymen, facing what seemed to be an increasingly uncertain future, rebelled against their puritan master-weavers. Those citizens of the Worcester suburbs who cried 'Down with the Roundheads', as Richard Baxter passed through in 1642, may have been using the rising tide of conflict as a means to vent their more general frustrations.[4] The biased Richard Baxter described the Parliamentary supporters as being the most intelligent rather than 'the ignorant peasants that are like brutes, who will follow any that they think the strongest, or look to get by'. He believed that the countryfolk were wholly for the king, following the particular loyalties of their landlords.[5] But, it cannot be surprising that most ordinary folk in areas of shifting fortunes such as Worcestershire had everything to lose by expressing any opinion too loudly. The property of Sir Rowland Bartlett, a noted Royalist, at Castlemorton was plundered twice in 1642 and three times within the next year.[6]

Extremist minorities from both sides tried their best to sway the rest. Although many of the common people might not have sought to affect the course of events, few could easily escape the consequences. Up to one-quarter of the male population may have served in the opposing armies. Few people went into the war willingly. The heady idealism and enthusiasm of the early months soon evaporated under the harsh realities of civil war, and many from field and workshop had to be conscripted and even kept in custody until they agreed to serve. The High Constable of Worcestershire in 1642 was described as being 'very active for pressing men for the late king, and haven got together a great many psons and pent them in churches for that purpose'.[7] In 1645, 15*s* was spent by Henry Alexander (the constable of Droitwich) to pay for guarding pressed men held in the town. By virtue of the fact that the county was under Royalist

The preacher Richard Baxter of Kidderminster (1615–91) was one of the most outspoken Puritans in the county. He was hounded out of Kidderminster by the mob, but took satisfaction in the fact that 'all of these drunkards went into the King's army and were quickly killed, so that scarce a man of them cam home again and survived the war'. (Almonry Museum, Evesham, with permission.)

occupation, most local recruits were probably conscripted into the Royalist armies. But by the end of the war, as Parliament increased its sphere of influence into Worcestershire, local Parliamentary regiments started to make a significant impact in the fighting.

On both sides there were still many who undoubtedly continued to fight out of an ideal or conviction (see below). There were also professional soldiers: mercenaries on both sides who had seen service in Sweden or in the Low Countries. Although none in Worcestershire showed the fickleness of Colonel Massey of Gloucestershire (changing sides from Royalist to Parliamentarian to Royalist again), many were criticized for sacrificing local needs to their future careers. This included the 'reformado' officers in Worcester during the siege of 1646 and the garrison commanders of Madresfield and Hartlebury. Far from being fervent in support of a 'faithful' city, it is clear from the accounts of 1646 that the loyalty of Royalist troops in the siege of Worcester had to be bought. Desertions from one side to the other were common, and it was also a common practice for captured soldiers to swap sides to avoid imprisonment. A particular problem faced by commanders was the considerable difficulty in getting men to march outside their home regions. Nevertheless, fight they did – often without food or adequate equipment.

When popular feeling exploded in the county during the 'Clubmen' movements of 1645 it was on the lines of 'a plague on both their houses' and a demand to the occupying (Royalist) power to fulfil their promise to preserve law and order. Likewise, there was little local involvement in the famous battle of 1651. With the exception of the militia (who supported Parliament), popular interest at the time seems to have been confined to attacking the retreating forces of both sides as occasion allowed!

Far from being a romantic interlude in Britain's history, this was a period of deep tragedy as the inhabitants were drawn inexorably into war. How had this situation come about?

Economics and politics

There had been a background of widespread complaints regarding King Charles' government for much of his reign. These grievances affected the whole country, whether those areas eventually sided with king or Parliament. The Crown was financially weak and, in trying to rule without Parliament from 1629–40, had been driven to rely on a number of extraordinary forced loans and taxes that were imposed without parliamentary consent. The levy of 'tonnage and poundage' (duties on imports and exports) reduced profits for merchants. Not surprisingly, therefore, the trading classes, including many in Worcester, were among the fiercest opponents of the Crown. This opposition in itself also created a suspicion among some sections of the gentry that the merchants were trying to usurp their traditional position in society and so helped further polarize opinion.

Objections to the Ship Money Tax (intended to pay for a refurbishment of the fleet) eventually affected a very broad section of the community as the tax was extended from coastal ports to the whole country. Worcestershire ranked sixteenth in the Ship Money Tax of 1636. Baxter described how this had caused 'a wonderful murmuring all over the land, especially among the county nobility and gentry'.[8] But the greatest problems in collecting the tax within the county appear to have been among the poorer classes rather than the gentry, with the escheater of Worcester stressing that it was not the gentry of Worcestershire who were to blame for the deficits. One of the justices who had proclaimed the legality of the tax was Mr Justice Berkeley, a Worcestershire man, who was subsequently arrested by Parliament for high treason and fined. His house was burnt at the Battle of Worcester in 1651 and he had to live thereafter in his stables until his death in 1656. The Ship Money Tax was extended by 'Coat and Conduct' money in 1639 to pay for the army's campaign in Scotland, but it was the Ship Money that remained the focus of agitation. Worcester was assessed at £266, Evesham had a particularly high Ship Money assessment for its size of £84, Bewdley was assessed at £70 and Kidderminster at £30. It may be no coincidence that all the towns had significant Parliamentary factions during the war. The Ship Money Tax was difficult to collect, although most was eventually gathered in Worcestershire before it was abolished in 1641. Baxter, with a characteristic disdain for the lower classes, explained how 'The poor ploughmen understood but little of these matters, but a little would stir up their discontents when money was demanded'.[9]

Complaint at one level was simply against what was considered unfair and excessive taxation during a time of economic uncertainties. But the imposition of taxes without the consent of Parliament during the eleven years of 'personal rule' from 1629 to 1640 was also feared as a signal of the absolutist ambitions of Charles I in wanting to rule completely without Parliament. Despite the widespread discontent that these measures engendered, there were many who still believed that the king's majesty was, nevertheless, sacrosanct. The role of Parliament in this conflict was similarly questioned. Did it exist to serve the interests of king or people? Political conflict came to a head with the king's attempt in January 1642 to remove five of his worst critics, by force, from the Houses of Parliament. Parliament retaliated by trying to seize control of the armed forces through the Militia Ordnance of March 1642. This helped polarize opinion, but for many in Worcestershire their innate moderation now saw Parliament as the unwelcome element in unbalancing the constitution.[10]

Religion

Such distrust over the method of fiscal government was closely linked to similar fears about the direction that the established Church was moving in. There was suspicion at both ends of the religious spectrum: on the one hand that greater ritual in the Laudian reforms was heading towards Roman Catholicism, and, on the other, there was fear of those promoters of radical puritan reform. Religion played a central part in the life of the country and could arouse immense passions, with the clergy heightening the tensions through partisan sermons. Most of the clergy in Worcestershire, appointed by Royalist Bishop, Dean and Chapter and gentry, were 'High Church' and this provided an important power base in trying to maintain the countryside for the establishment. Indeed, one of the first units of troops raised in the county was a troop of cavalry formed in January 1643 by the clergy to serve under Sir James Hamilton.[11] The church of St Michael Bedwardine in Worcester continued to ring its bells on the king's accession as late as 1647. This was a poor living, whose rector was 'very barbarously plundered' by Essex's troops in 1642.

There were some pockets of Catholicism, associated with noted families, such as the Sheldons of Beoley and the Lyttletons of Frankley, or with others who were more content to keep a lower profile, such as the Russells of Little Malvern. But the numbers were not great and few others would have supported outright Catholicism. Fear of 'papists' led to a rash of rumours about plots in the county. At Bewdley in November 1641 rumours 'caused them all in the town to be up in arms, with watch all night in very great fear'. The massacre of Protestants in Ireland had heightened the fear of Catholic plots against a reformed Church of England and was a major factor in the outbreak of the Civil War. As King Charles, with his own personal sympathies and a Catholic wife, tried to raise an army to quell the Irish rebellion the fears intensified as to whether he could be trusted with an army – which might ultimately be used against the English Parliament and Anglican Church.

Fear of Catholicism did not necessarily mean that people would support a swing to the other extreme of puritanism. The mood in the county was very much one of cautious conservatism in favour of the existing Anglican worship and against both extremes. There were petitions in the county to defend the bishops against moves to have them abolished. But local loyalty to the established Church may have depended greatly on the quality of the incumbent clergy. The drunken and adulterous behaviour of the vicar of Alvechurch has already been described. At Kidderminster, some influential parishioners, again unhappy with their drunken vicar ('a weak and ignorant man who preached only once a quarter'), passed a number of by-laws with a distinct puritan tone and appointed the radical lecturer Richard Baxter in 1641. He was to provide a teaching based on the Bible rather than the increasing ritual of Archbishop Laud's High Anglican Church. But such activists in the town were probably in a minority of the 'ignorant, rude and revelling people' as the partisan Baxter described the greater part of the population of Kidderminster.[12] When the churchwarden tried to take down a crucifix on the cross in the churchyard, in accordance with orders from Parliament, 'a crew of the drunken riotous party of the town . . . run altogether with weapons to defend the crucifix, and the church images'. A similar mob in Worcester ran amok, crying 'Down with the Roundheads'. It was the same conservative instinct towards their church that came to the fore in Worcester as Essex's men desecrated the cathedral in 1642. Despite the initial Parliamentary leanings of a large part of Worcester, it was the behaviour of Essex's occupying army against both church and secular property that seems to have driven the city finally into the king's camp. Strains in this relationship surfaced throughout the war, but were, by then, constrained by the presence of a large Royalist garrison.

The Royalists had, therefore, a great deal of potential influence over popular opinion. The county was governed by the Council in the Marches (based in Ludlow), whose jurisdiction gave the king considerable powers over the population and their property. The High Church establishment clearly was also able to act as one of the main propaganda organs for the Royalist cause. The county land-owning gentry, around 350 families, with a stake in the status quo, also had great sway over their tenants and labourers. But for many, there was little choice during the war, and the rather ambivalent population of the county acquiesced to whichever army was occupying their land. This makes it difficult to assess accurately the true strength of any popular feeling towards the Royalist cause. Both sides were able to recruit in Worcestershire, but often only under duress.

The Parliamentary lobby

If the majority in the county tended towards protecting traditional loyalties of king and Anglican faith or were indifferent, there was also a strong Parliamentary lobby that should not be disregarded. This was centred on the manufacturing and trading elements in the towns, but was also found among some of the gentry. There was the Presbyterian Rous family of Rous Lench near Inkberrow, the Lygon family of Madresfield, the Lechmeres of Hanley Castle and part of the Wilde family. Edward and Thomas Rous, together with Nicholas Lechmere, formed the core of the Parliamentary Committee for Worcestershire (also including William Lygon and a number of other minor families, some newly moved into the county). Edward Rous and William Lygon, as colonels in the Parliamentary army, were also given a licence by the 'Committee of Both Kingdoms' to 'beat up their drums in Warwickshire for volunteers for the service of Worcestershire'.[13] A number of Worcestershire men who might be considered potential recruits had fled into Warwickshire at the beginning of the war. The High Sheriff of Worcestershire in 1641, Daniel Dobbyns, became a captain in the Parliamentary army and was also a member of the County Committee. Five of the nine MPs elected in the county in 1640 were Parliamentarians: two were the MPs for Worcester, one of the members for Evesham and the two county MPs.

This truly was 'a nation divided'. Sir John Wilde of Droitwich was a committed Parliamentarian and one of the MPs for the county. His nephew, Robert, lived at the Commandery in Worcester and was an equally fervent Royalist. The Worcestershire branch of the Sandys were active Royalists but a member of the Kentish branch of the family was killed on the opposing side at Powick in 1642. The father of the noted Parliamentary commander, Lord Denbigh, was killed on the Royalist side at the battle of Camp Hill, Birmingham, in 1643.

The strongest local pockets of Parliamentary supporters were mainly in what might now be termed the middle classes of yeomen, craftsmen, clothiers and traders in the towns. Supporters of Parliament in Worcester were therefore dismissed as 'but of the middle rank of people, and none of any great power or eminence there to take their parts'.[14] This view is contradicted by Townshend, however, who wrote of Worcester in 1646 that 'the middle and lowest sort of citizens be cordially bent for to stand out courageously [for the Royalist cause], yet many of the best rank draw very backward'. The city had a strong trading class (well represented on the City Council) that typically supported the Parliamentary cause, and was under lesser domination by Royalist gentry.[15] There had been a strong puritan element on the Worcester Corporation before the war and on 14 August 1640 the Council paid 5*s* 8*d* 'to a Companie of players . . . to prevent theire playeing in the Citie'.[16] The City Council had objected in 1640 to the altar and altar rail erected by Dean Mainwaring, which was part of a much wider antagonism between City and Chapter, including the latter's contribution to maintaining the poor and the highways, and the licensing of alehouses within the Close.

But the puritans never achieved mass support in the city. The radical Wharton (who cannot be regarded as objective) described Worcester as 'papistical' and worse even than Algiers or Malta! The city's antipathy to the county was also an important factor in its early antipathy to the Royalist cause. Worcester was still jealous of its privileges won through its charter of 1621 and it therefore tried to get independent control of its militia in 1641. This factor may have coloured the city's initial resistance to the county-dominated Commission of Array and a refusal to participate in the muster. But in the end, many inhabitants may have simply deferred to the Royalist gentry and, most importantly, to the Royalist garrison that came into the city. This was, however, never a happy alliance.

A significant number of the established clergy joined the Parliamentary cause, including a majority of those in the towns. The former Bishop of Worcester, John Thorneborough (d. 1641), actually encouraged people to attend the puritan lectures as part of his personal dispute with the Dean and Chapter. Only one of the Chapter supported the Parliamentary cause. This was the bishop's nephew Giles Thorneborough, later praised as 'a man very well deserving, and the only man of all the Prebends who opposed the rest in their superstitions and their Actions for the late King'.[17] There was more support for Parliament from the parish clergy. The parsons of St Helen's and St Nicholas's in Worcester (Henry Hacket and John Halater) were described in 1642 as seditious and 'actually joined to the rebels'. Humphrey Hardwicke, the rector of St Mary Witton, Droitwich, was another local clergyman who joined the army of the Earl of Essex.[18] Mr Burroughs, rector of Oldberrow, was described as a 'great promoter and stirrer up of this horrid and unnatural rebellion'.[19] In Bromsgrove, Charles I ordered the parish to turn out the vicar, John Hall, as a rebel. The parish register records how 'The Warres beganne in England in the yere 1642, which was the occasion this register was neglected for the minister was faine to fly and divers ministers were placed in his roome until he could returne which was not until May 1647'. In Bewdley, the curate fled to the garrison at Coventry, as did the lecturer, Richard Baxter, in Kidderminster.

The war could make strange bedfellows and all classes were split by the issues. If there is some evidence to support the contention that loyalties developed on class or cultural lines, then the direction that these took in a particular locality could be shaped by individual circumstances. In Kidderminster, the Parliamentarians appear to have been an alliance of relatively better-off master-weavers and some of the minor gentry, against the journeymen and agricultural labourers allied to the rest of the local gentry. The former had appointed the radical puritan lecturer, Richard Baxter, in 1641. The weavers were firm puritans, described by Baxter as being 'of such a trade as allowed them time enough to read or talk of holy things'.[20] Nationwide, the clothing industry felt particularly under threat from the Royalist government and were among the most fervent supporters of Parliament. The clothiers of both Kidderminster and Worcester would have been able to take a close interest in the political arguments brewing in London as many kept stocks there. One Kidderminster clothier, Abraham Plimley, became a quartermaster in the artillery. His brother was an ensign in the cavalry. A dyer, John Freestone, also eventually served in the cavalry. He was imprisoned by the Royalists on a number of occasions, had goods to the value of £1,000 plundered and was reduced to poverty by the war.

But the poorer workmen in Kidderminster – 'poor journeymen and servants' – took a different line, whether out of genuine conviction or simply as a reaction against the views of their sober employers. The latter had been using cheap apprentice labour rather than that of the journeymen and objected to the rowdiness of their employees. The journeymen were then ripe to follow the lead of the Royalist gentry in the area. Not surprisingly, Baxter had a poor opinion of such men, who shouted abuse at 'Roundheads', knocked them down and otherwise threatened those 'who were accounted religious'. He described them as 'like tied mastiffs newly loosed' and tells, with evident satisfaction, how 'when the wars began almost all of these drunkards went into the King's army and were quickly killed, so that scarce

St Mary's Church, Kidderminster where Richard Baxter preached. Kidderminster itself saw fighting in 1642 and 1645.

a man of them came home again and survived the war'. They may simply have been poor men looking for a quick reward and an escape from the humdrum of ordinary life.[21] In London, such men would have been at the forefront of the Parliamentary cause. Ironically, the radical views of Baxter may well have turned many others from a passive conservatism into a militancy which saw its expression in supporting the Royalists.

At nearby Bewdley, later a noted centre of Baptist and Quaker nonconformity, local government also supported Parliament, although the MP, the courtier Sir Henry Herbert of Ribbesford (Master of Revels to King Charles I), was a relative of Lord Herbert, one of the most notable Royalist commanders in the war. In an unprecedented move in the county, the bailiff was hanged in March 1645 by Prince Rupert.[22] Some further indication of the scale of support for Parliament here comes from the fact that at the Restoration, twenty burgesses were removed from the Council for refusing to take the oaths of the Corporation Act and six others for the sake of 'public safety', including former officers in the Parliamentary army, such as the maltster Richard Inett and the gunsmith Samuel Gosnell.[23]

Evesham also retained a distinct Parliamentary allegiance during the war – being fined by the king in 1644 for helping Waller's army. The town had suffered a particularly high Ship Money assessment and also had strong puritan leanings; later becoming a noted centre of Quakerism. Evesham was also one of the centres of the Worcestershire tobacco-growing industry. This was an industry that tended to support the opposition party of the day in order to protect its interests against the government-supported Virginia plantations. Troops had to be regularly called in to destroy the crops until 1689, when the plantations were finally suppressed.

The prosperous iron-working areas of north Worcestershire might also have been expected to have an aversion to the high taxation of the Royalist government. Bromsgrove was later a strong centre of nonconformity, though there is little evidence of its loyalties during the war. But the iron-masters showed mixed loyalties; one of the most influential of the iron-working mill owners was Robert Porter, who steadfastly refused to supply blades to the Royalists. On the opposing side, Sir Walter Blount had his house at Sodington burnt down because he refused to make arms at his forge for Parliament. The Royalists relied heavily on the area for military supplies, having been deprived of the main arsenals at Hull and London. Between February and June 1643 alone, five convoys of iron were taken from Worcestershire and Shropshire forges. Many would have come from the forges of Richard Foley who, later in 1645, was contracted to cast 'iron ordnance, grenades, shot, and other instruments of war for our service' to the total value of £1,000.[24]

Loyalties shaped by war

At first, it appeared that the county might actually give active support to Parliament in its struggle for authority with the king. In July 1642, the Midsummer Quarter Sessions refused to support the orders of the Royalist Commission of Array to raise the Trained Bands (militia) and bring them to Worcester on 13 July.[25] The two Worcester MPs, Humphrey Salway (of Stanford-on-Teme) and Sergeant-at-Law John Wilde had rushed back from London to bring successfully their influence to bear to pack the Grand Jury and raise an alternative petition to support the Parliamentary Militia Ordinance 'with a great acclamation of the company then present'.[26] This early success was short-lived. The Royalist gentry then applied pressure in turn; a new Grand Jury was impanelled on 3 August and warrants were issued to search suspected Parliamentarians for arms. The Sheriff of Worcester, justices and leading gentry, including members of the City Council, now subscribed to a loyal Declaration for 'putting the County in a posture of Arms' and denounced the previous stance.[27] But this was a declaration of moderation in favour of constitutional monarchy calling on the king to 'preserve the freedom and just priviledge of parliament' and 'attend His Majesty in all lawfull ways'. It is significant that this Declaration falls short of outright support for the Commission of Array. This change of stance was not unanimous and a counter-petition was collected in favour of Parliament, but the judge rejected it.[28]

The county militia eventually mustered on Pitchcroft, just outside the walls of Worcester, on 12 August.[29] Not everyone was impressed by the turnout. It was described by William King as being attended by 'a great number of men – of mean and base quality as they seemed to me – and having hedgebills, old calivers [an early type of musket], sheep pikes and clubs'.[30] They were rumoured to be trying to ambush the two MPs, Wilde and Salway. We can perhaps imagine the mixed emotions of high excitement at a possible adventure to relieve the tedium of farming life and dread of war that ran through their minds. Offers were made by the gentry to raise other troops for the king. Sir Thomas Lyttleton of Frankley offered to raise a regiment of foot and a troop of horse.[31] Another c. 500 volunteers were being raised to train in Worcester, Bewdley, Pershore and Droitwich. In all, the total number of troops raised for the king in Worcestershire in the first year of the war has been estimated at c. 7,000 men, out of a total estimated population of only 57,000.[32] Meanwhile, on 5 August, Sir William Russell had compiled an inventory of the ammunition stocks held in the county. This amounted to 44 barrels of gunpowder, $1\frac{1}{2}$ tons of lead (for casting musket balls) and 2,276 lb of match (lengths of cord dipped in saltpetre used to ignite the charges of muskets) in the magazines of Evesham, Bromsgrove, Droitwich, Bewdley and Kidderminster. In addition there were 5 barrels of gunpowder, 500 lb of lead and 112 lb of match in Worcester. The total at the latter would have been greater had not John Wilde removed some of the stocks to Droitwich, fearing the direction in which the city's loyalties might turn.

Worcester remained less forthcoming than the county in raising forces for the Crown. The Commissioners of Array complained that 'the ill entertainment of the citizens of Worcester have so scattered our thoughts, that they cannot be so suddenly recollected'.[33] The 'middle rank of people' so ridiculed in the news-sheet clearly had some influence. There was apparently no reply to the Commissioners' enquiry of 20 August as to what number of volunteers the city might raise, how many troops could be billeted, and what number of armourers could be supplied. King Charles was forced again to order those 'factious and disorderly persons' that supported Parliament in Worcester to be disarmed.[34] Indeed, the city took an opposing position. In early September the citizens and Trained Bands of Worcester delivered a petition to the mayor, Edward Solley. They complained that:

> Cavaliers and soldiers in divers parts of the kingdom
> (where they come) have plundered the towns, bloodily
> killing the king's peaceable subjects, rifling their
> houses, and violently taking away of their goods and
> in some places deflowered women.

They wanted the 'strangers, gentlemen, delinquents and papists' who had arrived in the city expelled.[35] Correctly as it emerged, they feared their presence as a prelude to the arrival of a Royalist army – to be described in a Parliamentary tract as 'the birds of darknesse and prey'.[36] They also wanted the Commission of Array, described as 'unlawful', barred from the city, and an end to recruiting and billeting of troops there. The mayor, although he had signed the Royalist Declaration of

August, replied sympathetically to the demands, which did not, however, prevent him later being arrested by the Earl of Essex for supposedly aiding the Royalists. Unable to rely on Worcester, the Commission of Array were forced to meet just outside the city boundary, at the Talbot Inn in Sidbury.[37] The city maintained this independent stance from the county and turned once again to Parliament. On 13 September, the House of Commons approved a declaration of loyalty from the Council and a request to raise city militia under Captain Rea.[38] Rea (or Ray) was probably the same Thomas Rea who had signed the August Declaration – a measure of the confused loyalties of the time.

In the end, it was the arrival of the Royalist army in September that kept the city to a semblance of loyalty, but it was a strained relationship. Prior to the arrival of Prince Rupert in 1644, the garrison of Worcester was reduced to 200 men due to desertion and the town regiment was described as being slovenly and inefficient.

At the mercy of all

As the armies of both sides moved back and forth through the county it made no difference what one's personal feelings might have been: one's property was likely to be seized by 'friend' and 'foe' alike. The recorded instances of plundering of cottages are probably merely the tip of an enormous iceberg of unrecorded events. From February 1644 every parish in the county was assigned to one of the three main Royalist garrisons to help pay for its costs and also to provide labour for the defences. But both sides tried to raise taxes from the area, collecting whenever the opportunity arose as control of territory shifted. In the convention of the time, both claimed this in the king's name. The Royalists levied an initial tax of £3,000 'to be paid monthly towards the payment of His Majesty's forces sent and raised for the defence of the County of Worcester'. Parliament's County Committee, with the rest of the county occupied by the Royalist army, was forced by circumstances to sit first at Coventry and then at Evesham. Nevertheless, it demanded levies 'for raysinge and maynteneing of horse and foote for restoring and continuing the County and City of Worcester into and under the obediance of King and Parliament', and tried to collect these where it could, first on the east side adjacent to the operations of its garrisons in Warwickshire and then on the south border with Gloucestershire.[39] Strensham, on the west bank of the River Avon (five miles north of Tewkesbury) was assessed at £12 10s 0d by both sides in 1644. Assessments were backdated to take into account the periods under the opposition's control so that, after Massey's troops took increasing command in 1645, the assessment of £10 per month for Elmley Lovett (four miles east of Stourport) was backdated for twelve months. To give some idea of what these sums meant at the time, a ploughman might be paid 35–50s p.a., a pint of beer cost ½d and a cow £1–3. The taxes were used to buy muskets at 10–15s each, musket balls at £17 a ton and cavalry mounts at £7 10s. Locally, woollen 'Monmouth caps' were made at Bewdley for 2d each and sold for 2–4s.[40]

In some instances, orders were made to try to protect sympathizers from troops not overly sensitive to individual allegiances. Parliamentary troops were ordered not to plunder the property of Thomas Littleton, parson of Suckley, because he was 'a laborious, painfull minister, and well-affected to the parliament'.[41] On the opposing side, Prince Rupert ordered his men 'to doe no maner of violence, injury, harme, or detriment, by unlawfull plundering', to Sir Henry Herbert of Ribbesford and his family and property.[42] But these were the exceptions.

Both Royalists and Parliament tried to stop trade between London and Worcester for their own reasons, to the equal detriment of the local interest. Initially, the king did forbid interference of trade (8 December 1642) in an attempt to preserve a semblance of normality. This position was reversed in July 1643. The cloth merchants of Worcester were left to petition the king that if they were not able to trade with London they would be unable to pay the taxes designed for the support of the Royalist army. Parliament took a similar position but was not averse to bribery. In April 1644 Worcester clothiers paid £29 15*s* 0*d* to the Earl of

Not just the menfolk were drawn into the war: women played an important part in Worcester in maintaining the defences. Large numbers also followed the armies as wives or camp followers. One camp follower of the Royalist army was mortally wounded at Naseby in 1645 and was buried at Kidderminster as the shattered army passed through the town. (Copyright: Paul Lewis Isemonger.)

Denbigh to allow free passage of cloth to London. The Parliamentary troops were supposed to give a warning and turn back traders before seizing their goods, but in February 1646 the Committee of Both Kingdoms was forced to complain to Colonel Fox that he had seized goods from Bewdley merchants without proper cause and was ordered to return them.[43] Farmers had their crops destroyed by passing armies, or their plough teams requisitioned so that they could not bring in the harvest. Tenants were unable to pay rents and threatened to surrender their leases. The road systems, in a poor state before the war, deteriorated further during the war, hindering further trade. No route was safe: Colonel Massey from the Parliamentary garrison at Gloucester used a frigate on the Severn to mount a river blockade, cutting the trade route to Bristol.

The ordinary people were therefore caught in a vicious circle. They were plundered because the soldiers were not properly paid through the taxes. But there was no money to pay the taxes because of the looting and by the imposition of additional levies. The cavalry and dragoons gained a particularly bad reputation. As horse thieves, they could strip a local economy of an essential resource: horses were used for ploughing, harvesting and general haulage. In June 1643, men of Amscote and Blackwell in the parish of Tredington (then in Worcestershire) complained to the king that troops of Sir Thomas Aston's forces had stolen forty of their horses, beaten up the owners, and then deliberately rode 140–60 cavalry through their fields of beans and peas. The horses were tracked down to quarters at Black Burton, near Burford, in Oxfordshire – but the messengers who tried to negotiate for their sale back to the village were also robbed.[44] Doddingtree hundred had to pay its share of the normal tax and then pay additional amounts to help cover the cost of arms convoys to Oxford, the carriage of the mint from Shrewsbury to Oxford and work on the Worcester defences.[45] Ultimately, such experiences contributed to the 'Clubmen' leagues who wished to defend their locality against all comers (Chapter 7).

CHAPTER THREE

THE COUNTY OCCUPIED:
1642

Our food was fruit, for those that could get it; our drink, water; our beds, the earth; our canopy, the clouds, but we pulled up the hedges, pales, and gates, and made good fires; his Excellency promising us that, if the country relieved us not the day following, he would fire their towns. Thus we continued singing of psalms until the morning. Saturday morning we marched into Worcester . . .

(Nehemiah Wharton of the Earl of Essex's army, 26 September 1642)

Worcester hurriedly bought weapons during August 1642 'for the general use and defence of the cittie and not to be imployed but by consent of the chamber' and on 29 August collected funds to repair the derelict defences.[1] The Council was clearly determined to try to keep a control over events, but, in the confused emotions of the time, it was not totally clear on whose behalf the weapons would actually be used. On 16 August, King Charles wrote to the sheriff 'whereas the . . . Lord Byshop of Worcester hath bin menaced to be sent for in a disgracefull maner to the parliament, as if he were a notorious malefactor and delinquent' and requested the city officers to be 'ayding and assisting unto the said Lord Byshop of Worcester and by no meanes to permitt or suffer him to be forcibly or otherwise taken out of the See or County by any power, authority, order, or ordinance whatsoever, not warranted by us'.[2] Although the county militia had eventually been raised for the king, Worcester itself had been more ambivalent in obeying the king's commands. It was events rather than beliefs that crystallized alliances as the country drifted into war.

The Royal Standard was raised at Nottingham on 22 August to formally begin the Civil War. There was fighting in Warwickshire on the following day.[3] The conflict soon spread to Worcestershire for on 13 September it was reported that Royalist troopers had plundered the house of William Stephens of Broadway. The troops took money and two silver bowls, and set fire to his hay ricks. This was an ominous precedent for village life in the future. The soldiers then fled to Pershore and on to Bridgnorth, pursued by Nathaniel Fiennes (an MP, and son of Lord Say and Sele) and his cavalry which were an advance guard of the Earl of Essex's army. Some of the Royalists were captured and sent to Gloucester prison. Then, on 16 September, Sir John Byron and a 150–200-strong detachment of dragoons (mounted infantry) arrived at Worcester from Oxford, with a convoy of treasure destined for the king (who was then at Shrewsbury). Although he met no resistance from the city militia, Byron was otherwise received with scant sympathy from the city. In large part, this was probably due to their nervousness in the knowledge that Byron was being chased by the Earl of Essex's army of up to 20,000 men, then only twenty-five miles away. The citizens, whatever their personal loyalties, would have seen little attraction in the likelihood of Worcester becoming a battlefield between the two forces.

The Earl of Essex arrived at Pershore on 22 September with his tired army of London apprentices: dyers, butchers, weavers, tanners, shoemakers, bakers and saddlers. One of his officers, Colonel John Brown, dashed ahead of the main column with around 500–1,000 horse and dragoons, including Nathaniel Fiennes' troop, attempting to cut off Byron and his precious cargo from any further progress towards Shrewsbury. There was an abortive attempt to link up with 150 of the Gloucester militia and volunteers, but they failed to make contact. The Gloucester men then satisfied themselves with withdrawing to Castlemorton (thirteen miles to the south of Worcester) where they plundered (not for the last time in the war) the house of Sir Rowland Bartlett.

Clarendon described the gates of Worcester as being 'weak and rotten', without locks or bolts, but an opportunity to take the city easily through the poorly defended Sidbury Gate was bungled. Brown's men then withdrew and crossed over to the west bank of the Severn (presumably at the nearest bridging point of Upton-upon-Severn) and advanced back up to Powick Ham, three miles south of Worcester and on the south bank of the River Teme. His purpose, now reinforced with troops under Colonel Edwin Sandys, was to block the line of retreat of Byron's men to Shrewsbury, expecting them to try to flee Worcester as Essex's army approached from the east. As a consequence, he kept his men in the saddle all through the night, tiring both men and horses.[4] Edwin Sandys should not be confused with the Worcestershire Sandys family who were fervently Royalist. He was a relative from a Kentish branch of the family, but had local connections as brother-in-law to Nicholas Lechmere of Hanley Castle and had estates in Gloucestershire.

The skirmish at Powick

On the afternoon of 23 September, hearing a rumour from the town that Byron was decamping from Worcester, Brown prepared to intercept the Royalists. He drew down his dragoons who had been keeping watch on the ridge at Powick to form up on Powick Ham while Colonel Sandys assembled an advance party of troopers to cross the narrow Powick Bridge, and head up towards Worcester. But as the leading troops crossed the bridge – only wide enough to take four men marching abreast – they unexpectedly came face to face in the next field with part of a force of Royalist cavalry under Prince Rupert, sent by Charles I to assist Byron. The 22-year-old Prince is one of the best-known personalities of the Civil War. He was a highly intelligent soldier but was equally arrogant, quarrelsome and capable of great

The skirmish at Powick was not the first fighting in the Civil War but was seen by contemporaries as marking the beginning of serious conflict. The skirmish also established the reputation of Prince Rupert as a dashing cavalry commander as his troops unhesitatingly charged the Parliamentary forces as they crossed over Powick Bridge. (Copyright: Paul Lewis Isemonger.)

cruelty. The *c.* 700 Royalists, including a number of French mercenaries as well as the local Sir William Russell from Strensham, were resting after their hard march from Shrewsbury, and both sides seem to have been equally surprised. The Parliamentarians later claimed that they had been betrayed into an ambush by some of the citizens of Worcester, but the mutual surprise suggests that this was mere propaganda (see Appendix 1). It was the Royalists who recovered first and, not waiting to put on their armour, charged.[5] The area is that now occupied by modern houses in Lower Wick, north-east of Powick Bridge. They met, and both sides fired their carbines at point blank range before taking to the sword. A Parliamentary officer reported the first clash thus:

> We let them come up very neere that their horses noses almost touched those of our first rank before ours gave fire, and then they gave fire and very well (to my thinking) with their carbines, after fell in with their swords.[6]

It was a desperate skirmish: few of Prince Rupert's officers escaped unwounded and the troop of Sir Lewis Dyve was badly mauled by the carbine fire of Nathaniel Fiennes' men. However, it was the Parliamentary troops that broke ranks. The

Powick Bridge 'where England's sorrows began'. The wider arches on the right-hand side of the bridge were the result of repairs carried out on the bridge after it was partially demolished prior to the battle of 1651.

resultant confusion was hopeless as they stampeded back along the narrow bridge and lane behind. The confusion is reflected in the differing accounts of the fight. Some contend that Colonel Sandys vainly tried to restore order before being mortally wounded, whereas Fiennes and Brown fled. Others describe Brown dismounting with his dragoons to hold the bridge as a rearguard. One Parliamentary account even claims the whole affair as a victory for Fiennes.[7] Some men were trampled to death in the lane and others were pushed into the swollen River Teme and drowned. Indeed, they retreated right back via Upton-upon-Severn to Pershore – where, by their sudden arrival, they panicked the bodyguard of the Earl of Essex. But Prince Rupert had more urgent plans than pursuing them more than a mile or so. Each side put its own gloss on the result. Nehemiah Wharton, a sergeant in Colonel Denzil Holles' regiment of the Earl of Essex's army, put the total casualty figure at only twenty-eight (see Appendix 1). The official Parliamentary figure was given as thirty-six dead and twenty-one wounded. The Royalists claimed to have killed eighty. According to Wharton, many were buried in St John's parish on the west side of Worcester. Prince Rupert gathered up his men and they successfully escorted Byron's convoy back to Shrewsbury via Tenbury and Ludlow.

In reality, the skirmish at Powick was quite a minor engagement. But it had a great psychological effect and was considered by contemporaries to mark the first real engagement of the two field armies.[8] The war was now well and truly begun. It was also this action that established the reputation of the Royalist cavalry and, in particular, Prince Rupert's reputation as a dashing, formidable figure.

The occupation of Worcester

The Royalist victory was only temporary. The departure of Byron and Prince Rupert left Worcester an open city and at noon on 24 September, Essex was able to march into Worcester with no opposition. The citizens' worst fears were to be realized. Worcester had shown only half-hearted interest in the war so far

True and happy Newes From *WORCESTER*.

Read in the Honourable House of Commons, *Septem.* 24. 1642.

Sent in a Letter from His Excellencie the Earle of *Essex* upon Saturday the 24 of *September*, 1642. to the House of Commons.

Wherein is declared a Famous Victory by Mafter *Fines* a Member of the Houfe of Commons over Prince *Rupert*, who came to the faid City with 500. Horfe, upon Thurfday laft.

Relating alfo the fame Defcription of the Battell and the number that was flaine on both fides,

Likewife the proceedings of His Majeftie fince his comming to the faid City exprefsfed in the faid Letters.

Together with His Refolution concerning the City of *London*,being happy tydings for all thofe that with well to this happy Refolution.

London,printed for *Tho. White, Septem.* 26.

Parliamentary propaganda, 1642. Even though the Parliamentary forces fled the field of Powick in complete disorder, some propagandists still tried to convince their audience in London that, in fact, the skirmish was a 'Famous Victory'. (Hereford and Worcester Record Office, with permission.)

and had even sent a petition to the Earl of Essex via Captain Rea of the Worcester Trained Bands begging 'that the Earle would not be offended with the Towne, for what they did was meerely through compulsion, and feare of the Cavaleers, who had done the Towne great injuries, as likewise most places wheresoever they came'.[9] This transparent plea for mercy was to no avail. Taking a jaundiced view of such claims, rankled by their first experience of defeat in combat at Powick and no doubt irritated further by the pouring rain, it was decided to make an example of 'this base town and country'. This was to deter any thought of resistance from other towns. Nehemiah Wharton recounted in his letters initial stories of atrocities on the Parliamentary troops taken at Powick; on 26 September 'Our wounded men they brought into the city, and stripped, stabbed, and slashed their dead bodies in a most barbarous manner'.[10] He wrote again on 30 September recanting such stories but one can imagine the effect such rumours had already made on the temper of the advancing Parliamentary army (see Appendix 1). It is also an example of the way in which false accounts might be easily fossilized, uncorrected, in the historical record.

Wharton told how the army entered Worcester 'the rain continuing the whole day, and the way so base that we went up to the ankles in thick clay'. He was not

Robert Devereux, Earl of Essex (1591–1646). He commanded the Parliamentary army that occupied Worcester after the skirmish at Powick. The behaviour of his men in treating Worcester as a conquered city, when many of the inhabitants actually had Parliamentary sympathies, or were at worst equivocal in their support of any side, was a major factor in shaping future attitudes. (Worcester City Library, with permission.)

impressed with the city. He described it as, although pleasantly situated, 'so vile, and the country so base, papisticall, and atheisticall and abominable, that it resembles Sodom . . . a very den of thieves, and a receptacle and refuge for all the hell hounds of the County'.[11] Most of the Royalist leaders in the county had already fled the city. It was left to the mayor, Edward Solley, to beg on his knees for Essex's pardon for having surrendered the city without a fight to Byron's Royalists. Essex was not in a forgiving mood. The mayor and Alderman Green were arrested and taken to London. Other aldermen were removed from office and replaced by Parliamentarians.[12] A worse fate was to befall those townsfolk who were thought to have helped trick Brown at Powick by spreading the story that the Royalists were retreating to Shrewsbury. Wharton tells of gallows being erected to hang them if identified. There was also a financial penalty: £5,000 was collected for Parliament as well as 2,200 lb of plate. Adding insult to injury, the citizens had to provide a hogshead of wine and sugar loaves to the value of £8 as an offering to Essex, as well as quartering his hungry and lice-ridden men.[13] On 31 October the City Council were obliged to vote a tax of 'two double fifteens' (*c.* £72) towards the costs of providing coal and other fuel and other expenses for accommodating the soldiers, the defence of the city and the entertainment of the governor.[14] This established a pattern of hospitality for the rest of the war which the citizens were forced to offer to the armies of both sides as occasion demanded.

The irritable Parliamentary army was no great respecter of property. The number of constables in the city had to be doubled in October in an effort to try to preserve order, but this probably had little effect against the soldiery. In St Michael's parish accounts there is a record of a payment of 17*d* for repairing 'Widow Ward's chimney broken down by the soldiers'. The soldiers were bribed to prevent further damage. Another 10*s* 4*d* was 'Given to captain and soldiers for preserving our church goods and writings'.[15] Stories of the misdeeds reached London to be reported in the news-sheets. The *Weekly Intelligence* of 10–18 October told how one soldier had to be 'well-horsed' the week before. The news-sheet also reported how two gallows were to be set up to dissuade further outrages, probably the same gallows as Wharton reported being erected, given a different gloss for the London audience.[16]

On the Sunday, the puritan army chaplains took over the pulpits to harangue the local population. The cathedral was desecrated – the organ, windows, vestments destroyed. Derisory troops danced in the streets wearing the despoiled vestments. The anger of the troops was exacerbated by finding a cache of Royalist arms in the crypt (11 barrels of gunpowder and musket-balls). Horses were stabled in the nave, the choir and aisles used as latrines. The puritans lived up to their reputation as killjoys – on 17 November, John Browne's waits (musicians) were ordered to stop playing in the mornings.[17] To make matters worse, smallpox broke out among the wounded men brought from Powick (among the casualties was the wife of the ill-fated Colonel Edwin Sandys who had arrived to tend her dying husband – both were buried in the cathedral). In confident mood, Essex sought to strengthen the defences of the city with a new series of earthworks, but it was the citizens who had to bear the brunt of much of the work involved (Chapter 5).

It was not just the city that suffered. Essex's army had to range far and wide in order to maintain itself. Once again, the house of Sir Rowland Bartlett at Castlemorton was plundered. Soldiers 'take away good store of bacon from his roofe, and beefe out of the powdering tubs; they steal his pots, pannes, and kettles, together with his pewter to a great value, they seize on all his provisions for hospitality and house-keeping, and then breake his spits, as unnecessary utensells, they expose his bedding to sale, and presse carts to carry away his chairs, stooles, couches, and trunks'. It is likely that many other similar attacks on the local population went unrecorded in order to provision this army of 20,000 men.

While eleven regiments remained at Worcester, detachments of the Earl of Essex's army, comprising another five regiments, were sent to occupy Kidderminster, Stourbridge and Bewdley on 11 October, in case Charles tried to march back from Shrewsbury to London via Worcester.[18] The troops took five cannon, fifteen wagons loaded with ammunition and other items, including what were described as 'swan's feathers', which were probably what are better known as 'swedish feathers' or 'swine feathers' – 5 ft long stakes with pike heads mounted at each end. They were intended to be set into the ground at an angle to protect musketeers against cavalry charges, and were considered especially useful for dragoons who rode into battle and then dismounted to fight as musketeers – but without the protection of pikemen. Troops under the Earl of Stamford were also sent to occupy Hereford to block Charles's route into South Wales. But the Parliamentary forces were outmanoeuvred. Prince Rupert marched into north Worcestershire to mount a diversion and keep the Worcestershire troops occupied, while Charles tried to get between the Earl of Essex and London. By 14 October, Prince Rupert had reached Stourport and stayed with the iron-master, Richard Foley, while his troops were quartered around Wollescote Hall. A ring given to the owner, Mr Millward, as payment was later redeemed by Millward's son from

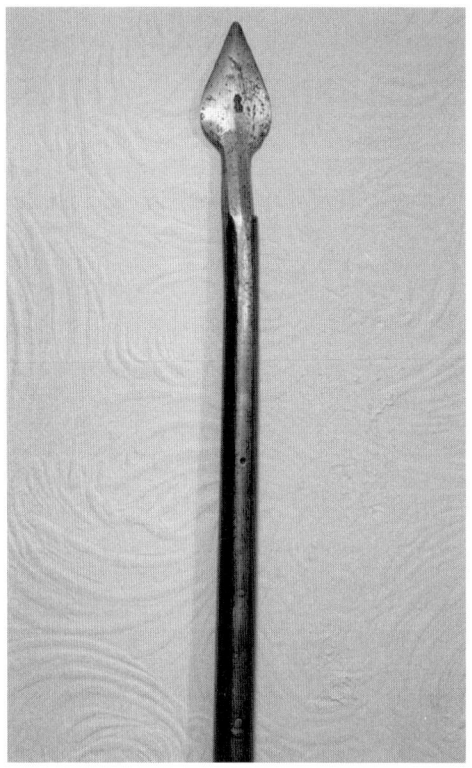

Civil War pikehead, showing the langets used to strengthen the shaft. The pike could be as long as *c.* 18 ft, although a shortened version only 5 ft long and with a pikehead at both ends (a 'swan's feather') was carried on horseback by dragoons (mounted infantry). (Private possession.)

Charles II. This movement threatened the flank of the Kidderminster garrison and, thinking that the Royalists were about to march on Worcester, Lord Brooke's regiment of 500–700 men were forced to flee the town. Brooke himself described this as a 'soldier-like' retreat, but other commentators took a different view, describing the panic as the men were forced, out of 'haste or feare', to leave their baggage and three or four cannon behind.[19] Richard Baxter tells how some of the Royalist sympathizers in the town hurried to the Royalist army to inform them of events so that they could capture the weapons.[20] In the rush to evacuate, one man fell down the cliff, the parish register for St Mary's Kidderminster recording how, on 14 October, they 'Buried, one Thomas Ringe, a Pliament souldier, that brake his necke, falling down the rocke towards Courfield into the Holloway that leads to Bewdley'. One skirmish took place on 17 October, somewhere between Stourbridge and King's Norton – 'a praty uplandyshe towne'. Local tradition has this at Ludeley, in a field where folklore says 'the King's men' were buried and where musket-balls, cannon-balls and seventeenth-century pottery have been found.[21] According to a Parliamentary tract (and therefore not entirely reliable), Lord Willoughby, with 800 horse and foot met Prince Rupert with 8 troops of horse and 300 foot in a battle that was 'very fierce and cruel'. It claims 50 of the Royalists were killed and 20 taken prisoner, to the loss of 17 of their own.[22] Prince Rupert then appears to have retreated towards Frankley Manor, which despite it being owned by the Royalist Lyttleton family, was later burnt down to prevent it being garrisoned by his enemies. The evidence of other, less well-documented, skirmishes is seen in the burial registers of local churches around Kidderminster.

Lord Willoughby was now in a position to take intelligence of the Royalist strategy back to Worcester. King Charles therefore took the opportunity to strike off for London. The Earl of Essex quickly set off in pursuit, leaving his artillery to

A skirmish documented as being fought between Stourbridge and King's Norton on 17 October 1642 may have been at Ludeley. A number of small-calibre cannon-balls, musket- and pistol-balls have been found in a field there. The iron cannon-balls, weighing just over 2¼ lb, are from a small 'Falcon' or 'Falconet' with a range of up to 800 m. (Private possession.)

follow, but the latter was delayed because of a lack of co-operation from local carters, no doubt fearful of ever being able to recover their draught animals. The parish accounts of Powick and St John's, Worcester, contain a number of complaints about ox teams and carts being requisitioned for the march to Edgehill in Warwickshire.[23] At first, the stratagem seemed to work and Charles did manage to get in front of the Earl of Essex. The road to London and victory seemed clear. However, Charles could not risk leaving an enemy army intact at his rear and so, at Edgehill on 23 October, he turned to face Essex at the first major battle of the war. The result was confused, with massive desertions on both sides, but was at least a technical Royalist victory. Not for the last time, the king missed an opportunity to strike out for the capital. Instead, he moved to plunder Banbury, giving the Londoners a chance to prepare their defence. Locally, the Royalists were now able to seize Bewdley and Evesham, which made the new Parliamentary Governor of Worcester, Colonel Thomas Essex, begin to feel very isolated. Consequently, and despite the recent work on the defences, he decided to abandon the city and withdraw his two regiments (his own and Merrick's) of *c.* 1,800 men to Gloucester. The owner of the house where he had been staying, the town clerk, Francis Street, was paid £5 'for the spoiling of his goods by entertaining the governor, Essex'. The rest of the city paid £40 to avoid being plundered by the withdrawing soldiers.[24]

Thus the county was now entirely held for the king and Parliamentary supporters fled. On 10 November 1642, Sir William Russell (who had fought at Powick and whose house at Strensham had consequently been pillaged 'unto the bare walls' according to Nehemiah Wharton) was rewarded by being made governor of the newly installed garrison at Worcester. This, and the occupation by the Royalists of Hereford, freed the supply route from Wales and enabled Lord Herbert to march an army of 4,000 to the king's headquarters at Oxford. In December, Sir William Russell ordered the chief constables of Doddingtree hundred to supply twenty carts and horse teams to the Talbot Inn in Sidbury. These were required to transport the Aberystwyth mint, under the Worcestershire man Thomas Bushell, to Oxford.[25] But calls for such assistance were as unwelcome as previous Parliamentary requests had been. The carts were not delivered and had to be hired from elsewhere. In January, the Doddingtree hundred was ordered to pay the hire costs at a rate of £3 per team.[26] This critical routeway, which also blocked the route from Parliamentary Warwick to Gloucester, was further secured by constructing new defences at the bridging point of Evesham, following the appointment of Samuel Sandys from Ombersley as governor on 20 January 1643 and his commission to raise troops. Evesham lies in a loop of the River Avon, giving natural protection on three sides. The loop was now closed on the north side by an earthen bank topped with timber palisade and with a large ditch on the outer side. The ditch may have been up to 10 m wide on the higher, drier ground to each side of the main road, with lesser, but wet, ditches (2–4 m wide) bounding the river (see plan, p. 87 below).

The county was now firmly put on a war footing as industries were turned towards munitions production. On becoming Governor of Worcester, Russell immediately ordered the casting of shot and ordnance. In the year from December 1642 he spent £152 on making saltpetre liquor (potassium nitrate and sulphur mixed with powdered charcoal as the key ingredient in gunpowder), paid three powder-makers £55 11*s* 5*d* for making gunpowder in the mills and spent other amounts on casting and boring cannon and making gun carriages.[27]

However, this apparent Royalist strength concealed a flaw that was to remain throughout the war. The local commanders were expected to pay for their troops from local resources, a burden the local communities were not able or prepared to bear, loyal or not. King Charles was evidently aware of potential problems of creating a military government alongside the existing civilian structures. His commission to Samuel Sandys at Evesham included a command 'not to meddle with the civil government of the said town of Evesham, but leave the same in the Mayor or chief Magistrate to whom it properly belongs'.[28]

CHAPTER FOUR

THE BATTLE OF RIPPLE AND FIRST SIEGE OF WORCESTER: 1643

The Royalists now had an opportunity to consolidate their hold on the county. Parliamentary supporters were removed from local government and a new County Commission was established in January 1643 to oversee the war effort – it became the Committee of Safety in March. Its role was to pass on the orders of the king's Council of War at Oxford and act as an intermediary with the garrison commanders. The commissioners were to meet weekly in Worcester and as often elsewhere as was deemed necessary.[1] Part of their duty was also to arrest subversives and provide lists of serving Parliamentary soldiers from the county so that their estates could be fined. They were also to levy taxes, arrange loans, pay the troops and punish any soldiers who had wronged civilians.

It was clear that the war was going to be expensive. In addition to voluntary donations expected from the gentry, and haphazard seizures from the estates of known Parliamentarians, the Grand Jury of Worcestershire agreed to pay a *monthly* levy of £3,000 to support the local Royalist troops, which was to be collected by the County Commission, who would also audit its expenditure. This sum should be compared with an *annual* grant of £6,167 15s 3d levied from the city and county in 1641. In the circumstances, it would have been difficult to oppose this demand and it cannot therefore be taken as representing a committed vote of support. Some may have hoped that it would be a protection against more forcible exactions or pillage. Despite this pledge, there were considerable difficulties in raising the money from the people. By 4 April, the money had still not been raised and payment of the levy was ordered to be continued for a further three months. In return, the Grand Jury asked that they be freed from the burden of providing free-quarter for the men and horses: free-quarter was a detested arrangement by which householders were obliged to provide board and lodging in the expectation of some future payment. The fact that this plea had to be repeated throughout the war suggests that it was not successful.

The demands were piled on. An additional monthly contribution of £180 was set for Worcester 'towards the fortification and other publique uses of the Cittie as the Governor shall appoint'.[2] The commissioners were then ordered to construct powder mills (for the manufacture of gunpowder) 'out of the public monies . . . over and above the £3,000 Monthly Contribution' and to borrow 100 draught horses.[3] The twenty-three appointees of the commission were all well-placed local Royalist supporters but they were not the normal peacetime government of the county. The City Council, to some degree pushed aside by the new body, pleaded on 11 March to be allowed to make their own arrangements to fortify the city rather than pay this amount. Their suggestion was to raise 40*s* for six days a week (Sundays excepted) in order to pay sixty men to work on the fortifications. Those of the citizens who volunteered for the militia (under Captain Martin Sandys, the brother of Samuel Sandys) were to be excused this contribution, but this was to no avail and the city was indeed rated at £180 per month on 16 March.[4] Colonel Dud Dudley (from Staffordshire, inventor of the use of coal in iron-smelting) was put in charge of the work on the fortifications. Other parts of the county were required to contribute to the defence of the city: in April the inhabitants of the Doddingtree hundred were ordered to supply hay, oats and bread to supply the garrison.[5] Arms were also collected up, either to reinforce the garrison or to prevent them being used against the Royalist troops.

The city continued to try to distance itself from wholehearted support for the Royalist cause. In 1643 it elected the clothier Thomas Hacket as mayor, although his son was a preacher in the Parliamentary army (formerly the rector of St Helen's). The king objected and Hacket was replaced. Nevertheless, the city again elected him in 1644, but Hacket was no radical and was then content to serve in the City Trained Bands.[6]

The number of troops in the county was rapidly increasing. It has been estimated that the local Royalists may have raised around 7,000 men down to October 1643 (*c.* 12 per cent of the total population), including a garrison of around 1,500 men in Worcester.[7] In May 1643, Sir James Hamilton raised three regiments (one of horse, one of foot and one of dragoons). The Sandys family made a notable contribution to the Royalist cause when Colonel Samuel Sandys of Ombersley also raised three regiments. Colonel William Sandys raised a regiment of horse and his uncle, Colonel Martin Sandys, the volunteer regiment of 800 foot from the citizens of Worcester. A regiment of the field army under Sir John Beaumont also came into the county in April, with part being sent to reinforce the garrison at Dudley Castle.[8] The problems of paying the wages of such an army were a constant problem. Indeed, some troops had to be disbanded during the year through lack of funds. Sir William Russell actually paid higher wages than were normally expected, which may have been an attempt to limit the tendency to plunder in his home county.[9]

The Committee of Safety tried to limit expenditure by only agreeing to pay costs when the troops were actually within the county boundaries, but this was little comfort for the troops themselves or for the unfortunate territories through which the unpaid men passed. This was true of the three weeks that Sir James Hamilton's regiment operated in the Forest of Dean during April, or the month that Worcester troops spent at the siege of Gloucester in August. The reverse was also true of course. In all, the movement of other Royalist armies through Worcestershire during the year cost the county £1,813, and was a major headache for Sir William Russell to try to collect, with Droitwich alone being forced to spend £312 on helping to clothe regiments passing north in November.[10]

Battle of Ripple

The southern border of the county was very insecure. The Royalists had failed to take Gloucester in March and its commander, Colonel Massey, went on to take Tewkesbury in April. As from February, Parliament had even tried to reimpose a weekly assessment for the county and establish committees for the county and city. But these can only have been paper committees; either because they could not raise enough men of status, or deliberately to cause mischief, the published list of members included the names of three who were actually Royalist Commission members at the time. Meanwhile, Prince Maurice was appointed to command the Royalist forces in Worcestershire and was sent against the Parliamentary general, William Waller ('William the conqueror'), who had come to Gloucester's aid in March with around 2,500 men and had subsequently captured Monmouth, Chepstow and Ross-on-Wye. They manoeuvred around each other in the Forest of Dean until Prince Maurice was in a position to cut Waller's communications with

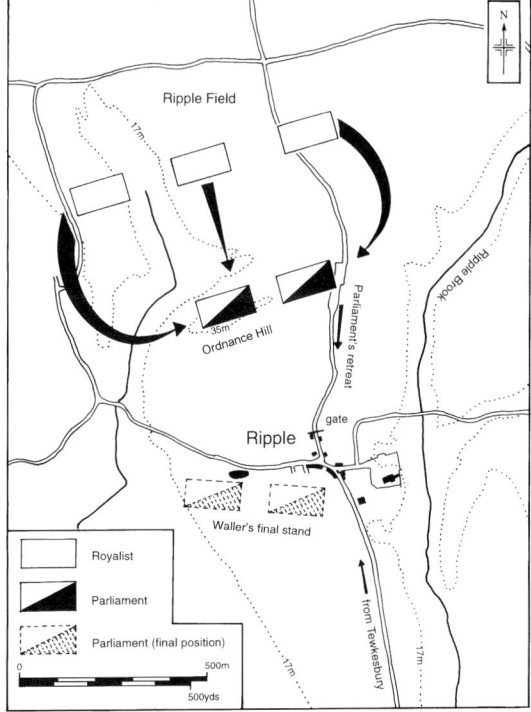

Map of the Battle of Ripple. The Battle of Ripple on 13 April saw the defeat of the highly experienced tactician William 'the conqueror' Waller by the young Prince Maurice. The Royalists attacked out of the sun in a pincer movement that forced the terrified Parliamentary army down a narrow lane into Ripple itself. Here, Waller vainly tried to make a last stand but was only saved by the arrival of fresh reinforcements from Tewkesbury.

Sir William Waller brought up his artillery to Ripple but the inexperienced gunners had brought the wrong calibre shot. Reproduction 'saker', or cannon capable of firing a 5 lb cannon-ball a range of 1000 m. (Commandery Museum, Worcester, with permission.)

Gloucester. Waller then had to extricate himself from potential disaster and retreated to the haven of Gloucester. Taking the offensive again, Waller re-occupied Tewkesbury (Russell's garrison retreating to Worcester) and, to prevent Prince Maurice from following him, sent on troops to break down the bridge at Upton-upon-Severn. But his demolition team was forstalled by the arrival of the Royalist army. The Parliamentary troops were forced back across the bridge on to the east bank of the Severn and were then pursued by Prince Maurice's army. Waller was already riding with an army of *c.* 1,500 troops to reinforce his men, and met up with the retreating Parliamentarians at Ripple (three and a half miles north of Tewkesbury). It was here, on 13 April, that Waller decided to make a stand against the young prince.

Accounts of the battle vary – not uncommon in the Civil War. The opening positions seem clear. The two sides met first at Ripple Field, on the north side of the village. Waller had advanced through the village on to a ridge known as 'The Bank' or 'Old Nan's Hill' (Ordnance Hill) which runs east to west between Uckinghall village and Ripple Brook. To the north was the large flat plain of Ripple Field, where Prince Maurice's army of *c.* 2,000 men formed up. The enclosures at the foot of the ridge were known from the later seventeenth century as 'Deadland Furlong' and 'Scarlett Close' as possible reminders of the skirmishing that took place here between the two sides. Corbet believed that, although outnumbered, Waller had initially intended to face Prince Maurice in open battle, having brought up his artillery, but this failed 'having neither shot prepared nor cannoneers that understood the businesse'. Some of the shot was found to be the wrong calibre! But the usually skilful strategist had again been outmanoeuvred by Prince Maurice. Although Waller had the advantage of the higher ground, he soon realized that he faced the danger of encirclement, with his officers discovering Royalist musketeers hidden all around in the hedgerows of Ripple Field, and with his flanks vulnerable.[11] Waller therefore decided

Sir William Waller (1597–1668) was considered a brilliant tactician but was outmanoeuvred by Prince Maurice at Ripple.

to beat a retreat back to Ripple itself, although some contemporaries claimed that this was to tempt Prince Maurice into an ambush. It was possible that if he could encourage the Royalists to follow his rearguard into the long, narrow, sunken lane leading back to Ripple then he could harry them from the hedgerows until they tumbled out of the lane into a large open field beside the village. Here they would be confronted by the main body of Waller's troops, lying in wait. In effect, this would have been the skirmish at Powick in reverse. The Royalists would then be expected to try to retreat in confusion back up the lane, and be cut to pieces in the process.

Whatever the original intention, the actual course of the battle is clear. As Waller tried to extricate his men off Old Nan's Hill and down the lane, Prince Maurice attacked. His men tore down on the Parliamentarians from the front and both flanks. The cavalry on the right flank of the Royalists had swung towards Uckinghall and come back up the gentler gradient on to the top of Old Nan's Hill, so seizing the initiative of the high ground. The fury of the assault, coming out of the sun and from three directions, completely panicked the Parliamentary troops at the head of the lane. Whatever their plan might originally have been, they retreated in complete disorder. The dragoons sent to cover the retreat also broke and rushed headlong into the musketeers fleeing in front of them. In an attempt to slow the

At the Battle of Ripple, the retreating Parliamentary army fled down this lane into the village itself, pursued by Prince Maurice's cavalry. Their advance is reported to have been slowed by a quick-thinking soldier closing a gate across the lane (just beyond the barn).

The centre of Ripple village. The Parliamentary troops desperately tried to reform in Ripple itself but were broken again by the Royalist cavalry.

Royalist advance, Haselrig's heavily armoured cavalry, the 'lobsters', were then sent in, but this was to be of little avail against the overwhelming might of the Royalists as they charged down the lane and crashed through the hedgerows on each side. The 'lobsters' were said by the Royalist press to have lost fifty men out of their total strength of seventy. Still the Royalists came on. Their passage down Coach Road was only stemmed by a ditched watercourse (from Cockshot Pond to Ripple Brook) and apparently by a soldier who managed to take a gate off its hinges and set it across the lane as a desperate barricade. (The position of the gate was shown in a map of 1778.) Massey, who had arrived with reinforcements, managed to re-form his men on the open ground on the other side of Ripple to try to make a stand, but Maurice charged again against the panic-stricken Parliamentarians who broke once more. The day was finally saved for Waller, himself said to be unhorsed in the battle, only by the arrival of new reinforcements from Tewkesbury. Only then was he able to extricate himself from a near total disaster and retreat south to safe hands in the recently captured Tewkesbury. Maurice's victorious army in turn headed for Evesham and then was ordered back to Oxford. A Royalist newspaper, *Mercurius Aulicus,* claimed that eighty of Waller's army were killed, and an equal number drowned in trying to swim back over the River Severn. By the following week they had inflated the death toll to over 500 men. The Royalists were said to have lost only two men.[12] Interestingly, there is no mention of any casualties in the Ripple parish register.

This was a humiliation for Waller, but on 25 April – smarting for some victory in the area – he retook Hereford in an unexpected 'smash-and-grab' campaign. Sir William Russell responded by instantly calling on Doddingtree hundred to supply further provisions for the Worcester garrison in case of a siege. This included thirty loads of hay, thirty quarters of oats or peas, bread and cheese. All able-bodied men between the ages of sixteen and sixty were also ordered to hurry to the city as soon as it was heard that Waller was marching on the city.[13] This command received an unenthusiastic response from the citizens and had to be repeated on 29 April, with the men supposed to muster on Pitchcroft on 2 May. Despite threats of 'the strictest punishment the lawe can inflict', this had little effect and was repeated again on 9 May.[14] Waller did not have enough men even to garrison Hereford, so after plundering the area he returned to Gloucester. On 20 May, Hereford was once again occupied by the Royalists. The taking of Hereford and subsequent raids in the south of the county had seriously worried the Royalist command in Worcester. Fearing a new attack on themselves, on 28 May they again tried to raise the militia, who were to come to the city with whatever weapons they could find together with provisions for three days. Once again, they got a very half-hearted response for the muster ordered on the Pitchcroft. There was already considerable discontent in Worcester about the expense of the war and the lack of discipline of the Royalist troops, and this disquiet may have been encouraged by the continued presence of former city officials dismissed by a Royal Warrant of March 1643 under suspicion of being disloyal. It was also due to rising tensions between the military and civilians and with some local scores to settle within the gentry. The Parliamentarian troops of Essex had not been alone in desecrating the cathedral: the Royalist garrison stripped lead from its roof to make ammunition. All of these factors combined to make the citizens unwilling to serve in the militia.

Devastation was spreading throughout the county. In June, Sir Thomas Aston's cavalry rode through the county on their way from Chester to the king at Oxford. Their progress was followed by complaints of 'plunderins and abuses' from Droitwich, Bromsgrove, King's Norton, Alvechurch, Beoley and Abbots Morton. On 15 June the king was forced to write an angry letter to the commissioners, who were supposed to act against such outrages, complaining of the disorderly conduct of the troops in Worcestershire, but they could do little, and problems were already exacerbated by power struggles variously between the military officers and the governor, the latter and the commissioners and with the City Council.[15] In Worcester, Lieutenant-Colonel David Hide, a former mercenary on the continent, had run amok at a New Year celebration – he had demanded a gift from the mayor, had thrown a plate at him, insulted his wife and assaulted another woman after arrest. When his commanding officer, Sir William Russell, tried to intervene he was called a 'sonne of a bitch'. There were soon considerable desertions from the new town regiment under Martin Sandys, as the local volunteers tired of the war. Some of Sandys' men were also accused of a 'mutinous and seditious carriage' towards the governor. This was part of an old family feud between William Sandys and Sir William Russell over the latter's opposition to Sandys' plans for the navigation of the Avon. The conflict also emerged in disputes over Russell's handling of the financial accounts, together with charges of him slighting the Committee and turning troops on them. It has been suggested that within this conflict there may also have been factions between the gentry of north and south Worcestershire, led by Sir Ralph Clare in the north and Sir William Russell in the south.[16]

First siege of Worcester, 1643

Waller's forces raided all around Worcester in the spring as a prelude to a siege proper. On the morning of 29 May, and following the distribution of propaganda leaflets the previous evening, he arrived with a force of around 3,000 men and 8 cannon, demanding that the city, with a garrison of around half that number, should surrender. Colonel William Sandys (acting as temporary governor while Sir William Russell was in Oxford) haughtily told him 'he was not at Hereford'. The herald did not regard this as a suitable reply and there was an exchange of words which ended in him being shot in the thigh by the Royalists. Clarendon attributes this refusal to consider the summons to surrender to the courage of the inhabitants, but the decision actually lay with the military government. The citizens were probably also reminded of the treatment meted out by the last Parliamentary occupying force in 1642. The Parliamentary attack began immediately, concentrating on the east and south sides, with Waller's centre on Green Hill and his right flank on St Martin's Gate. It started with an artillery barrage and then direct attacks towards Friar's Gate and Diglis – both of which failed. The house of the cathedral organist was destroyed in the cannon barrage. The Royalists replied with their own fierce cannon fire (using eleven barrels of gunpowder to fire 200 shot) and there was a desperate battle as they tried to dislodge Waller's men from just outside the city walls below Castle Hill at the converted blockhouse at William Berkeley's house (rebuilt as Diglis House). They tried a cavalry sortie from St Martin's Gate to disrupt the flank of the besiegers, and managed to clear the east side of the city. Casualties were high and it was clear that this was going to be no easy victory. Waller knew he needed a quick result as Prince Maurice was known to be marching to the relief of Worcester and Waller could not risk being caught in a pincer movement between the city garrison and the relief army. So on the morning of 31 May, after a siege of only two days, Waller retreated back to Tewkesbury and sent his wounded back to Gloucester by boat. Before he did so, he scoured the countryside around for fresh horses – particularly targeting the Sandys estates at Ombersley in revenge for his defeat, but also not being averse to taking them from less 'royalist' areas such as Pershore.[17] In all, he may have lost around 160 men. Not even Tewkesbury was now considered safe and so, after ordering Sir Robert Coke from Highnam (Glos.) to slight its defences, Waller retreated further to Gloucester.[18]

The dangers of allowing an enemy to approach close to one's defences had been made apparent both to the garrison of Worcester and also to Waller. Worcester immediately began to level the suburbs outside the walls so that they could not be used as cover by a future besieging army, and a band *c.* 600 m wide was cleared outside the Fore Gate. An extensive programme of improving the city defences was also immediately begun, partly paid for by the county. In July Doddingtree hundred was ordered to supply fifty labourers with supplies for three days to 'perfect the bulwarks and fortifications about the said city'.[19] Waller also took this lesson back to Gloucester, which embarked on a similar operation of levelling the suburbs. There was one other more ominous lesson to be learned: captured Parliamentary soldiers informed on a number of citizens and soldiers of the garrison who were alleged to have assisted Waller. They were arrested but it was an uncomfortable reminder of the precarious loyalty in Worcester that was to remain throughout the war.[20]

On the march again

The war was going badly for Parliament and not only in Worcestershire. In July there were significant defeats at the battles of Lansdown and Roundway Down and at the end of July came the fall of Bristol. The Royalists clearly had the upper hand in the west midlands and only Gloucester remained to prevent the whole of the Severn Valley from falling into their hands. Victory here would, in turn, allow the Royalist troops to concentrate on the war in the north and west, but their plans were foiled by the unexpected success of the citizens of Gloucester in holding out against quite overwhelming odds during the siege of 10 August to 5 September.[21]

There, the besieging force of up to 30,000 men, under the king himself, included 800 foot and a regiment of horse from Russell's and Sandys' troops at Worcester. Gloucester was relieved on 5 September by the army of the Earl of Essex, and Charles I withdrew with his army, first to Sudeley Castle and then to Evesham, where the annual fair was cancelled as a consequence. The retreating soldiers helped support themselves by sheep-stealing.[22] Townshend, a Royalist himself, believed that the looting by the 700 cavalry (from King Charles's Lifeguard) sent to protect Worcester at the time cost more than the bill for feeding the entire field army of 20,000 men then in the shire, but the faults were shared equally. On 23 August Parliamentary troops under Captains Croxton and Venables raided Droitwich 'and cutin pieces all the pans, pumps, saltpits, and works, carried some of their pans off; so their salt-making was spoiled'. Although this is the only reference to such destruction and the accuracy must therefore be questioned, there is archaeological evidence for a major repair of the brine pit and pumps during the seventeenth century which adds some weight to the story. The lead pans (cut from a single sheet measuring 1.68×0.91 m) would certainly have proved a tempting target for melting down into shot. The attempted destruction of this vitally important industry was said to be taken in revenge for Lord Capel's proclamation to boycott the saltworks of the Parliamentary-held Nantwich.[23] While at Evesham, King Charles demanded a loan of £4,000 from Worcester and £3,000 from the county. The Worcester Council claimed that they were unable to raise such a sum 'in respect of decay of trade of clothing, the weekly burdens and taxes laid on the Inhabitants for making fortifications and scouring the ditches, etc'. They claimed that the cattle were dead and complained of the costs of free-quarter and those of producing and carrying ammunition to Oxford. Sir Samuel Luke described the city as being filled to bursting point with troops.[24] The Royalists had expected Essex to follow into the county with the possibility of a major battle to follow. Additional cannon had been quickly brought to reinforce the defences of Worcester. One was mounted at Sidbury Gate, one on the Severn frontage and another on Severn Bridge itself. Other ordnance was placed on Castle Hill.[25] But after a diversion towards Upton-upon-Severn, Essex reversed tracks and marched to Cirencester, took it, and then made back for London. Charles managed to intervene on the line of march and the two sides came to battle at Newbury (Berkshire), where the king was defeated but managed to return to his capital at Oxford.

The withdrawal of the opposing field armies did not mean a respite from war for the border districts of Worcestershire. The Royalist plan to secure Gloucestershire was now to mount a remote blockade from surrounding garrisons against Gloucester. The Parliamentary forces under Colonel Massey countered with an aggressive policy of raiding parties into south Worcestershire to prevent the Royalists from concentrating their forces for a new assault. To the east, Parliamentary troops from Warwick also assisted by raiding the Royalist garrisons in east Worcestershire in order to relieve the pressure on the tortuous supply route from London to Gloucester via Warwick. The home of the noted Catholic Sheldon family at Beoley, near Redditch, was taken in a savage assault in which the Irish defenders were (on the admittance of Parliament) ruthlessly put to the sword. Redditch itself was plundered, possibly around the same time.[26]

The continuing internal squabbles among the Royalist administration and military establishment meant that there was a much more insidious threat to the stability of the county. Sir William Russell was replaced as Governor of Worcester by Sir Gilbert Gerrard in December. The appointment of an outsider added to the resentment felt in the city towards the military. It is notable that there is not the same evidence of civic entertainment towards Gerrard as with earlier, local, post-holders.

Re-enactment of a Civil War battle. (Copyright: Paul Lewis Isemonger.)

CHAPTER FIVE

THE CIVIL WAR DEFENCES
OF WORCESTER

Strenuous efforts were made to improve Worcester's defences throughout the Civil War. A considerable body of documentary evidence records work on the defences but not the form that the various episodes took. Little physical evidence of this activity has been identified in the surviving parts of the city walls, but new information has been collected through archaeological investigation on the

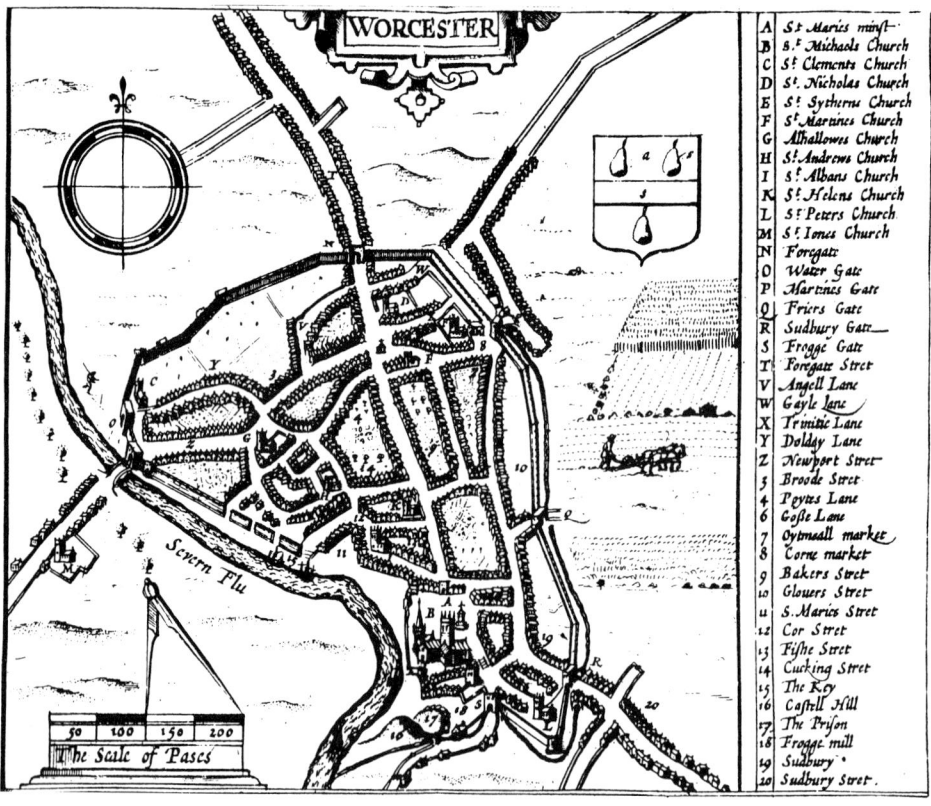

Speed map of Worcester, c. 1610, showing the dilapidated condition of the defences prior to the Civil War, and the extent of the suburbs that were later destroyed.

line of the defences on the north, east and south sides. Inevitably, however, this leaves much of the chronological sequence as speculation.

Speed's map of 1610 gives a schematic impression of what Worcester was like prior to the Civil War. It shows a city with a mixture of high-density occupation and large open spaces, particularly on the north and east sides. The medieval town walls and gates, leaving the bend in the river undefended, are also shown, and the remains of the castle motte (the castle itself being demolished by the mid-sixteenth century). There are extensive suburbs stretching along the main approach roads. Nehemiah Wharton describes the defences as the Earl of Essex arrived at the end of September 1642 as 'The wall in the forme of a triangle, the gates seaven, the bulwarkes [towers] five, but much decayed: no castle, only a mount of earth . . . This citty hath also a stronge stone bridge over Severne, consistinge of six arches, with a gate in the middle of the bridge, as stronge as that on London Bridge, with a percullis'.[1] The basic defences were therefore in a state of bad repair and the south side in particular was very vulnerable. England had seen no need to construct the highly organized citadels that continental towns had been turned into by the long-running wars. What the plan and descriptions do not convey is the siting of the city in the valley of the Severn. The city occupies a strong position on a ridge of high ground above the River Severn, but it is overlooked by further high ground on the north, east and west sides. This put Worcester in a dangerous situation, as future events were to show.

Work on restoring the defences had actually begun before the war broke out. The City Council voted a double-fifteenth tax (a fifteenth being calculated at £35 11*s* 8*d*) in 1641 for the repair of the walls and bridge, but the Parliamentary occupation in September 1642 led to an immediate strengthening of the defences in expectation of future siege and battle.[2] Wharton describes how 'Wensday morninge I went to view the soildiers workes, who have pourtrayed out the severall formes of their scaunces, half moones, redouts, etc., beginninge at Severne on one side of the city, and goe round the city unto Seuerne againe'.[3] This suggests an elaborate system of earthworks was being constructed on the basis of the pre-existing defences. The *Weekly Intelligence* for 10–18 October also describes the construction of 'some small workes upon the hill neere Worcester betweenus and London' which may be a precursor of the more elaborate Fort Royal built in 1651.[4] The Earl of Essex was reported by Wharton as offering 12*d* a day to soldiers who would help with the digging.[5] The work was continued after the Royalists occupied the city. Droitwich tried to avoid contributing and paid £1 to a captain at Worcester to avoid paying a £40 contribution to the cost of the works. This was all in vain. The borough accounts record payments of £100 for 'the payment of labourers and pioneers working at the fortifycacons of Worcester'.[6]

The map of defences of 3 September 1651, published by Vaughan in 1660 on a superimposition of the Speed map, gives the clearest impression of the final scheme the Earl of Essex's soldiers were beginning to develop. It shows the medieval walls with six four-sided bastions added on the north and east sides. The major additions built during the course of the war are the defences enclosing the castle on the south side, the defences of the east suburb and Fort Royal.

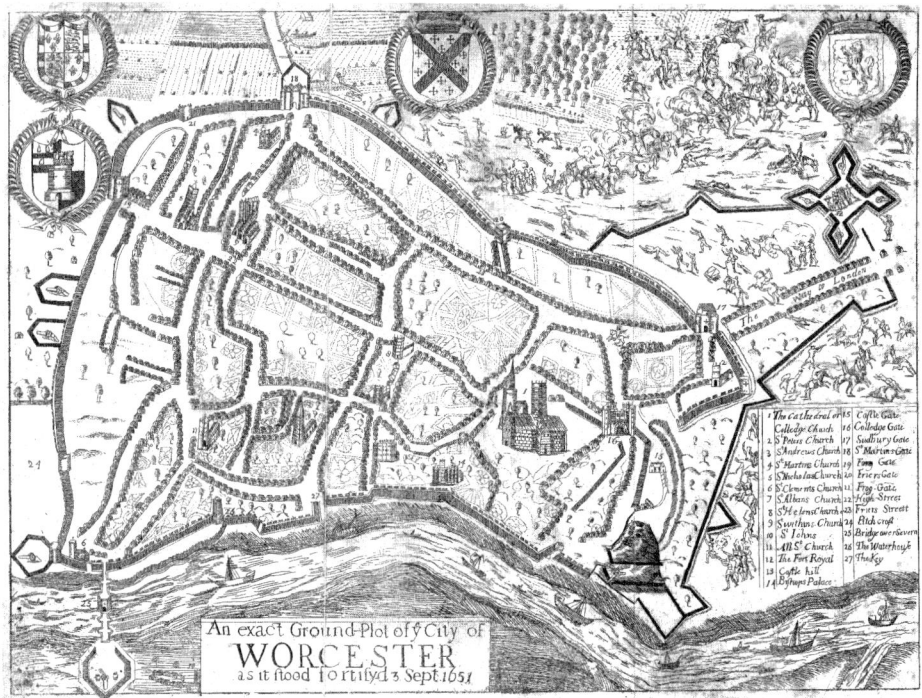

Plan of the defences of Worcester at the Battle of Worcester 1651, as published in 1660. The circuit of defences was probably complete by 1645, with Fort Royal rebuilt in 1651. Although the line of defences is correct, the bastions are not drawn to scale. (Worcester City Museum, with permission.)

The defensive plan

The defensive plan consisted initially of three main elements:

1. Strengthening of existing defences
2. Bastions
3. Clearance of the suburbs

Strengthening of existing defences

The existing medieval defences of stone wall and ditch were strengthened. The intention was to line the stone walls with thick banks of earth to deaden cannon shot. But Townshend, writing of the siege of 1646, complained that this had still not been completed. The castle motte was also refortified in 1643, with stockades and terracing to produce fire traps and a guard room on the top. It is shown in the plan of 1660 as having artillery mounted there within a small sconce. The main medieval gates of Foregate, St Martin's Gate, Sidbury Gate and Bridge Gate were probably the

Recording of the medieval city wall of Worcester during construction of City Walls Road. The medieval city walls were refurbished in the Civil War, with a bank of soil built-up behind to help deaden the cannon shot. The walls were largely demolished in 1652. (Photograph by J. Bennett.)

strongest surviving elements of the former defence, with gateways flanked by stone towers. The 1660 plan shows that Sidbury Gate was flanked by three-storied towers. Additional structures were simpler postern gates and five stone bastion towers.

The best evidence of the physical scale of the main defences now comes from archaeological sections of the city ditches. On the north side at The Butts, evidence was found for the recutting of the medieval ditch, to form a ditch over 16 m wide and at least 3.5 m deep. Apart from its sheer scale, it is likely that further obstructions would have been created by the use of 'storm-poles' – sharpened stakes projecting from the rampart or set at an angle within the ditch – to hinder advancing troops. The ditch was 5.5 m outside the line of the city wall and there was some evidence to suggest that the ground level between ditch and wall had been dramatically reduced, possibly as part of the operation of clearing tenements that were known to have been built against the city wall prior to the war.[7]

Reference was made in 1643 to scouring out the ditches, but the work on restoring the city defences appears not to have been completed. There was no evidence from the Bowling Green Terrace excavation of 1967–9 to suggest that the ditch on the east side had been cleaned out or recut in the period, despite orders to 'cleanse and scour' the ditch in 1638.[8]

Bastions

In line with seventeenth-century military planning, four-sided bastions comprising earthen ramparts with ditches were progressively added to the north and east sides of the city, linked to the existing circuit of stone walls, and are shown (not to scale) on the plan of 1660, probably having been completed by 1646. At some stage, a bastion may also have been constructed at the St John's side of the Severn crossing, as shown on the 1660 plan. St Martin's sconce, outside St Martin's Gate on the north-east side, is specifically referred to in the accounts of the siege of 1646. The straight line of a defence on the south side, with two bastions, was part of a new addition during the war. The outline of the bastion built below the castle can still be detected on the south side of Frog Lane.

These bastions were a rudimentary form of a Dutch style of defence whose ideal was to provide a platform for enfilading (crossing) fire for musketry and artillery which could rake along the whole line of the defence. The simplified version used at Worcester (and elsewhere in the Civil War) was designed to provide some limited flanking fire and to protect the medieval gates. The earth ramparts were more effective at deadening cannon shot than were the existing stone defences, built for warfare of a different age. A possible ditch associated with a bastion at Farrier Street on the north side of the town was excavated in 1990.[9] Although on the correct alignment for one of the bastions shown in the 1660 plan, this ditch with a stepped profile was only 2 m wide and survived to a depth of only 0.7 m. This is too small a scale for a usual Civil War ditch but may conceivably represent merely the truncated bottom of a much larger feature or outer defence. Its fill contained sixteenth- and seventeenth-century building materials, possibly reflecting clearance after the Civil War.[10]

The bastion beside the Friar's Gate on the east side was known as 'the blockhouse'. It was built in 1643 using lime worth £11 13s 9d. Outside it, the marshy ground could be turned into a bog by damming up the Frog Brook if necessary.[11] This 'blockhouse', along with the newly defended Castle Mound, was described by Sir Samuel Luke as the main strong point of the city in 1643.

Clearance of the suburbs

In April 1643 Hereford fell to Waller, and the garrison at Worcester became understandably nervous. The city was briefly under siege in May of that year. This experience provided one important lesson – the need to maintain a clear field of fire outside the defences even at the expense of demolishing houses. On 13 June 1643 reference is made to houses of Mrs Fleet which had been pulled down to make way for the fortifications. On 30 October 1643 a visit was organized by the Council to inspect the site of the demolition of houses belonging to the town clerk, Francis Street, outside Sidbury Gate; he was awarded 20 marks in compensation.[12]

This process continued throughout the war. In June 1645 arrangements were made to rehouse the almsmen in Mr Inglethorpe's almshouse when it was pulled down for the fortifications.[13] This would have been traumatic for the residents – and also for those who were then expected to provide temporary accommodation. There are numerous references in the survey made in 1649 to houses 'Burnt down by the cavalleers' which reflects this clearance. The entries are concentrated within the parish of St Nicholas in Foregate and Northgate Street, but also in Cripplegate, Wennall Street and across the river within St John's in Hilton Lane.[14] On Cripplegate was the property of Humphrey and William Downe 'which house was burnt by the Cavaleers, and nothing remains but the plot of ground'.[15] St Thomas More's charity also suffered. The introduction to its rental of 1670 states 'all the houses without St Martyns Gate were Burned Down and Destroyed in the tymes of the Late unhappy warr'. Only one house, in the High Street, was said to have survived.[16] The Vaughan map of the defences in 1651 shows the suburbs as having been completely cleared, although this may be an oversimplification. One man at least was able to think ahead to save his property: in June 1645 Thomas Vale asked his landlord (the City Council) for permission to dismantle his house and rebuild it elsewhere – one advantage of a timber-framed building![17] Not all of this destruction was unwelcome. The mill on the north side of Frog Lane, outside the Frog Gate and adjacent to the old defences surrounding the castle, was demolished in 1643 and its millpond allowed to dry up, removing a source of noxious pollution flowing from the city ditch, and the inhabitants of the parish resisted subsequent attempts to rebuild the mill.

A new line of defence

Work on strengthening the fortifications of the city went on throughout the war and included a wholly new line of defence on the east and south sides in *c.* 1644–5. Dudley claimed that the work carried out in 1643 on rebuilding the city walls and fortifications was under his direction; but it was Sir William Russell who sent to Bewdley for stone and timber to make new drawbridges, including one inserted into the bridge over the Severn by demolishing the central span. The work did not go smoothly. One (otherwise unconfirmed) story tells of the engineer and workmen being beaten up by Colonel Sandys men. If true, it is a further example of the tensions and jealousies between the leaders of the garrison. The work was not completed, and a considerable amount of further construction was undertaken in 1644 at the instigation of Prince Rupert. The details of the work are not recorded but it all clearly demanded tremendous organization. On 19 February 1644, Prince Rupert ordered 300 workmen to be provided every day to work on the fortifications, with the city divided into six to maintain a rota. Every householder was directed to work on the defences in his turn or pay a fine of 1*s* a day. Each man was to bring his own spade, shovel or pickaxe.[18] A similar order was repeated in

August, with High Ward and St Nicholas's Ward working on Monday, St Martin's and St Peter's on Tuesday, All Saints and St Clement's on Thursday and St Andrew's on Friday. Mr Gatten was paid £10 on 22 August 1645 as the engineer for the fortifications.[19] This effort was probably concentrated on the new defence lines on the east and south sides. We can imagine what that work entailed: without the benefit of machinery they had to clean-out and re-dig the defence ditches up to 3.5 m deep. They scraped up or quarried soil to line the backs of the defences and build new ramparts, and filled large wicker baskets ('gabions') with soil and stones to protect cannon emplacements.

The new defence constructed after 1643 to the east and south was built in order to protect the London Road suburb, command the high ground and regularize the derelict medieval defences on the south side. It incorporated a sconce built at the site of later Fort Royal to command Red Hill and the London Road. This may have been the 'small workes' built in October 1642 but later described as the 'great sconce' visited by Colonel Rainsborough after the siege of 1646.[20] The hill on which Fort Royal was built was only 200 m from the South Gate, which it overlooked, and it would have been extremely dangerous to leave such a strategic position undefended.

The original sconce was now linked in to the rest of the city by an impressive new earthwork joining the medieval city defences south of Friar's Gate on one side and an earthwork on the south side extending to the River Severn and enclosing Castle Hill. The bastioned lines may have made use of the outflow from the former Frog Mill (demolished 1643), running off the Frog Brook. On the south side, the end bastion, on the south side of Frog Lane, was planned in Young's map of 1779 and is still visible on the site of the Bowling Green. The 1966 excavations on the King's School site on Severn Street (below the castle), recovered a section across the defence ditch. Further work was undertaken to the west in 1991. A large U-shaped ditch, 8–10 m wide × 2.4 m deep was found running east to west, with some evidence for a classic seventeenth-century layout. The bulk of the fills appeared to have been pushed in from the city side, suggesting that this material had originated from the main rampart. A line of post-holes on the outer edge may have been to retain a glacis bank or outer rampart, and a pebble surface represents an intervening, narrow, covered way. Musketeers would have tried to protect the outer line of the defences from here until their position became untenable and they were forced to retreat inside the main earthworks. There was some slight evidence of the inner bank, which may have been up to 7–8 m high originally, provided with a fire step to protect musketeers.[21]

In 1972, an excavation on City Walls Road revealed a dump of made-up ground against the city wall, at the junction of the earthwork leading from the later Fort Royal to the city defences. This may have been the vestigial remains of the earthwork. Parts of the lower courses of the city wall contained traces of sockets which were then interpreted as possibly having held timbers for the framework of a breastwork over the junction of the two defensive lines, although this now seems more doubtful.[22]

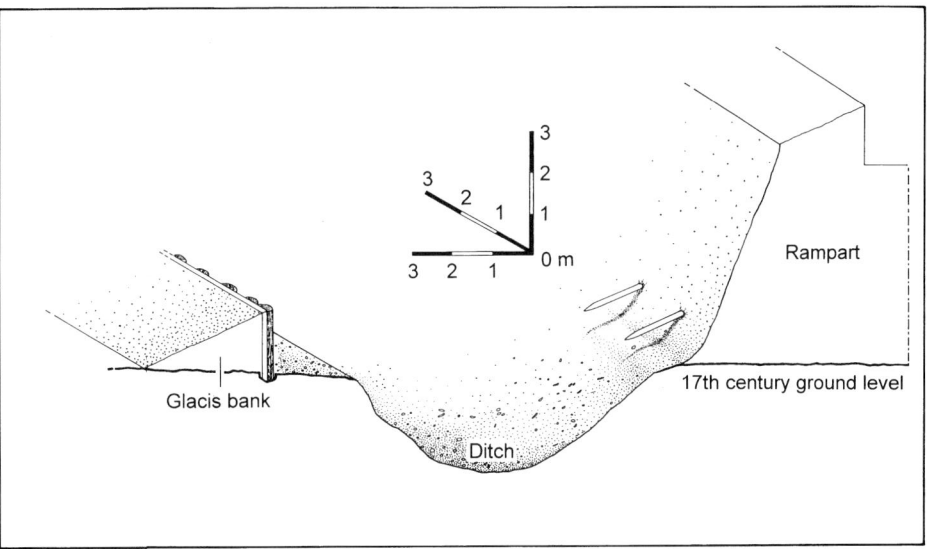

The defences of Worcester were rapidly refurbished 1642–6. The work was started by the Parliamentary garrison and completed by the Royalists when they occupied the city. Excavation of a section on the south defences at King's School, Severn Street in 1966 revealed the 8–10 m wide and 2.4 m deep ditch and important evidence for what has here been interpreted as an outer 'glacis' bank. 'Storm poles' have been shown protruding from the bank as a common additional defence on such works. (Reconstruction based on a section by P. Barker.)

Within this defensive circuit, the old motte or castle mound was re-fortified with a star-shaped sconce on the top (to carry artillery) with the sides protected with storm poles. A terrace was made on the mound to cover the lines of defence east and west.[23] In addition, between July and September 1645 a new drawbridge was made for the bridge to St John's, probably connected to a new bridgehead defence (as shown on the plan of 1660).

All were expected to play their part in these efforts to protect the city. After the withdrawal of Waller in May 1643, the women of Worcester played a notable role in helping protect against a future siege. According to Henry Townshend:

the ordinary sort of women out of every ward within the city joined in companies and with colours and drums striking up with spades, shovels, and mattocks did begin to work on Tuesday last, the 30th day of June, who were to the number of 400 on a day, going in a warlike manner like soldiers, and did so behave themselves there in levelling all such fortifications as were left by the Earl of Essex, and throwing down ditches, that by their own industry and free service . . . as they within one week perfected the levelling of the same . . . .

The work included the uprooting of 'all the trees, hedges, mounds and fences which might prejudice the City and help and succour the assailants or enemies and likewise all Houses or buildings be immediately plucked down and levelled'.[24]

In 1645, Richard Symonds described how Prince Maurice built an additional defence outside the main ditch on the north-east (Droitwich) side. Extra protection was needed here because the ditch was not water-filled as on the rest of the circuit. The new work was described as 'a low breast work, and a stockade without: the top of the breast work is not a foot about the ground outside. Very necessary to safeguard a dry ditch and wall'.[25] This probably refers to the addition of a sloping glacis bank on the outer edge of the main ditch, in order to provide an extra depth to the ditch.

Last ditch defences, 1646

Despite all this effort, the defences were still not completed by the time of the siege of 1646. Townshend complained that the city walls had only been lined to a thickness of 6 ft (1.8 m) on the bottom, rather than the 15–20 ft (4.5–6 m) thickness to the top as recommended, and including a firing step to the rear. Defences had to be made during the siege itself. One inner defence – literally a 'last ditch' defence – was made behind The Cross. Another stockade was built between Castle Hill and 'Mr Hall's garden wall thrown up to stop the Enemy's passage if he should force the line'.[26] The defences on the bridge were also improved during the siege, with the side walls raised in brick to provide better protection for musketeers and the incorporation of gun loops.

One addition to the defences during the siege was made at St Clement's sconce and between St Clement's Church and Foregate, behind The Butts on the north side of the town. Documentary evidence for 23 July 1646 identifies the construction of a 30 yd (27.4 m) long defence stated as being between St Clement's and Foregate, on the brow of the hill, consisting of a 15 ft (4.5 m) high barricade or 'blind' made of poles, rafters, roof trusses, etc., with the spaces filled with earth and horse manure.[27] Its purpose was to 'prevent the enemy's clearing the wall from their works at St John's, No-one being able to stand on the walls'. This therefore appears to have been intended to act as a shield to block the line of fire from across the river along the length of the north defences. As such, its axis must have been north to south rather than east to west as stated. An explanation for this discrepancy comes from archaeological work carried out inside the line of the north medieval defences on Blackfriars in 1985. A large ditch, aligned east to west and 6 m wide and 1.6 m deep, was found, containing some human remains; remains of an associated rampart survived to a height of 1.7 m, including the post-holes for a surmounting palisade. This is almost certainly the works described by Townshend as lying between St Clement's and Foregate, behind The Cross. Townshend appears to have conflated the construction of a north to south 'blind' (running off St Clement's sconce) and this east to west inner defence line. The ditch appears to have been quickly backfilled after the siege with material pushed in from the rampart of the main defences to the north, leading to disappointingly few finds being contained within the fills.[28] This is not

Defensive ditch dating to the siege of 1646, excavated on Blackfriars, Worcester in 1985. During the siege, an inner line of defence – literally a 'last ditch' – was created inside the line of the north defences. A section was cut through this ditch in 1985, showing it to be 6 m wide × 1.6 m deep. (Scale in half metres.)

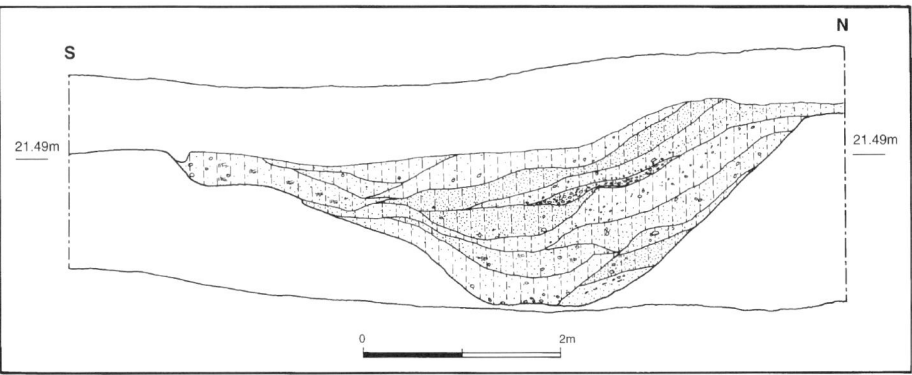

Drawn section through the Blackfriars defences, showing the layers of rampart and rubbish pushed back into the ditch.

View of Fort Royal from the cathedral. This may have originated as a defensive work during the First Civil War but was certainly built in its present form in 1651. It was built to command the east approaches to the city but was itself overlooked by the hills to the east. The fort was stormed during the battle of 1651 and its guns then turned upon the city.

unusual: in general, most finds from within such features do not date from their actual period of operation but rather from their subsequent abandonment, when many were used over a considerable period as convenient rubbish tips.

Fort Royal

The impending arrival of Charles II and the Scottish army in 1651 caused a feverish attempt to renovate the defences (ordered to have been levelled only in the previous year) and this work was continued by the Scots themselves. They only occupied the city for eleven days, but the major new addition to the defences was a rebuilding of what has been suggested as the 'Great Sconce' of the First Civil War as Fort Royal to command the eastern approaches to the city. The shape of this four-sided fort can still be seen within Fort Royal Park, although the corner bastions have been softened and rounded off as part of garden landscaping. Eighteenth-century plans show an outer defence line on the east side, including a small diamond-shaped bastion. The line of this became the road of Fort Royal Hill. Men from Ripple were commandeered to help build the fort in 1651 (still unfinished at the time of the September battle), and six months later were recalled to level it!

Siegeworks

Less detail has survived for the scale and form of any siegeworks that would have been used to help blockade and assault Worcester during its sieges of 1643, 1646 and the battle of 1651.

The 1643 siege only lasted two days and was too short for any sort of proper emplacements, as the anxious Waller tried to take the city by direct assault or storm. The accounts of the longer siege of 1646 do, however, contain a number of references to defence 'lines' and trenches as the Parliamentary army tried a more cautious assault. There would have been a rudimentary system of communication trenches and other positions hidden behind hedgerows linking camps and artillery positions. The cannon were set within earth-banked emplacements or were shielded by large stone- or earth-filled baskets or gabions. A great deal of this work seems to have been undertaken by labourers commandeered from surrounding villages. Other troops were quartered well to the rear, and forges would also have been set up to replenish ammunition and equipment. If Worcester had not surrendered, it is likely that the city would have been approached by a series of zigzag trenches or 'saps' that would have been extended out from the surrounding trench lines to provide the basis for a final assault, supported by advanced artillery positions. Excavation elsewhere has shown such trenches to be *c.* 1.2 m deep and 1 m wide.[29] In the final stages, mines may have been used to blow up the defences. Fortunately for both sides, the city surrendered before such an attack had to be mounted. According to contemporary theory, there should also have been a 'line of circumvallation' facing outwards from the city to protect the besiegers in case they were attacked by a relieving force, but this was only rarely carried out in practice and the circumstances in 1646 made such a precaution unnecessary (the Royalist field army having already been destroyed).

Prior to the battle of 1651, Cromwell's army quickly built encampments and artillery positions on the lower slopes and summit of Red Hill and Perry Wood, but this was not to be a long drawn out siege of occasional bombardment and negotiation as was that of 1646. This was a much more mobile battle as the Royalist positions were overrun and turned during one day's bitter fighting. Consequently, there is little surviving evidence of this enormous army of 30,000 men camped around the city. The features popularly identified as 'Cromwell's Trenches' at Perry Wood are part of a former natural stream course, although it is likely that a battle developed along its length as the most easy access to the gun positions at the edge of the wood, when Hamilton attacked on 3 September. There is better evidence for an artillery emplacement further to the north-west, off Tamar Close (270 m to the south-east of Shrub Hill Station): it is a rectangular enclosure, 73 m × 82 m, with banks and ditches surviving on three sides, with the one towards the town having been backfilled and that side also protected by the steep slope of the hill. This side would originally also have been protected with gabions set between the cannon. Unfortunately, it is not possible to date the original construction of this definitely to either 1651 or, perhaps more likely, to 1646.

The defences after the Civil War

In 1652, Cromwell ordered the city walls to be levelled, so that Worcester could no longer offer up any resistance to the state. The gates survived but were clearly in a very battered condition and were later restored. It took four weeks to repair the Fore Gate and £50 was spent after the Restoration of Charles II on restoring Fore Gate, St Martin's Gate and Sidbury Gate.[30] They were finally demolished in the eighteenth century.

The surviving ditches soon became a health hazard as they filled up with stagnant water and it was normal to use them as convenient refuse tips. Indeed, plague broke out in the crowded city during 1644–5. On 6 February 1645 it was agreed to spend £35 11*s* 8*d* in bringing the water from Barbourne Brook into the town ditch, 'for the keeping sweet of that watercourse'.[31] It is likely that the inner defences were backfilled quite quickly as they would have been particularly inconvenient, and this was suggested by the thick homogeneous fills pushed into the ditch excavated at Blackfriars. But the lowest fills of the ditch excavated at The Butts in 1992 dated to the late seventeenth century, suggesting that it had remained open for some time and had been used as a rubbish tip.[32] The fills contained chicken, fish, eel and horse bones, together with charred cereals.

Map of 1795 showing the plan of Fort Royal and part of the east defences of the city, after the map of 1660. Note the additional defence just to the east of Fort Royal. The line of this ditch became Fort Royal Hill. The sconce built on top of the castle mound is also shown.

CHAPTER SIX

UNDER ATTACK: 1644

Royalists under pressure

The year began with Royalist control of Worcestershire being probed along its north, south and east borders. To the east was the Parliamentary garrison of Warwick, to the north-west the garrison of Bridgnorth and to the south that of Gloucester. The latter, under Colonel Massey, also tried to block access up the supply artery of the River Severn, using a frigate. In January 1644 he seized a ship laden with wine, tobacco and ammunition, essential supplies destined for the Worcester garrison.[1] The Royalists were under pressure, especially after Prince Rupert drew off troops from the garrisons to meet the new threat of a Scottish army in the north of England. As a consequence, they had difficulty in drawing together enough troops from their garrisons to meet the cut and thrust of the raids from the surrounding Parliamentary garrisons. Parliamentary news-sheets gleefully (and probably with some exaggeration) reported increasing unrest in the county, claiming that Worcester had called for the expulsion of its garrison.[2] The Royalists did certainly encounter increasing problems in trying to recruit men from the county, and the garrisons of Hereford and Worcester both resorted to pressing men forcibly. An order was given to impress 267 men from the county in March.[3] Symonds estimated in June 1644 that the Royalist forces in the county amounted

A royal mint was established in Worcester in May 1644 and there may have been another mint at Hartlebury. The reverse of this coin bears the county privy mark of three pears and HC for Hartlebury Castle. (County Museum, Hartlebury, with permission.)

to 3,000–4,000 men. An idea of the problems that were faced comes from the attempt of Sir William Russell in April 1644 to raise new regiments of horse and foot from the county; 400 subsequently deserted for lack of pay.

A new impetus was clearly needed in the Royalist camp, still wracked by the squabbles of the previous year between Sir William Russell on one hand and the commissioners and Colonel Samuel Sandys on the other. The new governor from December 1643, Sir Gilbert Gerrard, had found the Worcester garrison reduced to only 200 men and described as 'slovenly and inefficient'. He tried to force Worcester to pay an earlier promise of £2,000, to the great resentment of the city.[4] Prince Rupert took charge of the area in February 1644 and held a council of leading officers at Bewdley (which cost Bewdley Corporation £5 11s 8d in providing refreshments, including a hogshead of claret for Prince Rupert, bottles of sack and claret for Lord Herbert and a quart of sack and claret for Colonel Sandys).[5] He then began a programme to overhaul the administration and military, trying to resolve the conflict between troop numbers and money to pay them. This programme tried to *reduce* the number of troops in the county to 2,000 foot and 500 horse – but *raised* the monthly levy to £4,000 for a period of three months. He did, however, offer the concession that half the amount could be supplied in kind. The contribution of each parish was to be assigned to one of the garrisons of Worcester, Evesham or Hartlebury; free-quarter was to be abolished and plunderers were to be executed. He also commanded a new programme of fortification for Worcester, now defended by Gerrard's regiment of foot and the Town regiment under Martin Sandys. This was not to prove enough, and further change to the military establishment was to come later in the year. The system of contributions also proved to be an inadequate basis on which to finance the war, and in May the Excise Tax was imposed on Worcester.

The war became a deadly game of chess as the parties manoeuvred for position. The ruthlessness of the Parliamentary raiding parties caused complaints even among their most ardent supporters. Colonel John Fox wrote self-righteously of 'the many complaints of the country, by reason of Lord Denbigh's new garrisons exacting provisions, pillaging and issuing warrants for money in Lord Denbigh's name . . .'. There was no love lost between the two men. The property of no-one – friend or foe – was safe as the armies of both sides were driven by want of regular pay and supply to provision themselves by any means. In June 1644 Lord Denbigh, with Waller's army raging over the county in pursuit of Charles, was forced to order 'all commanders in the service of the king and Parliament to forbear to plunder the cloth in the fulling mills in Kidderminster and Hartlebury, belonging to Robert Willmott, treasurer for the Committee for the County of Stafford'. When Waller passed through Kidderminster in June 1644 he found it 'little better than an empty farm'.[6]

A new force on the Parliamentary side had entered the fray from December 1643 – John 'Tinker' Fox, a Parliamentary leader whose audacity was to rival even that of Colonel Massey in Gloucester. Fox was probably a swordsmith, although disparagingly called a 'tinker' by the Royalists. After Prince Rupert had sacked Birmingham in April 1643, the local population had rallied to the Parliamentary cause, with Fox becoming their leader. Despite his lack of experience, he was now given command of a regiment of 800 cavalry, with his son as major. Fox commanded by virtue of his strong personality, once writing to Lord Denbigh 'I cannot leave my men to wait on your Lordship, for fear of mutiny and general departure'. He seized Edgbaston and then began to raid all over north Worcestershire. Fox also set up a new garrison at Stourton under his brother, which was soon put under siege by the Royalists. Edward Broade, from near Kidderminster, tried to drum up local reinforcements for the Royalist force. He was later accused, in 1651, that he 'sollicited and earnestly pressed the country thereabout to rise together and go along with the said Sir Gilbert Gerrard'. The consequences were to be dire if they refused 'telling and threatening divers of the country people that they should be hanged at their own doors if they would not go with him against the said castle'.[7] In an abortive attempt to relieve Stourton, 'Tinker' Fox's men were 'piteouly bang'd' on Stourbridge Heath by Prince Rupert's men and the garrison surrendered. Fox also established another garrison at Hawkesley House, north of Bromsgrove (where he was accused of demolishing the church to build new defences).

In April, Fox launched a daring plan to take Bewdley and capture the governor, the royal favourite, Sir Thomas Lyttleton. The Royalist garrison consisted of at least 120 men and had already been under some pressure – four soldiers were buried

Eighteenth-century engraving of Bewdley. Bewdley occupied a strategic position as a bridging point on the Severn, at the point where cargoes were transferred from larger vessels into the smaller craft that journeyed into Wales. During the Civil War it was only defended by a gatehouse on the bridge, and by chains drawn across the roads. The Royalist troops housed here, and the royal favourite, Sir Thomas Lyttleton, were captured in an audacious raid by 'Tinker' Fox in April 1644.

there during March. Its main defence was the River Severn, the crossing guarded by a gatehouse on the five-arched stone bridge. Fox rode there from Edgbaston with sixty troopers, who on arrival pretended to be stragglers from Rupert's army (then on the march from Shrewsbury to Oxford).[8] They were allowed across the bridge and rode up to where a chain had been drawn across the main road. Again, the Royalists let them pass. Fox then divided his men to capture the sentries, and put guards on the billets of the garrison. Having isolated the defenders, he made each billet surrender in turn – all without giving a warning to the governor who was housed in the adjacent Tickenhill Palace. Fox was consequently able to ride there and take Lyttleton in his bed! The raiding party then escaped with their prisoners and booty (including forty-four horses) to Coventry.

To the south, Massey managed to take Ledbury. The Parliamentary plan was that, while so threatening the area to the south-west of Worcester, Lord Denbigh would simultaneously march on Worcester from Warwickshire, thus forcing the Royalists to divide their attentions. As expected, this caused panic in Worcester. Parliamentary news-sheets taunted the citizens as being ignorant – 'poore in purse as barren in knowledge' and even the governor, Sir Gilbert Gerrard, complained that many of its citizens were 'very base'.[9] There were evident fears as to the loyalty of the citizens under pressure, and the strains were intensified by an influx of refugees from the countryside and by the interruption of trade with London. Banned from trading with London since July 1643, the Worcester clothiers successfully petitioned the king in June 1644 to be allowed to resume their trade, but this was to be to no avail. The first wagon load of cloth was intercepted by Royalist troops, with 'His Majesties protection made only a stalking horse for their Insolencies and Robberies'.[10]

The military situation was saved by the arrival of Prince Rupert's army at Evesham which, by threatening a pincer movement in concert with Colonel Mynne at Newent to cut Massey off from his base at Gloucester, forced Massey to withdraw. The crisis over, Rupert then withdrew to Shrewsbury. To prevent the same situation arising again, the Royalists decided to establish a new garrison at Tewkesbury as a buffer to protect the county, but this once again proved to be too far out on a limb, and Tewkesbury was dramatically stormed by Massey on 4 June – the eighth time that the town had changed hands during the war.

Cat and mouse in the county

Meanwhile, in May the Parliamentary armies of Waller and Essex had been trying a pincer movement on the Royalist capital of Oxford. The king escaped the trap and, on 5 June, retreated across the River Avon into Evesham with an army of around 7,000 men and a baggage train including thirty carriages carrying the ladies of the court and their luggage. The army was tracked by a somewhat reluctant Waller who halted at Broadway. With good reason (remembering Ripple), Waller regarded Worcestershire as bringing him only bad luck. For the county, these events meant that the next month was taken up by a zigzag progress of both armies through it.

Charles arrived at Evesham the day after Massey had taken Tewkesbury. As a consequence, Charles was vulnerable to attack on his flanks (Massey from the south and Denbigh from the north) and the loyalty of the people of Evesham was also questionable. Apart from resentment at now having to feed the king's army as well as its garrison of 550 men, there was still considerable resentment at the level of Ship Money Tax that the town had been forced to pay in 1636 – it was among the nine highest rated towns in the country. Reflecting the overwhelming concern from most people to preserve normal economic life during the war, in 1643 there had been complaints that the presence of the Royalist field army had frightened people away from Evesham Fair. King Charles, therefore, withdrew further west to Pershore on the morning of 5 June, ordering the bridges across the Avon at Evesham and then Pershore to be destroyed behind him. The task was rushed at Pershore Bridge, so that around eighty of the local impressed workmen and forty soldiers were killed as the masonry collapsed with the men still on the bridge; it is perhaps noteworthy that Symonds does not bother to record the civilian losses.[11] The evidence of destruction can still be seen in the red sandstone patching of the widened central arch. One can imagine that this would do nothing to improve the area's sense of loyalty.

Charles reached Worcester on that night. The city was persuaded to advance him £1,000 and had to house and feed his army. Post-Restoration accounts suggest that King Charles was more impressed with the city's loyalty than Gerrard had been. Clarendon reported how, owing to the 'loyalty of that good town and the affection of the gentry of that county . . . he [King Charles] procured both shoes and stockings and money for his soldiers'.[12] But were the shoemakers and hosiers ever paid for this gesture? Was loyalty the motive for the gift, or fear of the newly arrived army? A Council of War attended by the king on 10 June tells a very different story. There, echoing the earlier fears of Sir Gilbert Gerrard, the Council was concerned as to the lack of recruits to the town regiment under Martin Sandys which 'doth not consist of any great number, nor is it proportionable to the greatness of this city'. The Council wished to double the number of recruits 'if the inhabitants would have putt themselves under that command for their own defence and preservation which seeming they have not already performed'. Martin Sandys was ordered to call up all men of an age to bear arms and 'signify to them that it is His Majesty's express pleasure and command that every of them list themselves to his regiment'. Any that refused were to be expelled from the city or arrested.[13] Worcester had now been given additional importance. Sir Thomas Cary had been authorized to establish a coin mint in the city on 22 May and Worcester may well have been the main Royalist mint in the region.[14] Despite repeated efforts, much still needed to be done on the Worcester fortifications, and King Charles ordered a further repair of the defences, involving the demolition of all the houses on North Street.

The king diverted some of his troops from Worcester on 10 June to try to lift a new siege of his men at Dudley Castle. This siege had been launched by Lord Denbigh with an army of 3,500 men (and a 32 lb cannon called the 'Stafford Great

Dudley Castle. Worcestershire troops were sent by the king to help relieve the Parliamentary siege of Dudley Castle in 1644. The castle was finally captured in 1646 and was partly demolished. (Dudley Metropolitan Borough Council.)

Piece') at the time that Charles had reached Evesham. There was a fierce battle and the Royalist cavalry under Colonel Wilmot were forced to retire to Bewdley and Stourbridge. Although the rescue attempt was unsuccessful in immediate terms, the Royalist effort caused sufficient damage to Denbigh's troops to force the latter to withdraw a few days later. Denbigh wrote to the Committee of Parliament on 15 June to complain that his men were now ready to disband for want of pay and arms.[15] The Royalists could not rest on their laurels and the castle was quickly repaired in preparation for expected further assaults.

On 12 June, Charles left Worcester for Oxford, having first given Governor Gerrard additional powers to help him defend the city, including more power to command over the disgruntled civilian commissioners, but his march was not to be straightforward. In the meantime, the rebellious citizens of Evesham had rushed to repair their bridge so as to allow the army of William Waller to pass over it. Clarendon described how 'the evil inhabitants received him [Waller] with willingness'. Waller had stayed there on 11–12 June and requisitioned further horses from Pershore as remounts.[16] Charles therefore decided to travel by a circuitous route to throw Waller off the scent. He stayed at Bewdley from 13 to 14 June at Tickenhill Manor. Two shillings were spent on ringing the bells to welcome him. For his part, Waller marched to Bromsgrove and, leaving the infantry there, sent the cavalry on to Kidderminster to watch the Bridgnorth road for signs of the king moving northwards. Others went to Stourbridge. There was some skirmishing between the opposing forces, and a number of officers (including Lieutenant-Colonel Stamford) were taken at Kidderminster.[17] The parish register for St Mary's, Kidderminster, records how they buried two soldiers on 15 and 21 June. But Charles then tried a blind, described by a contemporary journalist as 'a dance beyond Worcester'. While sending some of his cavalry up to Bridgnorth as a diversion to send Waller's army northwards, he marched back to Worcester, demolishing Bewdley Bridge behind him. On 16 June, after a service in the cathedral, he headed back to a no doubt nervous Evesham. Pausing there only an hour or so, he forced the town to pay a fine of £200 and provide 1,000 pairs of shoes (at approximately 1s 4d–2s a pair) for their action in repairing their so-recently demolished bridge on Waller's behalf. He also took the mayor and some of the aldermen as prisoners to Oxford. Once again he tried to demolish the unhappy bridge and went to Broadway and thence by Campden to Stow-on-the-Wold and Burford. It had been a close-run thing for the king.

Meanwhile, Waller had occupied Bewdley, repaired the bridge, and then marched on to Droitwich.[18] The latter had recovered from the plundering of the previous year but now, on 17 June, Waller's men were quartered in the salt cellars where they became so dehydrated and 'grew so drie, that we drunke the Towne drie' – probably a convenient excuse to explain the drunken excesses of his men. The army evidently took the opportunity to make running repairs. The Constable of Droitwich was ordered to deliver six tanned hides and five white hides to the collarmaker of the Train of Artillery.[19] The commander of the latter was the Scot, John Wemyss 'Master Gunner of England', who had served in the Swedish army. The next day, Waller marched on to Worcester, where he tried a brief, token, show of force, but this was not intended to mark the start of a serious siege. Waller's priority was still to trail the Royalist army. He therefore almost immediately followed the Royalist army back to Pershore and Evesham (arriving there on 18 June). During the march, Symonds accused Waller's men of breaking the stained glass east window of Fladbury church, three miles north-west of Evesham. Waller levelled the Evesham defences (a ditch and bank built across the neck of the loop of the Avon) but in trying to demolish the bridge at Pershore there was, by account, a similar collapse to that which had so recently befallen the Royalists – this time sixty men were killed. More despair for the locality! Waller then marched to Tewkesbury, received some reinforcements from Gloucester and then went on to do battle at Cropredy, near Banbury (Oxon), on 29 June – where he was defeated. Worcestershire was, indeed, unlucky for him.

There was but a brief respite for the county. The victory at Cropredy meant that the king could now turn back into Worcestershire as part of his campaign to collect

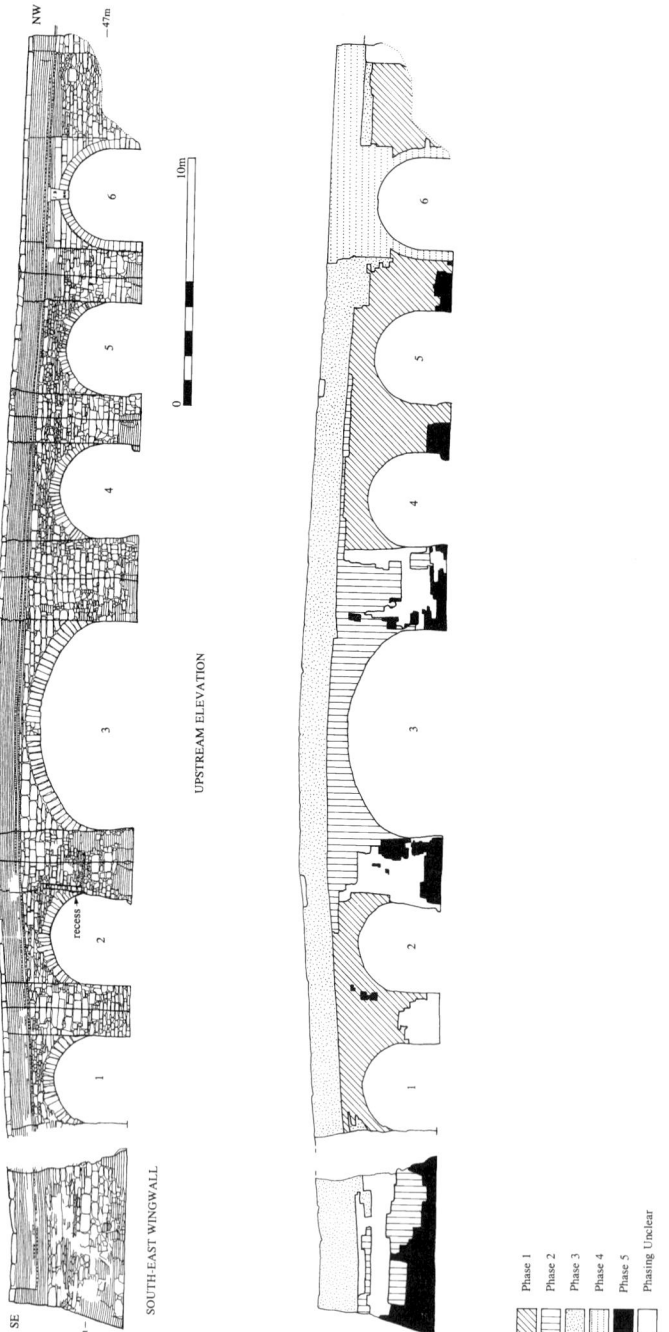

NW

—47m

UPSTREAM ELEVATION

10m

0

SE

47m —

SOUTH-EAST WINGWALL

Phase 1
Phase 2
Phase 3
Phase 4
Phase 5
Phasing Unclear

Elevation drawing of Pershore Bridge. The bridge collapsed in June 1644 during an attempt by the Royalists to demolish it. Up to 120 men may have been killed. The damage to the central arch is still recognizable in the different building materials used to repair it (phase 2).

View of Pershore Bridge from the north.

more recruits and supplies from Wales. He stayed at hard-pressed Evesham for nine days (to 13 July), residing at the house of Alderman Martin on the north side of Bridge Street (Langstone House). Many of his troops were billeted in and around Fladbury. This village must have been completely overwhelmed by the troops, who were regarded as much as foreigners as if they had come from another country. We can perhaps imagine them lounging around the village green or churchyard, after eating the villagers almost literally out of house and home and gazing upon the locals with mutual curiosity. Richard Symonds complained in his diary about the unseemly behaviour of the parson's wife in the village, 'a young woman often carrying a milk-payle on her head in the street, – so far from pride'.[20] One can also imagine the strain that feeding such an army put on the local village economy. The king had to send out for 10 tons of cheese from Bridgnorth to feed the troops. It was from Evesham that Charles made an abortive attempt at conciliation with Parliament, writing to try to find some means 'which by the blessing of God, may prevent the further effusion of blood, and restore the Nation to peace'. But this was all to no avail.

The strategic importance of Tewkesbury was well understood by both sides. Charles now tried to retake the town by siege. The plan was that troops from

Langstone House on Bridge Street, Evesham, where King Charles stayed for a period in July 1644.

Worcester would also secure the bridge at Upton so that he could then march with some security into Herefordshire and Wales, but the Worcestershire troops were defeated by Massey at Corse Lawn and so Upton Bridge fell instead into Parliamentary hands, thus blocking the king's line of march. Worse was to come. Massey could now move to relieve the Royalist siege of Tewkesbury. Rather than be caught in a possible pincer movement, Charles was forced to return to Evesham, his rearguard harried by Massey, and thence to Bath. Freed from the threat of the Royalist field army, Massey was now able to extend his operations and raided within four miles of Worcester. Colonel Mynne tried to relieve the pressure by countering with a march on Gloucester, hoping to take advantage of Massey's absence to take the city, or at least force Massey out of Worcestershire in order to defend his base, but the two forces met on 27 July at Redmarley on the Gloucestershire border and Mynne was killed. Part of the reason claimed for the defeat of the Royalists was that the contingent of troops ordered from Worcester arrived too late, otherwise the outcome might have been very different. As one of a number of similar, and possibly apocryphal stories from the war, the local inhabitants were described as having more urgent business in hand than matters of politics and therefore determinedly continued to gather in their harvest of wheat in the fields at Hazeldine while the battle raged. More definitely, entries in the parish register over the next week give testimony to the lingering effects of the fighting.

1644	Soldier slaine	9,	August 3.
	And more	5,	August 4.
	And	1,	August 6.
	And	2,	August 8.

Meanwhile, pressure was maintained from other directions. Lord Denbigh was keeping up the pressure on Worcestershire from the north-east. In August, Colonel Archer from Alcester (sixteen miles away) tried to capture the Commissioners of Array meeting at Sir Samuel Sandys' seat at Ombersley, six miles north of

Fladbury Church. Parliamentary troops were accused of breaking its east window. The village was later occupied by Royalist troops, when the vicar's wife was accused of being 'far from pride'.

In August, a raiding party from Alcester tried to capture the Royalist Commission of Array while it was meeting at the Sandys seat of Ombersley. The Kings Arms, Ombersley, is one of those places at which King Charles is reputed to have stopped for refreshment while being pursued by Parliamentary cavalry after the Battle of Worcester in 1651.

Worcester and four miles west of Droitwich. In the event, the latter were able to flee north to the nearby garrison at Hartlebury, presumably because they expected the route south to Worcester to have been blocked by the raiding party.[21]

The rise of parliamentary power

What enthusiasm there had been for the Royalist cause in the county was now definitely on the wane. There were still problems over providing pay and so from 22 July the number of troops had been further reduced to 1,000 foot and 400 horse, and the county was divided into districts to support them. Existing units were combined in an attempt to reduce the rivalries between the Royalist commanders. The cavalry was put under Samuel Sandys and the foot under Gilbert Gerrard, although Russell's men still appeared to remain aloof.[22] There were still further attempts to ban free-quarter and the situation was desperate enough for the military to buy support at almost any price. At the autumn session of the Grand Jury it was agreed that troops, unless marching through the county, could only be quartered in the garrisons or towns, and that county troops could remove 'any strange force' which quartered for more than a night on their march, and 'whensoever any soldiers, horse or foot shall commit any robbery or violence the County may rise upon them and bring them to justice'. If these conditions were not followed then the monthly contribution would cease.[23] In the event they were not obeyed but the contribution went on. In another attempt to keep the troops in order it was also stated that the men should be paid before the officers.

In August, Colonel Archer from Alcester reported how 'divers of Worcestershire offered to raise forces for the Parliament'.[24] Whether this was wishful thinking, a genuine response out of changed loyalties or simply an attempt to come to a clear outcome and rid the county of both armies is not clear. Parliament had tried to collect weekly assessments since February 1643, but from

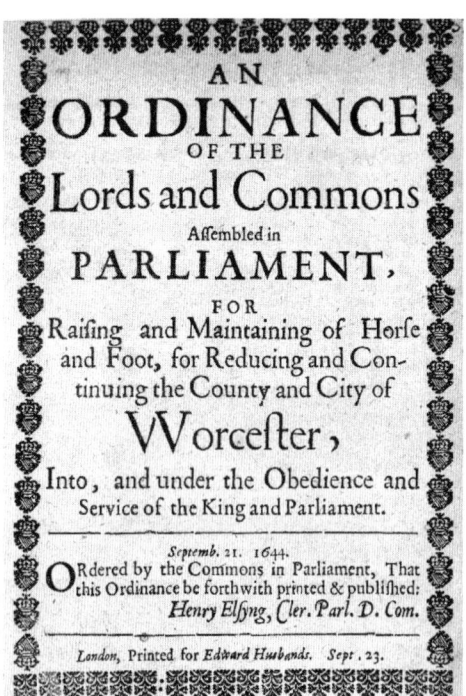

AN

ORDINANCE
OF THE
Lords and Commons
Affembled in
PARLIAMENT,
FOR
Raifing and Maintaining of Horfe and Foot, for Reducing and Continuing the County and City of

Worcefter,

Into, and under the Obedience and Service of the King and Parliament.

Septemb. 21. 1644.
ORdered by the Commons in Parliament, That this Ordinance be forthwith printed & publifhed:
Henry Elfyng, Cler. Parl. D. Com.

London, Printed for *Edward Hufbands. Sept.* 23.

Order for the raising of troops by Parliament in September 1644. Note the convention still being used that the army was required for 'Service of the King and Parliament', although they would actually be used against the Royalists. (Hereford and Worcester Record Office, with permission.)

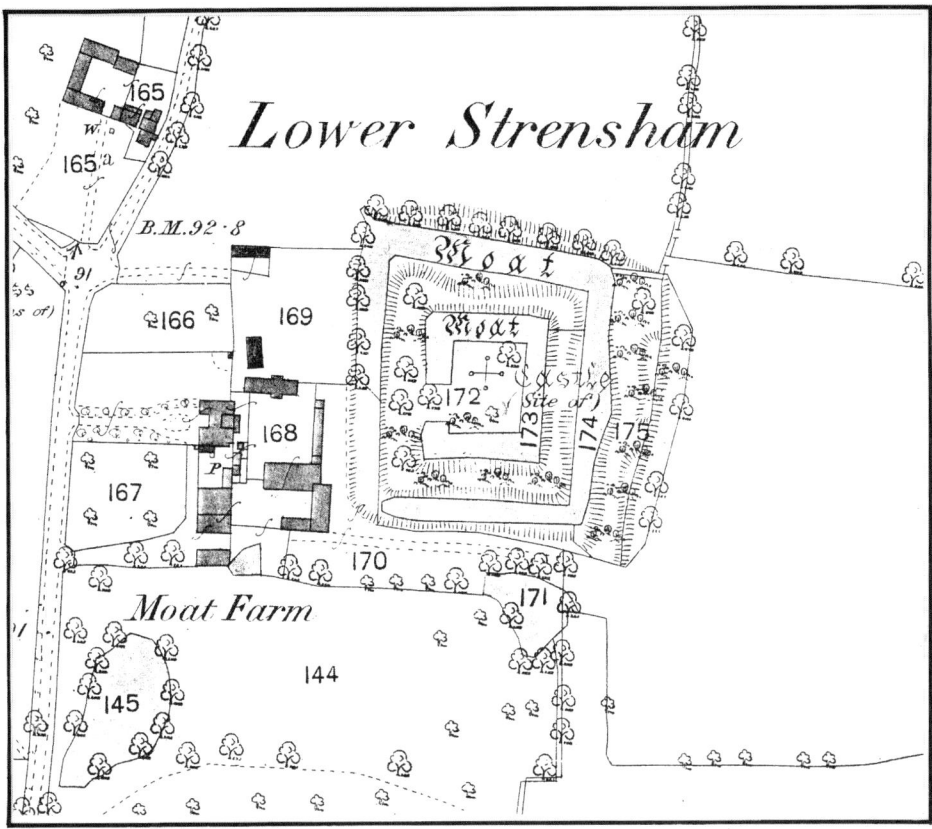

The medieval moated site at Strensham was converted into a small fort for the Royalist garrison. An additional rampart and ditch were added, with the rampart including artillery emplacements at the corners. (1st edn, Ordnance Survey map, 1885.)

September 1644 it felt confident enough to set up a new County Committee for Worcestershire. It was still forced to sit in Warwickshire until May 1645, when it moved to Evesham. Although it contained men of lesser status than its Royalist equivalent and only one JP, it now consisted mainly of Worcestershire men, including some important county names such as the Lechmere, Rous, Devereux and Salway families. It also contained representatives of burgesses and tradespeople such as Samuel Gardner and Edmund Young of Evesham and William Collins, a tanner of King's Norton.[25] It tried to increase the parliamentary assessment from the county to £3,000 and was authorized to raise 4,000 new troops. It is not clear how many men were actually recruited but, in October, one regiment of horse was raised by Colonel William Lygon and a regiment of foot by Colonel Edward Rous. On 8 October, Thomas Millward (possibly a Worcestershire man) was appointed to command a troop of horse under Thomas Archer and was then to take a very active role in events in the county, appearing later at Droitwich and Madresfield. Some troops were even raised from Worcester.

The warfare for the rest of the year now degenerated into a series of piratical raids from both sides, and there is a sense of rising exhaustion from the county. George Varney complained bitterly to Wilmot how his horses had been stolen first by Royalists and then by Parliamentarians.

> Besides all this, when the King's soldiers come to me they call me 'Roundhead,' 'Rogue,' and say I pay rent to the Parliament garrisons, and they will take it away from me. And, likewise, when the Parliament soldiers they reckon with me, and tell me I pay rent to Worcester and Winchester, therefore the Parliament soldiers say they will have the rest.[26]

A petition was sent to Parliament on 7 September complaining of the exactions of both sides, explaining how supporters had

> for the last two years been under the power of the enemy [Royalists], who have exacted large sums of money from the County, besides seizing cattle and horses without payment, Your petitioners have, besides, suffered at the hands of the Parliament forces, who in their inroads and requisitions make no distinction between the ill-affected and well-affected.[27]

Under an army of occupation, there was little that Worcester could do to show its frustration at the continuing war. The city was put under increasing strain by the refugees that continued to flock to its gates; in July it was described as 'abounding with people'. As a token of disenchantment, in 1644 Worcester defiantly elected Thomas Hacket as mayor, a man to whom the king had already objected (on the grounds that there were no objections to him locally). They went further. In December 1644, war-weary Worcestershire was discussing a joint petition with Shropshire for peace, to be delivered to king and Parliament. But this was actually part of a carefully manipulated royalist-inspired 'peace' movement that was designed to encourage more popular support for the king.

The Royalist Association

The king sought to channel the clear frustration in the county in favour of a defence of law and order against the Parliamentary raiding parties. He encouraged the formation of a new Association of neighbouring counties which, it was hoped, would be better able to mobilize local forces against Parliament and create a better general state of active opinion in favour of the Royalists. The particular advantage to King Charles was that this force would be prepared to serve anywhere within the bounds of the Association (Worcestershire, Herefordshire, Monmouthshire, Shropshire and Staffordshire) and avoid the usual parochial interests of the existing militias.

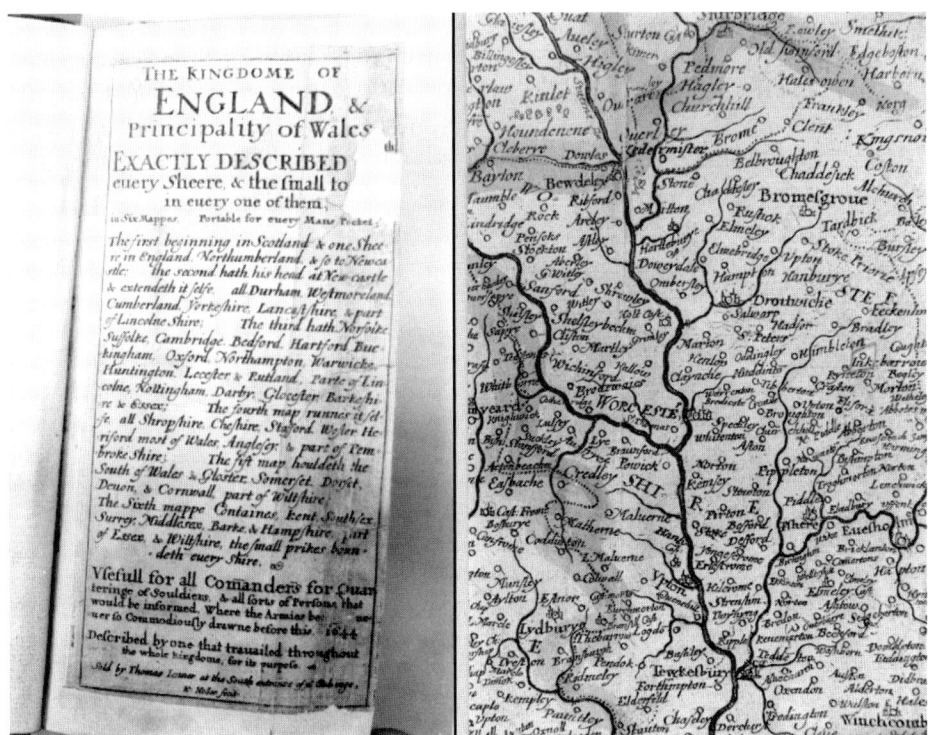

A book of maps (printed 1644) produced specifically for army officers and left by King Charles I at Inkberrow vicarage, when he stayed there on the night of 10 May 1645. (By permission of the vicar of Inkberrow and Hereford and Worcester Record Office.)

The possibilities were seen differently by the various interested groups. The local gentry had their own agenda and saw this as a means of wresting back control of local forces from the military. The Association was therefore to be appointed by the Quarter Sessions. The Association offered serious criticisms of the military: 'For the soldier assumes a liberty to rapine and violence . . . our fortifications neglected, our frontiers laid waste, And in the most inward parts of the County no man's person secured'.[28] The gentry of the Association were to be responsible for raising a new militia, officered by local men and subject to common (not martial) law. They further wanted exemption from free-quarter, the right to check for fraudulent muster rolls from the garrisons and a ban on garrison commanders making levies on the surrounding countryside. The Commissioner Henry Townshend was made muster-master to assist the sheriff in taking a monthly muster of the troops to ensure that accurate accounts were being presented by the officers. He was also assigned the duty of reporting on the state of the Worcester magazine to the Quarter Sessions.[29]

Unfortunately, rather than creating a new common purpose among the Royalists, the Association inevitably heightened still further the tensions between the professional officers and the local governmental establishment, and this restricted its effectiveness. The attempt to create more of a democratic local movement, ostensibly to preserve law and order, also raised the expectations of the ordinary folk and this was to backfire on the Royalists by encouraging the Clubmen Movement of the following year.

The provision of regular supplies of shoes for the footsore armies was a continual problem for the army commanders. King Charles persuaded Worcester to provide a supply in June and then fined Evesham 1,000 pairs after the town had assisted the Parliamentary army to cross the River Avon.
(Copyright: Paul Lewis Isemonger.)

CHAPTER SEVEN

THE BATTLE OF EVESHAM
AND CIVILIAN REVOLT: 1645

That the Country is fallen into such want and extremity through the number and oppression of the Horse lying upon free quarter that the people are necessitated (their hay being spent) to feed their Horses with corn, while their Children are ready to starve for want of Bread.

(Henry Townshend)[1]

The robbing of a county

The plundering by both Royalists and Parliamentarians showed no signs of abating. A committee of Parliament was established to consider 'These fruits of civil war; robberies, and innumerable wicked actions committed by the barbarous soldiers, to the unspeakable misery of the poor country'. In March 1645, some of Massey's troops were accused of setting fire to Pershore Abbey, fearing that the Royalists were intending to turn it into a garrison. In the same month, a memorial in All Saints Church, Worcester, records the death of the 'massacred gent: Mr Richard Chettel'.[2] The number of deserters was increasing rapidly in the county and some of these men turned to outlawry. Shrawley Wood, north of Worcester, was said to swarm with bandits and refugees as a result of the 'great distraction' in the county, including fifty men from one (unnamed) parish alone.[3]

The Royalists tried to tighten their hold on the countryside by improving the strength of their local garrisons, which formed, in effect, an outer defence around Worcester, under its new governor, Samuel Sandys. The recently levelled defences of Evesham were restored in early 1645 by the new Royalist governor, Colonel Robert Legge. Those of Hartlebury Castle, ten miles north of Worcester and now possibly used as a small Royalist mint, were also strengthened during that year and the next.[4] Bewdley men were pressed into service for the work on the Hartlebury defences in 1646. Unhappy with this, they bribed officials to be relieved of this duty: 'Pd. for wine for Mr Turton, to get off our men from going to work at the Castle'. Work was also undertaken on the fortifications at Strensham, with contributions drawn from Queenhill Manor, Longdon.[5] New garrisons were also built during 1645 at Campden House, Madresfield House and Leigh Court. Droitwich was forced to send carpenters to reinforce the Worcester defences and was itself garrisoned. It is possible that defences were constructed around St Augustine's Church on the high ground at Dodderhill at this time, or in the following year; this was a long-established strategic location, a Roman fort having been constructed there. In 1646, Parliamentary troops certainly camped up here and excavations on Dodderhill between 1977 and 1985 revealed a short length of a seventeenth-century ditch, 2.9 m wide and 1.25 m deep, with a flat bottom. There was little evidence of silting and the feature appeared to have been quickly backfilled.[6] All of this is typical of Civil War siegeworks or small-scale defences. Its location east of the church and on the top of the steep slope down to the river, possibly following the contour, suggests that the land around the church may well have been defended, with the intention of using the church itself as a final stronghold if required. Nevertheless, the inhabitants still had to pay Parliamentary assessments when Parliamentary troops also occupied the town or passed through it.[7]

The Royalists also began preparations to move a new army through the county. On 4 April, the Royalists demanded 3,000 bushels of wheat, 500 pickaxes, shovels and spades, hay, oats and beans to be delivered to the Cross Inn when the army arrived at Worcester. The county was also to supply twenty-eight teams of horses with carts and carters for each team, supplied with three days' rations, to be brought to College Green on 11 April.[8] Parliament countered with orders for these commands to be ignored, putting the local people in something of a cleft stick.[9] At the end of April, Prince Rupert from Hereford joined up with Prince Maurice at Worcester and their joint force (reputed to be around 5,000 men) marched to Evesham and then on to meet the king at Oxford; they met at Stow-on-the-Wold on 8 May.[10] Rupert and Charles then turned back into Worcestershire with a combined army of up to around 8,600. The inhabitants of Worcestershire must have groaned with despair at the arrival once again of the hungry field army. On 9 May the army was back at Evesham, meeting up with Lord Astley's army of 3,000 foot. The king and his bodyguard camped at Childswickham, two miles north-west of Broadway. They then continued their march and fanned out across east Worcestershire, not least to improve their chances of scavenging for supplies. On 10 May, Charles was at Inkberrow and stayed at Droitwich from 11 to 14 May, with his movements closely followed by Parliamentary spies. The Committee of Salop wrote to Brereton on 15 May that 'a boy, belonging to one of our commanders' had come from Worcester through the Royalist lines and reported on the Royalist movements around Bromsgrove and Droitwich.[11]

There was then a general rendezvous of the army at Bromsgrove (the king himself quartered at Droitwich) and Prince Rupert and Lord Astley were ordered to take the Parliamentary garrison of 100 men at Hawkesley (eight miles north of Bromsgrove). The Parliamentarians had little stomach for a fight against overwhelming odds and surrendered just as Charles arrived there, after a siege of only two days. The defences were then slighted and Astley was rewarded with the rights to pillage the house, after which it was set on fire. The army also took similar care to render any possible garrison sites at other mansions indefensible, which may have included the 'fair brick house' at Frankley (home of the Lyttleton family), if it had not already been destroyed.[12] They then marched on into Staffordshire, Warwickshire and finally into Leicestershire.

Battle of Evesham

However, Worcestershire was not to be left in peace. As the Royalist army left the county, Massey once again tried to step into the void. He seized the opportunity to try to block the well-established Royalist communication from Wales to Oxford, disrupt any line of retreat of King Charles' army to Oxford should they be defeated in the north, and also provide a safe haven on his own supply route from Warwick to Gloucester. This was to lead to one of the most dramatic incidents of the Civil War in the region when, on 26 May, Massey took Evesham 'in a storm of fire and leaden hail'.

Massey left Gloucester on 23 May with a force of 500 foot and a brigade of horse, gathering reinforcements from Tewkesbury on the way and rendezvousing at Evesham two days later with 200 men of the Worcestershire Committee, based in Warwickshire. In all he had a force of *c.* 2,000 men. By contrast, the garrison at Evesham had been reduced in order to provide reinforcements to the king's army and was probably only *c.* 700 men. The garrison clearly did not have enough men to defend the whole of the circuit around the town but the commander, Colonel Legge, was undaunted by Massey's threats of 'fire and sword' if he did not surrender 'being nothing terrified at the summons'.[13] Massey's plan was therefore to attack simultaneously from five points along the length of the north defences and across the bridge at Bengeworth. Careful preparations had to be made, and the countryside around was scoured for materials. Householders in Fladbury were forced to supply ladders and boards to help cross the wide defence ditches.[14]

Eighteenth-century engraving of Evesham, from the east. Evesham was basically defended by a broad loop of the River Avon, with a bridge leading from the adjacent hamlet of Bengeworth. A new defence was constructed during the war to close off the loop of the river.

Colonel Edward Massey (1620–74) was a Parliamentary hero in the First Civil War but supported Charles II in his attempt to regain the crown in 1651. The seizure of Evesham was one of his most famous exploits.

The initial assault was to be from the north, Massey crossing the Avon at Twyford Bridge (at Offenham Boat, two miles north-east of Evesham) and forming up on Green Hill. While he engaged the Royalists on the north defences, a second contingent was to try to storm Evesham Bridge from across the river at Bengeworth, enter the town and then attack the garrison in the rear. A troop of dragoons was also sent out three miles north-west to Fladbury in order to cover the approach road to Worcester and prevent any Royalist reinforcements from getting through. The attack began on the morning of the 26th. The previous night, Massey had given two false alarms to disturb the sleep of the defenders. Without the advantage of any artillery fire to cover them, Massey's men had to try to storm the ditch and palisade. Under heavy fire from the defenders, faggots were thrown into the ditch, the earthen bank scaled with the assistance of the ladders from Fladbury, and the wooden palisade on the top was torn down. The intention was then to dig through the rampart and open up an entrance wide enough for more troops and cavalry to pour through. The fighting was bitter. For a time it looked as though the musket fire of Colonel Legge's men might drive Massey's troops back across the ditch, and the attackers became pinned down on the top of the rampart. Colonel Legge mounted furious charges on the pinned-down Parliamentary soldiers and it looked as if he might actually succeed in driving the Parliamentary troops back off the defences. But the Royalists simply did not have enough men to do battle at each of the five points of attack and eventually Massey's men managed to effect a breach on the west side of the defences (probably where the ditch was narrower against the river). The dragoons were now able to pour into the Royalist flank. Legge retreated back into Evesham, still determined to rally his men. Against all the odds, it looked as though he might succeed when he managed to stem the Parliamentary advance and then actually forced them to retreat, but then the troops attacking Evesham Bridge managed to force their way across to attack Legge in the rear. As the Parliamentary cavalry charged down Broad Street, Legge's courageous troops could not hope to succeed in fighting the full force of Massey's army who now surrounded them, and they had no choice but to surrender. In this fierce battle of only an hour, marked by

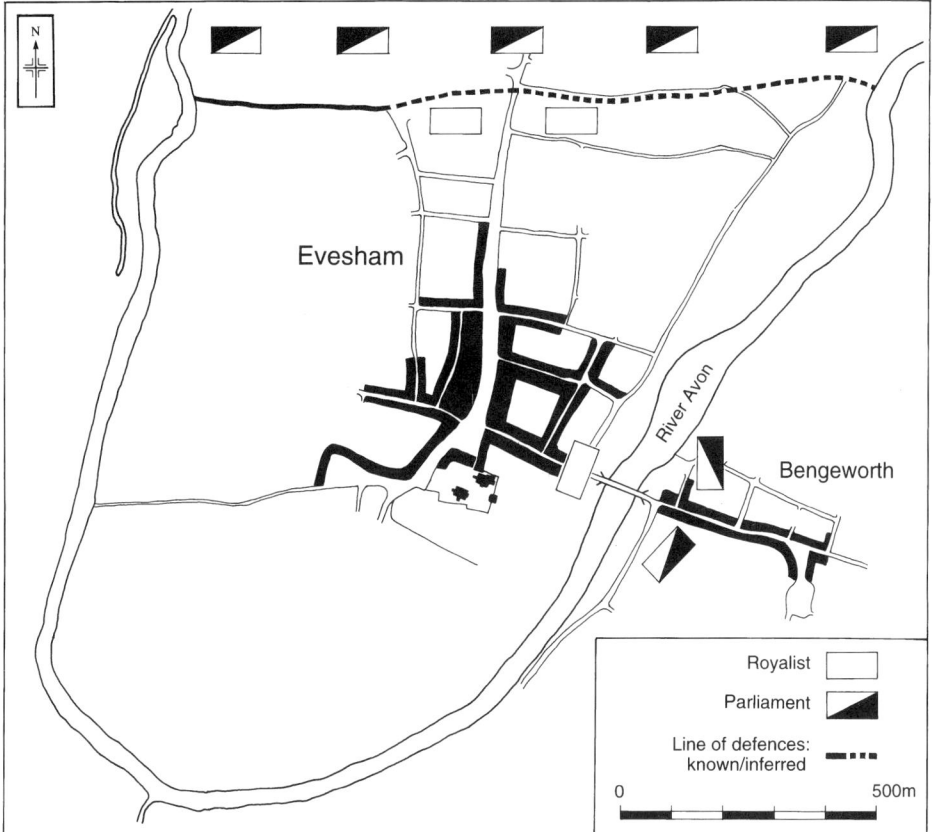

Plan of the Battle of Evesham, 1645. The Royalists had a garrison of around 700 men against an attacking force of 2,000. The defences had been repaired earlier in the year but the front that the Royalists had to defend was too long to protect properly. Nevertheless, the defenders put up a courageous defence.

the dogged determination of the troops on both sides, Massey took over 500 prisoners, including 70 officers (later exchanged for Parliamentarians captured at the fall of Hawkesley House). The town was now garrisoned by Parliament under the local man, Colonel Edward Rous (of the Rous Lench family), who ordered 6 new cannon and 500 muskets to help defend the place. As Massey had hoped, this cut the critical line of communication from Oxford, Worcester and South Wales and marked the start of a rising Parliamentary ascendancy in the county.

Apart from the military significance of this victory, the capture of Evesham was also important in allowing Parliamentary administrative influence to extend back into the county. Evesham now provided a secure base for the Parliamentary Committee for Worcestershire (previously forced to meet in Warwick) to collect

View of the surviving part of the north defences of Evesham. These consisted of a ditch originally with an earthen rampart topped with a timber palisade. On the river meadows the ditch was 2–4 m wide, but may have been up to 10 m wide on the higher ground across the main approach road from Greenhill. (Scale in half metres.)

After the fall of the north defences and the capture of Bengeworth Bridge the Battle of Evesham spread into the town itself. The marks of musket fire are still visible in the wall of the Abbey bell-tower.

intelligence and try to collect local taxes from at least the east side of the county – of course these places were already being taxed by the Royalists. In October, the constable of Elmley Lovett received a demand for twelve month's arrears of the Parliamentary assessment (£120) or face the 'perils of pillaging, and your houses fired, and your persons imprisoned'.[15]

By 17 June, and following the disastrous Battle of Naseby, Charles had come back briefly into the county. This had been the first major test of the reformed Parliamentary 'New Model Army'. The king's shattered army with its attendant camp-followers was still nursing its wounds and burying its casualties, and not just of the soldiers. The parish register for Kidderminster records on 1 July, 'A woman buried, wounded at the battle in Leicestershire'. She was probably the wife, widow or camp-follower of one of the soldiers. Some of the Royalist army retired to Oxfordshire, harried by Parliamentary cavalry. They had some minor successes on the way. Troops under the Earl of Northampton were returning to Banbury when they came across, and destroyed in a 'hard misfortune', a patrolling troop of Parliamentary horse at Church Honeybourne, east of Evesham.[16]

King Charles needed to try to raise a new army from Wales. He stayed at Bewdley (at The Angel on Load Street) and then moved to Hereford while he tried to rally his broken troops, and thence continued into Wales. A special Assembly was held in Worcester on 30 June to require the county to raise an additional £3,000 within ten days in order to mobilize 2,000 foot and 50 horse. But King Charles was being pursued: there now came a new threat to the stability of the county.

The arrival of the Scottish army

In early July a Scottish army under Lord Levan (that 'old, little, crooked soldier'), in support of their Parliamentary allies, began a march on Worcester as part of their chase of the king. They went from Alcester to Pershore but, finding the repaired bridge over the Avon was now unsafe, they had to go north to Droitwich and then to Bewdley in order to cross the River Severn and head further west.

On the urging of King Charles, Prince Rupert's force at Worcester was not drawn out to meet the Scots (thereby risking a weakened garrison with a governor whose loyalty was, at the time, under question). The Scots evidently thought the number of troops at Worcester too strong to risk a siege and turned instead for Hereford. They followed a tortuous route in order to gather supplies and massacred the Royalist garrison at Canon Frome on the way. It was easy for the Royalists to incite hatred for this foreign army which appeared like a swarm of locusts on an already ravaged countryside, although this backfired on them in 1651 (see Chapter 10). At Droitwich, after supplying the Scots while at Alcester, the inhabitants had to supply a further 100 cheeses and 288 loaves of bread.[17] At Tenbury the Scots smashed the font of the church and those of surrounding churches.[18] At Hartlebury they appear to have driven off most of the sheep in the district and trampled the crops.[19] Charles, then in Wales, now swung back with 4,000 cavalry and dragoons towards Worcester in order to gather further forces for the relief of Hereford.

Harried by the Scottish army, he left a troop of 'reformadoes' (men from broken regiments) under Lord Molyneux at Bewdley to defend the river crossing. Unfortunately, they were soon captured by the Scots during a skirmish in August. A testimony to the fighting there is found in the parish register of Bewdley, which records the burial of three soldiers during August and a further three at the end of September. In all, the parish registers of Bewdley record the burials of twenty-two soldiers during 1645.[20]

Charles was at Moreton-in-Marsh on 30 August and the following day had 'no dinner' on his rush to Worcester. While there, he took care to order a further improvement of the defences of the city, possibly the breastwork built on the Droitwich side of the city. He arrived at Hereford on 4 September but by then the Scots had withdrawn to Gloucester. The jubilant Charles was not, however, in a position to risk following the retreating army as it then moved north through Worcestershire, quartering outside Evesham at Wickhamford on 7 September. General Pointz had brought a Parliamentary army to occupy Evesham, covering the line of the Scottish withdrawal and blocking the line of any Royalist support from Oxford. So after returning to Worcester, Charles turned north for Ludlow, heading for a safe haven in North Wales, but it was not to be. On 24 September, the Royalist army was defeated at Rowton Heath.

Worcester was under increasing military and economic pressure during the autumn as supplies became more and more difficult to obtain. The city was blockaded by Parliamentary garrisons at Evesham to the east, the new garrison at Canon Frome to the west and Gloucester to the south. The Governor of Worcester, Colonel Samuel Sandys, tried to improve the defences, the *Weekly Account* of 16–30 December describing him as being 'very diligent in mending his worke', but a winter at war was hard for the citizens. Coal ran short because of the blockade on the River Severn and some further houses in the suburbs were demolished to extend the clear field of fire and also to provide fuel.[21] The Royalists ordered 100 loads of timber from Shrawley Wood, but the Parliamentary news-sheets claimed, dismissively, that these would be intercepted. There were, indeed, attempts to tighten the noose around the city. In December, there was a skirmish at adjacent Malvern. It is also possible that Parliamentary troops managed to occupy Ombersley, six miles to the north of Worcester (if Ombersley be equated with *Aunnersleth* in a letter of the Committee of Salop to Sir William Brereton, 26 December), so blocking a possible rendezvous of the Worcester garrison with those gathered at Kidderminster.[22]

The Royalist garrisons became more and more desperate as they found it increasingly difficult to collect taxes and supplies and also were prevented from mobilizing a relief force for Chester. The Parliamentary forces held a tight grip on the routes from Oxford to Chester, and in December they turned back a force of around 2,000 men on Broadway Hill. As usual, it was the local populace who took the brunt of the frustration. In a letter of 24 September, Anthony Langston of Sedgebarrow (one of the Royalist Commissioners) wrote to Lord Digby (Secretary of State) of the Worcester garrison that 'The hands it is in and their assistants are men

Civil War cavalry trooper. 'You are to expect an unsanctified troop of horse among you, from whom if you hide yourselves . . . they shall fire your houses without mercy, hang up your bodies wherever they find them, and scare your ghosts'. This was the answer of Col. Bard to the rising tide of opposition to the Royalist's demands for taxes in the county. (Copyright: Paul Lewis Isemonger.)

of very little care, and their reproaches are great upon all those that have any; the pressures and provocations are great upon the country . . .'. Taxes were imposed arbitrarily, the soldiers were incapable, the officers divided, so that 'Many gentlemen of great quality residing in the city full of distrust and discontent are desirous to remove if they knew Whither . . . and many of our country gentlemen daily taken and submitting to the enemy'.[23] Prince Maurice took up the same themes in October when he was driven to complain about his subordinates

> imprisoning and restraining the persons, and seizing the goods and Cattle of
> divers persons, and releasing them at their own wills; without giving any
> account of the same: which irregular proceedings have tended much to the
> grievance of the said Inhabitants of this County, and dis-service of his Majesty.[24]

But Prince Maurice was himself blamed for the development of this state of affairs. He was praised as being 'civil to all and wel-beloved of the citizens' but was 'too easy and facile to the troops of Reformadoes'.[25] The latter were notoriously badly disciplined. The Royalist, Henry Townshend, wrote of the exactions of free-quarter, threats, kidnapping, stealing so

> That all the country lying between Severn and Teme, and on the banks of the Severn (which are his Majesty's only secure quarters). And also the parishes adjacent within 4 miles of the City, are by free quarter of the Horse eaten up, undone and destroyed . . . That the Insolencies, oppressions, and Cruelties have already so disaffected and disheartened the people: that they are grown desperate, and are already upon the point of rising everywhere . . . .[26]

He wrote that all the hay had been used so that the people were forced to feed their horses on corn, rather than bake it into bread for themselves. If his account is to believed, a large part of Worcestershire was destitute.

Kidderminster seems to have suffered particularly badly at this time. Already garrisoned by Royalist cavalry, it was also described as being molested by troops under another member of the Gerrard family, Gilbert Gerrard (nephew to the late Governor of Worcester and brother of General Charles Gerrard) 'the most rude and ill-governed house . . . that ever trod upon earth', as a force passed through on its way to try to reach Chester via Ludlow.[27] Parliamentary troops were waiting for them. Those under Colonel Jones claimed to have attacked a Royalist force near Kidderminster, which was then reinforced, and a possible sconce (small fort) was made at Trimpley. This may have consisted of a refurbishment of the medieval moated site lying on the edge of Wassall Wood. In a second skirmish on 8 November, 120 Royalist cavalry from the garrison, on their way to Worcester, were defeated by Captains Stone and Backhouse after a failed attempt to ambush the Parliamentarians, in a 'little field' somewhere between Bridgnorth and Kidderminster.[28] Twenty of the Royalists were killed and over forty taken prisoner (including Sir Thomas Aston).[29] Fighting continued in the area, even within Kidderminster itself; the Kidderminster parish register records how on 11 December the town 'buried John . . . a souldier under Captain Denham. Dec. 14th buried another of his souldiers one Giles . . . slain in the town'. Captain Denham was himself killed in the following March. At Stourbridge in late November, a troop of cavalry from Stafford surprised a party of 200 Royalist troops in the town and took 100 horse and 80 prisoners – all apparently without bloodshed.[30]

Fighting in the year ended with the fall of Hereford to Parliament on 18 December. Worcestershire was now largely isolated in the midst of Parliamentary-controlled areas in England. An order had gone out to surrounding garrisons (on 10 December) to cut off the trade of Worcester from London.[31] Ironically, this supported a similar order from Charles I, trying to cause injury to London's economy. Neither may have been very effective but they illustrate the strain on the local economy from both warring factions. In any case, Charles no longer had a field army and increasingly the question was how long his beleaguered garrisons in the county, described as 'ragged and ravenous', could hold out.[32] The whole county was now under siege. The Parliamentary Committee of Worcestershire wrote to Sir William Brereton from Evesham on 11 December gleefully explaining that the Royalist troops seemed incapable of organizing for a march to relieve Chester. 'They draw out and march back again, stagger to and fro as if they knew not well whither to betake themselves'.[33] The Worcestershire Committee had done their part by ordering the demolition of bridges and digging up fords to make the route impassable. The garrison at Canon Frome raided Malvern in December and took 50 horse and 28 prisoners.[34] Unable to move out, by 18 December the Royalists (up to 4,000), were said to be occupying all of the villages between Bewdley and Bridgnorth, with 700 troops in Bewdley and Kidderminster.[35] By 26 December there were reported to be 200 'firelocks' (troops armed with the more modern flintlock musket) in Kidderminster, 200 horse at Bewdley and 50 at Rednal.

Spies

The Parliamentary army sent out spies to give early warning of any attempt by the Royalists to break out of their enclave.[36] On 6 November 1645, Gerrard Jones wrote to Brereton asking him to send the woman that lodged with Captain Booth (Mayor of Macclesfield) into Worcester to get information. On 9 December, the Committee of Salop wrote to Brereton informing him that the female spy that he had sent into Worcester had arrived back at Shrewsbury. She delivered her report on 11 December at Chester. On arriving at Worcester, posing as a bringer of news, she had been challenged and said she had come from Chester to visit John Onion, a citizen of Worcester. She was first summoned to Prince Maurice and then the governor, who asked her what information she might have of the Parliamentary forces and state of Chester. She then accompanied one of the Royalist officers – Sir William Vaughan – back to Bridgnorth where she had met a woman spying on the opposite side![37]

Internal dissent

The tensions between the military and civilians had intensified throughout the year as the military situation worsened. The Association of December 1644 had been an attempt by the civilian government to try to reassert themselves against the growing influence of the professional soldiers who had no connection to the county. This trend had also been apparent in the appointment, from December 1643, of outsiders as Governors of Worcester (rectified after January 1645 by the appointment of Samuel Sandys). King Charles had been ready to accept a number of the conditions of the gentry Association in order to raise more mobile forces, but the Association was outmanoeuvred by Prince Maurice, who is unlikely to have taken kindly to such civilian interference. He issued a charter to try to remove some of the sources of conflict by defining the role of military and civilian government, and launched an energetic campaign against indiscipline among the troops, but his position was getting desperate. On 17 February, the Parliamentary news-sheet *Perfect Occurrences of Parliament* reported:

Out of Wostershire it is certified that since they here [hear] in those parts of the strength of Sir William Brereton, and see the retreat of Maurice that they begin to fall off from him, and that his strength doth rather lessen than increase, especially such as were pressed by him, and forced to serve, many of whom do daily run away, and those who are left, have little to subsist with, but plunder; which doth harden the hearts of the countrey against them.[38]

That this was not simply propaganda is suggested by the fact that Prince Maurice had only written to Prince Rupert the previous day, complaining of desertions among his men.[39]

In April 1645, Prince Maurice reinforced his authority by making new demands for supplies without reference to either the Committee of Safety or Quarter Sessions and tried to impose a loyalty oath or 'Protestation' to be sworn by all commanders, soldiers, gentry, citizens, freeholders and others in the county. They were to swear that:

1. The king was the sole monarch.
2. Neither Pope nor Parliament could depose him.
3. Thomas Fairfax, William Brereton, etc. were rebels.
4. It was treason for anyone to deliver Worcester into the hands of Parliament.
5. 'All rendezvous lately kept within that county (though with his Majesties consent) is rebellion'.[40]

The latter is probably a reference to the assemblies of Clubmen (see below).

The Governor of Worcester, Samuel Sandys, supported the Prince and said that any who refused were 'not to be trusted, nor fit to live in the Garrison'.[41] But many loyal Royalists felt insulted by this: the Commissioners of Safety refused to sanction the 'Protestation' and Henry Townshend was one of those who objected. Ironically, it was Samuel Sandys who was himself to fall under suspicion for loyalty in July. He lost local support, according to Townshend, by 'rather attending his pleasures, than the true duty of his place'. The military were blamed for leading him astray! King Charles wrote to Prince Rupert on 5 July anxious about the safety of Worcester because 'I hear that Sam Sandys is at present highly discontent (having not yet worn his sword since his restraint)'. Sandys was too valuable an ally to lose. In September, the king wrote to try to restore good relations.

Sam. Sandys, I am told that some malicious person both to you and to my service, hath endeavoured to give you misapprehensions of my good opinion of you and value of your affections and integrity to my service, and although your knowledge of my justice to all those who have deserved so well of me as you have done ought to secure you. Yet, I have thought fit (as to a person of whom I have more than ordinary value) to assure you in this particular way, that there is no gentlemen in England upon whose faithfulness and entire affections to my person and cause I do more confidently reply, nor from whom do I expect with more assurance a good account whatever happen of that important place of Worcester where with you are entrusted, and whenever it please God to restore me you shall be sure to find the effects of my being

Your assured friend

Charles R.

Bridgenorth this 30th day of Sept. 1645.[42]

After the fall of Evesham, the military were able to use the urgency of the situation to tighten their hold on local government. The Committee of Safety lost much of its purpose and was attended by fewer than half a dozen members. Samuel Sandys had also evidently not been completely appeased and the king was still writing in November to reassure him of his confidence and calling upon him to ignore the gossip of 'whatsoever idle or malicious people tell you'.[43] This seems to have been to little avail, for Sandys was to resign his command in February 1646.[44]

If this conflict had been at an official level, affecting a small group of gentry and officers, a more populist voice of protest had also emerged during the year: the Clubmen.

The Worcestershire Clubmen

The despair of the local population in many counties, continually at the mercy of either side, whatever their original loyalty had been, led to the rise of the 'Clubmen Movements': associations or 'clubs' of local inhabitants who practised armed neutrality. The trend was also probably encouraged by failure of the officially inspired 'peace' movement of 1644, and by the breakdown of the Uxbridge peace negotiations in February 1645.[45] They were particularly strong in Herefordshire, where up to 16,000 men had risen in 1644, and Worcestershire, which had suffered from the repeated to-ing and fro-ing of the opposing armies and looting by the garrisons.

There were assemblies of Clubmen in the county throughout 1645. The best evidence comes from the west of the county, around Woodbury Hill and the Malverns, areas that had so far escaped the worst excesses of the plundering by both sides and that wished to continue to do so, and where the rise of the new Royalist Association might increase the risk of conscription of their menfolk for the Royalist armies.[46] They had seen some examples of what they might expect. In February, local men twice surprised troops of Royalists ransacking Leigh Court (owned by the Parliamentarian, Sir Walter Devereux). Each time the looters were brought before the Governor of Worcester but it was the captors who were rebuked – for interfering with the king's troops in the execution of their duty. A little later, the efforts of the Worcester garrison to raise recruits and money from this area were met by a rising of 800 countrymen who declared their neutrality in the conflict.[47] On

Bredon Hill from the west. In November 1645, 3,000 'Clubmen' from the area surrounding Evesham met here to formally declare their support for Parliament. They were daring enough to try to attack Prince Rupert and later probably took part in the siege of Madresfield.

5 March, in what was a period of relative calm, 1,000 men from north-west Worcestershire met on Woodbury Hill, under the leadership of Charles Nott of Shelsley, to protest the 'utter ruin by the outrages and violence of the soldier; threatening to fire our houses; endeavouring to ravish our wives and daughters, and menacing our persons'.[48] There is a particular venom in the language of the Clubmen declarations against Catholics. The by now familiar pleas to preserve the moderation of the Anglican Church was given additional fervour because one of the leaders of the Royalist Association was the noted Catholic, the Earl of Shrewsbury.

The Clubmen wanted to establish 'a mutual league for each other's defence', including provision to rescue members who were captured. Admission to the league was refused to any soldier or those marked for enlistment. This was not a revolutionary, or even Parliamentary movement, although the Parliamentary press naturally made what propaganda they could out of it. The *Kingdom's Weekly Intelligencer* of April 1645 claimed that, following a skirmish, the rescue of cattle by Parliamentary troops under Colonel Bridges (including men of the Committee of Worcestershire) had led to 'Divers of the inhabitants of Worcestershire, and Warwickshire, by the reason of the restoring of their cattell to them, are ready to rise upon all occasions to join with the Warwickshire forces'.[49] The Woodbury Clubmen, composed mainly of commoners, recognized the Royalist High Sheriff (Henry Bromley of Holt) and Grand Jury as the legitimate legal authority of the county and claimed that their league was to enforce the Royalist's own, oft-repeated and by now discredited, proclamation to improve the discipline of the troops. The practical consequence of this stance was, however, to seem to oppose the Royalist occupying forces. The profession of loyalty to the king was in itself a well-used convention during the war. In practical terms this movement benefited the Parliamentarians, as it was the Royalists whose armies were the principal occupying power. Some of the Malvern Clubmen joined the much larger armed rising in Hereford.[50] Nevertheless, the refusal of the Clubmen to offer outright support to Parliament meant that an irritated Massey (who supplied them with some weapons) still described them as traitorous rebels and Corbet declared them 'foolish neuters' who had given 'assurance that they were our friends, but could not declare for either side'.[51]

Nothing seems to have come of this first phase of the movement in Worcestershire although the Committee of Salop wrote to Brereton on 13 April that the Clubmen 'continue resolute to oppose the King's party'.[52] This was after the crushing of the much larger Herefordshire revolt. Despite attempts to track down the ringleaders, local constables refused to give the names of those attending meetings. After an abortive attempt to negotiate with the Clubmen at Tenbury, there is no recorded reaction to the demands of Prince Rupert in May for every man to forswear the leagues. The fortification of Madresfield House and Leigh Court may, however, have been partly a response to this threat from the Clubmen of Malvern, Mathon, Cradley, Leigh Sinton, Suckley and Powick (as published in a Parliamentary newsletter of 18 March).

Despite this ominous sign of popular revolt, the exactions of the Royalist army continued unabated. In addition, there was an absence of any firm Royalist leadership in the county. Prince Maurice had resigned in September in support of Prince Rupert who had been dismissed by the king, and a successor was not appointed until December. One can imagine the lack of central control on the bands of unpaid reformadoes that had fled into the county. By now, the ultimate defeat of the Royalists was becoming ever more obvious and this encouraged the waverers. A more politically calculating movement with a different power base therefore emerged in the winter, and was a more overt anti-Royalist movement. On 11 November, 3,000 men from the Evesham area (who had been the most reluctant supporters of the Royalists during the war) met on the heights of Bredon Hill to declare formally for Parliament and seek armed support. This time they were led, not by commoners, but by gentry who had realized that they had been supporting a losing cause and who may also have been nervous of such a popular movement getting out of control of the traditional leaders of society. Sir Edward Dineley of Charlton, formerly a Royalist Commissioner and then a member of the Parliamentary Committee of Sequestration (to investigate and seize the estates of proven Royalist gentry), was elected leader. This was a development which enraged the local Royalists. Colonel Bard, commanding the Royalist garrison at Campden House near the Warwickshire border declared to the constable and parishioners of Twyning (two miles north of Tewkesbury in Gloucestershire) on 21 November:

> Know you that unless you bring unto me (at a day and hour in Worcester) the monthly contribution for six months, you are to expect an unsanctified troop of horse among you, from whom if you hide yourselves . . . they shall fire your houses without mercy, hang up your bodies wherever they find them, and scare your ghosts.[53]

He declared that neither the twenty-one troops of cavalry at Tewkesbury nor the sixteen troops at Strensham would protect them. Twyning had been rated at £51 15*s* per month. Previously tolerant of a failure to meet the demands of the local taxes, even the Royalist Clarendon now described Bard as exercising 'an unlimited tyranny over the whole country'; his men were known as 'shirt-stealers' or 'cormorants'. King Charles was himself concerned at the strains being imposed on the people of Worcestershire. On 23 November he wrote, via Sir Edward Walker, a letter to Samuel Sandys, Governor of Worcester and the garrison commander:

> Trusty and welbeloved, wee greet you well. By our former letters wee expresst our care to prevent the inconvenience that might arise to the country and our service if our nephew Prince Rupert and Prince Maurice, with their trayne and followers, should make any long abode at Worcester, or other our quarters, which by your letters to Sir Edward Walker wee perceive was not without cause . . . Our nephewes stay in those quarters hath already been longer than wee expected . . . Our will and command is, that you declare unto them that our pleasure is, that they deliver to you a lyst of all their owne servants which they intend to take with them, whome wee will you to accommodate, as well you may, with quarters and other necessaryes for them during their residency with you, which wee presume will not be long. And that for all the others that adhere to them . . . Our command is, that you signify our pleasure unto them that they leave our quarters by the first of December next, for that wee may not beare the inconvenience of the eating out of our quarters by those who have so abandoned our service . . . .[54]

The hopes of the eastern Clubmen were short-lived. Fired with new-found enthusiasm they tried to blockade Royalist garrisons and, in early December, they rashly attacked Maurice and Rupert, who were on their way to Oxford, but were easily defeated and dispersed, at least temporarily. Nevertheless, the Committee of Salop wrote to Brereton on 14 December that the troops at Evesham 'joined with the country who rise so freely that Worcester is already much straitened for provision'.[55] Men from this force may have been in the contingent that attacked Madresfield and Leigh Court in January 1646.[56]

The area of the former Malvern Clubmen was now garrisoned to keep dissidents quiet but the Woodbury league re-emerged in early December. On 6 December they presented a new manifesto to the Governor of Worcester.[57] Details were given for systems of warning of danger, arranging help for any that were wounded and declaring any that did not answer the summons to be enemies who would be denied future protection. Every parishioner worth £10 a year had to provide himself with a musket. The new Royalist commander in the county from 6 December, Lord Astley, was ordered to 'keep the county from rendezvous and tumultuous assemblies of men without authority'.[58] He actually arrived in Worcester on 23 December. In his analysis of the composition of the Royalist Commission for Worcestershire in December 1645, Styles has pointed out the shift in composition away from the leading gentry families that was so evident in the early years of the war.[59] With this, the desertion of gentry from Worcester and the strength of feeling evident in the Clubmen movement, the king seemed to be running out of friends of any sort in the county.

CHAPTER EIGHT

THE COUNTY FALLS: 1646

From the plundering of soldiers, their Insolency, Cruelty, Atheism, Blasphemy and Rule over us, *Libera nos Domine* [God Deliver Us].

(Henry Townshend at the siege of Worcester, 1646)

The year opened with the launch of sieges against the Royalist garrisons of Madresfield House and Leigh Court (in late January), an operation designed by Parliament to tighten the noose around Worcester and one which involved substantial bodies of troops from Gloucester, Herefordshire and Evesham.[1] The latter, ordered to supply 500 horse and foot, may well have used contingents from the local Clubmen as well as the seasoned troops of the New Model Army. The intention was probably to overwhelm quickly the small garrisons with massive force, and then make the sites untenable, before the Royalists could collect an army

Parish accounts from Powick, detailing the losses incurred from the quartering of troops during the siege of Madresfield, 1646. (Public Record Office, with permission.)

against them. Ironically, the attack on Madresfield was led by its owner, Colonel William Lygon. Troops for the siege were quartered at nearby Powick and Newland: from Powick there was an account for '. . . in January, when Capt. Michelburne came against Madresfield, 10 men and horse quartered at several times 14 days . . . £7', and at Newland, 'Paid to Capt. Badger's troop at the leaguer against Madresfield, being 50 men and horses besides foot . . . £40'. There is a possible reference to the 'countrymen' Clubmen in an account for 'To Capt. Badger and Capt. Michelburne [when they] came with the countrymen against Madresfield, one half hogshead of perry . . . 8s'.[2] There are similar accounts relating to Leigh Court; in the nineteenth century two skeletons and 29 skulls were found in the vicinity which, with a number of cannon-balls, are popularly ascribed to skirmishing at the siege.[3] The garrison possibly managed to withdraw to Worcester after firing the house themselves rather than engaging in a serious siege. After the war, Sir Walter Devereux, the owner, claimed that the house had been burned by the Royalists.

Lord Astley had left Oxford at the end of 1645 to try to raise a Royalist army from the Royalist garrisons of the Midlands, which meant that relief was at hand for Madresfield and the siege was lifted in February. Nevertheless, with the fall of Chester in the same month (Worcestershire troops were part of the besieging army), Astley found himself almost surrounded. By the beginning of March he had raised around 3,000 men and set off for Oxford via Bridgnorth, Kidderminster and Worcester – this was the only Royalist field army now in existence. The wolf pack of the Parliamentary armies now gathering had the scent of victory. They had been recruiting hard for the final fray and troops raised from Worcestershire now began to make a serious impact on the war effort: nineteen men were raised from the parish of Longdon alone in February by Captain Badger – possibly that Captain Talbot Badger from Pool House, Hanley Castle.[4] Colonel Morgan from Gloucester and Colonel Birch from Hereford were waiting for Astley at Broadway, and behind them in the Cotswolds was Colonel Fleetwood. Sir William Brereton was moving up from Chester to Astley's rear while Evesham and its Parliamentary garrison was denied to him. Astley therefore marched back to Droitwich, where there was a sharp skirmish with troops under Captain Millward of Alvechurch.[5] He then made off across country via Feckenham and Inkberrow to Bidford and Cleeve Prior. Crossing the Avon, he reached Honeybourne and managed to outflank Morgan to reach Campden and Blockley and thence marched to Donnington, but such manoeuvres gave only a temporary respite. The Parliamentary forces finally caught and surrounded him on the Cotswolds. Astley's position was hopeless. On 21 March, at the Battle of Stow-on-the-Wold (thirty miles from Worcester), he was caught between Birch attacking from the front and Morgan from the rear. In the ensuing battle, 1,600 Royalists were taken prisoner and the rest were killed or dispersed. Some of the wounded were taken to Droitwich.[6] Astley sat down on a drum and prophetically addressed the Gloucester troops: 'You have now done your work and may go to play, unless you will fall out among yourselves'.

The Civil War was now effectively over, although this was difficult for many in the surviving garrisons to accept. In January, Worcester had protested at the demands to pay reformadoes at £70 per month but the latter had nowhere else to go. Parliament now had to persuade the surviving Royalist garrisons to surrender. Some men still held out hopes that a Scottish army might support the king, but in truth, the time for vengeance against the Worcester garrison, and therefore by association, against Worcester itself, was nigh.[7]

The jubilant Parliamentary army under Brereton quickly marched to Worcester and on 25 March demanded its surrender in order to 'prevent your houses from spoil, your estates from ruin, your persons from restraint, the effusion of blood, and such other miseries as inevitably will fall upon yourselves, your wives and children'. But they were in no hurry and did not intend a proper siege at this time, perhaps expecting that the city would recognize the hopelessness of the situation and surrender without a fight. But the new governor since March, Henry Washington (a Leicestershire soldier who was a former Governor of Evesham and brother-in-law to the prominent Worcestershire Royalist, Sir John Pakington), was in no mood to surrender. He had half a thought towards his reputation with future employers when he must once again serve as a mercenary overseas, saying 'I owe so much to my Reputation which I gained, and must hereafter maintain abroad, when these wars shall cease, as not to be persuaded to the least unworthy action'.[8] After a little desultory skirmishing, the Parliamentary army drew off to Droitwich, to give the garrison a few days' grace to think over the consequences. Brereton's men camped around St Augustine's Dodderhill while the inhabitants had to supply them with beer, tobacco and candles.[9] While the bulk of the Parliamentary army was diverted towards the siege of Lichfield, and the Gloucester contingent returned home, the Worcester garrison prepared for the battle ahead. The latter, containing men who now saw little hope for the future, had no intention of surrender without clear orders from the king. It foraged for supplies and on 30 March began to again clear the suburbs, including demolishing the church and hospital of St Oswald on the north side, in order to ensure a clear field of fire. The entry in the Parliamentary Survey says 'Burnt by the Cavaliers'. Only the stone buildings at the Whiteladies were left intact – spared because they could be used as billets for up to 500 men.[10] The two sides did, however, still range around each other. There was a skirmish outside Worcester on 19 April and one of the casualties – 'John Jones, a parliament soldier, slain at the skirmish at Worcester' – was buried at Kidderminster.

Charles himself gave up the fight and surrendered to the Scots on 5 May. As part of the initial terms of surrender, Charles ordered the garrisons at Banbury and Newark to surrender, which they did on 6 and 8 May, which meant that more troops were available to deal with Worcestershire, and the troops from Gloucester were also summoned back to the fray. Thus it was that the garrisons of Dudley, Hartlebury and Madresfield surrendered to sieges in quick succession. The siege of Dudley began on 27 April. The garrison of up to 340 men was well supplied and seemed determined to make a last stand, burning the buildings around the castle (including the church of St Edmund), but this resolve did not last long and the castle surrendered on 13 May. As a measure of how quickly loyalties might change,

The excavation of Civil War destruction levels at Dudley Castle. The castle was captured by the Parliamentary forces after a siege beginning 27 April 1646, and surrendered on 13 May. (Dudley Metropolitan Borough Council, with permission.)

at the start of the siege the Parliamentary army expressed surprise when the citizens did not try to rescue their burning houses, destroyed to deny the Parliamentary troops cover as the Royalist forces retreated to the castle. If this was meant as a sign of support from the garrison, the mood quickly changed when the castle fell. Richard Persehouse wrote how the garrison commander, Colonel Leveson, had to 'gallop away with manie thousand curses of the cuntrie people, whoe would certainly have killed him had hee not beene strong guarded with two troops of horse of the Parliament'.[11]

Aerial view of Hartlebury Castle. The defences of the medieval moated site (the Bishop's Palace) had been extensively refurbished during the war and probably included the enlargement of the original ditches, described as a 'huge moat' in 1646. Townshend regarded its fortification as an 'excessive charge' by the 'covetousness of the governor and officers'. (Copyright: Aerofilms Ltd.)

The minor Worcestershire garrisons surrendered with some ignominy. The 160-strong garrison of Hartlebury surrendered to the Gloucester troops without a fight on 16 May, despite having ammunition and stores for a year – in return for secret terms being given to Colonel William Sandys. He accepted a bribe of £3,000 and a promise to protect his estate at Ombersley from sequestration. Townshend was particularly bitter about the surrender because the governor had 'sharked' the countryside around to fortify the place.[12] Also captured there were the other members of the influential Sandys family: the former Governor of Worcester, Samuel Sandys, and his brother the captain of the Worcester militia, Martin Sandys. Samuel Sandys had resigned the governorship of Worcester (involuntarily according to Townshend) at the end of February, after a long-running period of disenchantment with the Royalist command. The final straw was the perceived subordination to Astley (who tried to restore some authority to the civilian commissioners at the expense of the military) and a reduction in pay.[13] It then appears that the family had decided to make their own stand outside Worcester, within William's command at Hartlebury (Martin Sandys's responsibilities to the Worcester militia notwithstanding). It is not clear when Strensham fell; it probably occurred without a fight, as nothing is said about it.

There were no immediate plans to besiege Madresfield again until the siege of Worcester was well underway. Parliament had, however, raised concerns as to the activities of the garrison, raiding in the immediate area and also into Herefordshire.[14] There seems, therefore, to have been some skirmishing around Madresfield House, probably with the intention of isolating it. There are references to wounded soldiers in the parish accounts of Newland: 'Paid to soldiers which lay wounded under the chirurgeon's hands, belonging to Capt. Cannon . . . 5s.' Townshend, in Worcester at the time, was scathing in his assessment of the garrison. On 18 June, the garrison seemed full of bravado. Sending a message to Colonel Washington in Worcester, it offered to hold out either for at least a month (and then seek further orders), or alternatively until terms had been agreed for Worcester. Captain Aston, the garrison commander, boasted of being able to hold out for three months, but his confidence seems to have been shaken the very next day, after Parliamentary reinforcements arrived from the siege of Worcester, bringing with them two cannon. The garrison actually surrendered on 20 or 21 June, apparently without a further struggle; which was, no doubt, much to the relief of Colonel Lygon, the owner of Madresfield, who would otherwise have been forced to order the cannon to pound his house to rubble. In return, £200 was given to Captain Aston (who reportedly also sold the garrison cannon to Colonel Lygon), 30s to each trooper and 10s to each foot soldier. The governors of the four garrisons were denounced for giving up their commands 'traitorously, cowardly and basely'.[15] Captain Aston, a Lancashire gentleman, was another mercenary, 'a soldier of fortune, who having raised himself plentifully, loved not to hazard the loss of it, but rather his loyalty which will be a bar to him in his honour'.[16]

The second siege of Worcester, 1646

Dealing with Worcester was to be a different matter. Colonel Whalley, fresh from the siege of Banbury, was ordered by Parliament to 'straiten the garrison of Worcester until such time as the army was at liberty to march against it'. As a consequence, therefore, this was to be a siege of protracted negotiation, truces and military action consisting largely of artillery barrages and occasional sallies from the city, rather than a direct assault. Until July, the besiegers were content to simply contain the garrison, as per their orders, and take advantage of the evident tensions between the soldiers and the city. Many people in Worcester, despite an oath of 1 May proclaiming mutual support and unity, saw no point in supporting what had become a lost cause. Townshend reports how 'Many gentlemen went out before the siege to stay at home'.[17]

The governor, Henry Washington, wrote to the king on 13 May asking for

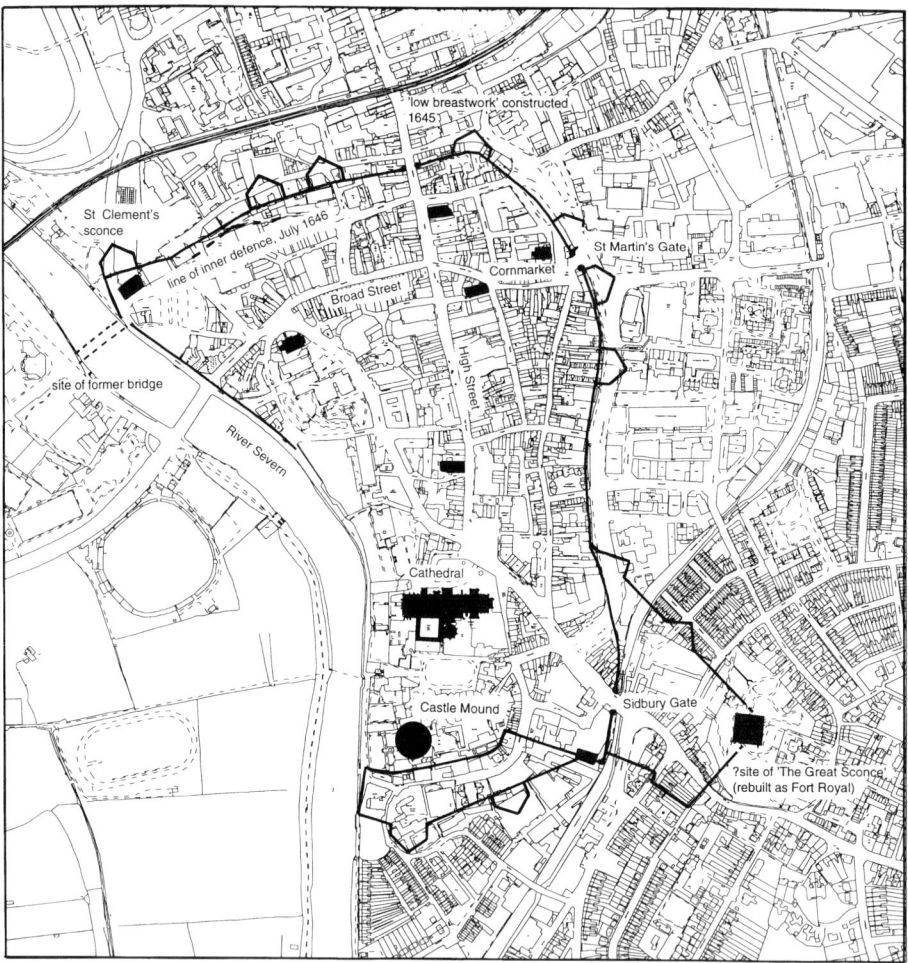

Plan of the defences of Worcester at the time of the siege, 1646 (based on Young's map of 1779 and Vaughan's map of 1660). Many of the details remain speculative. (Background based on the Ordnance Survey 1:1250 digital mapping, with permission of the controller of HMSO.)

instructions, but was himself clearly determined to hold out until all honour was satisfied. On 16 May Fairfax, the Parliamentary general, called on the city to surrender. Washington, although a brave officer, could be rash, negligent and subject to extreme tempers. He had a garrison of 1,507 men, including the governor's regiment, and the depleted ranks of the local regiments of Sir William Russell, Colonel Samuel Sandys, reformadoes and 224 cavalry plus the city's Trained Bands, now lacking their captain, Martin Sandys. Many of the troops were

Irish. The garrison also had 28 cannon and 6 lighter drakes, together with other 'sling-pieces', manned by 58 cannoneers and matrosses (assistant gunners) under the command of Dud Dudley.[18] The sum of £224 16s 8d had been spent in February for purchasing 'iron guns, bullets and grenadoes' for the garrisons of Worcester and Hartlebury.[19] The 'master gunner' was mathematician Nathaniel Nye, who used his experiences in the siege to write *The Art of Gunnery* in 1647.

This was to be against a force of around 2,500–5,000 of the New Model Army, and new forces which continued to be raised from the county.[20] On 21 May, the day after the fall of Madresfield, the Parliamentary army under Colonel Whalley began to encamp on Wheeler's Hill (Rainbow Hill) on the north side of the city. Their initial aim was clearly to occupy the high ground on the north and east sides of the city and so win tactical advantage over the Royalist garrison below. They were confident enough of their strength for Morgan to march his men back to Gloucester.

Whalley formally demanded that the city surrender on 25 May and therefore save itself 'thousands of pounds' of damage. There was then a pause in the action, in order to give the besieged another chance to surrender, but, in fact, Washington took the opportunity to strengthen his defences further and bring in more supplies while he could. In the event, Worcester was able to continue foraging for supplies out of the south side of the city for another month, until Kempsey was occupied by the Parliamentary army on 23 June. Meanwhile, the besieging army was starting to dig trenches and to prepare positions behind the hedgerows, and labourers were brought from surrounding villages to help with the work. The constable of Flyford Flavell was paid 3s for bringing labourers to the siege lines. Carpenters were also brought from Droitwich.[21] Washington therefore also tried to relieve the military pressure by trying to disrupt the efforts of the encircling Parliamentarians by mounting raiding parties (sallies) out of the city. Townshend tells how, on 24 May, 'About 7 at night a strong sally, with 50 horse, fell on their foot that lined the hedges and were stationed about Roger's Hill, beat their guard there back, and killed and hurt at least 40. 2 of ours killed and 3 hurt, 3 taken'. (Roger's Hill is just north of Rainbow Hill, in the angle with Landsdowne Road and the canal.) But the building of the siegeworks continued.

It was vital to ensure the loyalty of the Royalist troops in what, conceivably, could be a long and bloody siege. One of the most pressing needs, therefore, was to ensure that the grumbling troops were paid. No longer able to collect taxes from the countryside, the city would be forced to rely on its own resources. On 23 May it was agreed that the city provide an assessment of £240 a week for one month in order to pay the soldiers – on the understanding that this would cease if the Parliamentary army withdrew (and amounts paid could then be reclaimed out of an assessment levied on the surrounding county). This amounted to 2s 6d per man per week for a month – the alternative was to risk mutiny; the soldiers were already 'muttering and ready to run away for want of bread and provisions'. But this assessment had to be reduced in early June to a payment of 1s in money, 1s in corn and 6d in bacon or cheese.

The besiegers began to settle into their camps on 26 May with a line of ditches and emplacements (sconces) defending the camp on Roger's Hill and linking forwards towards Rainbow Hill (Wheeler's Hill). The possible remains of one of these camps on Elbury Mount, consisting of an enclosure 200 × 100 yds, survived into the nineteenth century. They also requisitioned supplies from the surrounding countryside. Parishioners of Wichenford supplied beer, bread, cheese and bacon to a contingent from Shropshire, while Edmund Andrews paid 5s to the 'Evesham foot' in order for them to buy provisions.[22] Unfortunately, the troops in the new Parliamentary camp managed to burn down their own huts in some drunken revels on the night of 28 May. By 3 June, the siege lines that were designed to enclose the city on the east side stretched from Windmill Hill (Green Hill, Bath Road) on the south side to Barbourne on the north and then through fields to the river. Workmen were drawn in from the countryside to help carry out the work, defended by a force of 500 foot and 200 cavalry against sallies from the city. The defenders were also busy digging in; on 5 June the City Council ordered all shovels, spades and mattocks to be seized and brought for use in strengthening the city's defences. Houses around the inside of the walls were swept away in order to allow troops to be moved from one place to another with ease. All the fuel and lime was brought into the city from St John's on the exposed west bank of the river.

Eighteenth-century engraving of Worcester Bridge, showing the gatehouse. It was the scrawling of the slogan 'Civitas Fidelis Deo et Rege' ('City Faithful To God and King') on the drawbridge of Severn Gate during the siege of 1646 that led to the romance of the 'faithful city'. (Worcester City Museum.)

There were over 7,000 people in the city to feed, a number swelled by refugees from the countryside, and people unnecessary to the war effort were given permission to leave. But there was a condition that if any who left gave aid to the Parliamentary army, their effects would be seized and their families turned out of the city. Yet another call to surrender had been made on 30 May, and Whalley pointed out that Worcester was now 'the only Troublers of this Kingdom'. As a consequence, he believed that they deserved 'to be dealt with in an exemplary way, even to be made a prey to the soldiers'. Some took heed. Townshend tells how, around 4 June, 'Many foot have run out of the City to the enemy for want of pay, and some servants have stole their Master's Horses, clothes and money and gone away to them or to their own country'. As a poor omen, there was one early disaster. On 2 June a culverin (a large cannon firing a 19 lb ball) exploded at St Martin's sconce, killing the city's best cannoneer – the cannon had been aimed at the emplacements on Roger's Hill and had possibly been overcharged to meet the range.

Whalley continued his steady progress to tighten his grip on the city. On 9 June, now reinforced by troops brought from the successful siege of Ludlow (which fell on 27 May), the besiegers had pressed forward on the west side of the Severn with 1,500 men to Henwick and St John's. Townshend claimed that the city managed to beat them off. Even after almost four years of fighting, there was still an attempt to hold on to gentlemanly behaviour between the opposing gentry. A Parliamentary officer was killed and a truce was arranged to allow his body to be brought out of the battle zone. This turned into something of an extraordinary party between the two sides. The governor Colonel Henry Washington, a number of gentlemen and 100 horse went out with the body to the foot of Roger's Hill where they were entertained for two hours by the opposition, drinking wine which both sides had brought. Richard Baxter, the former lecturer of Kidderminster and now chaplain to the Parliamentary commander, engaged in a philosophical discussion with the Royalist Dr Warmestry, later Dean of Worcester. A number of Whalley's men may well have been local, from Kidderminster, and this was therefore a rare opportunity to socialize with friends from what was now a bygone age. Colonel Whalley himself remained aloof and coldly refused to join in with this fraternization.[23]

On 10 June, King Charles (now a prisoner of the Scots) issued a general order from Newcastle to those garrisons still holding out. Referring to Colonel Washington and Worcester by name, he commanded 'to evidence the reality of our intentions of settling a happy and firm peace, to require you upon honourable terms to quit those towns, castles and forts entrusted to you by us, and to disband all the forces under your several commands'. There was a considerable delay before the garrison became aware of this order. By 11 June, Whalley had been able to bring up his heavy artillery of culverins and demi-cannons and the bombardment began in earnest from both east and west sides: the cannon could fire shot of up to $31\frac{1}{2}$ lb and had ranges of up to 1,200 m. One penetrated 2 ft into the earthen rampart of St Martin's sconce. The city returned fire but failed to dislodge the artillery from its positions.

Civil War cavalry trooper's armour of three-bar 'lobster pot' helmet, breastplate and backplate. Note the dent of the proofmark on the breastplate. Reputedly found in a barn at Lulsley, 7 miles west of Worcester. (Private possession.)

On 12 July, the besiegers managed to occupy St John's. It is not clear if this bridge was already defended by the bridgehead bastion as shown on the plan of 1660. Certainly, in 1643, the garrison had improved the bridge defences by demolishing the central span. The city needed to relieve the mounting pressure and a sally of around 700 men (nearly half the garrison) managed to drive them out temporarily and tried to burn down Cripplegate in order to provide a clear field of fire from the city. The garrison claimed that 100 of the Parliamentarians were killed and three colours taken (hung up on the bridge and tower of the cathedral to mock the besiegers). Many of the latter were said to have been drunk as they celebrated moving up into new quarters, but the respite for the city was only temporary. By the next day the Parliamentary artillery was once again firing cannon from St John's on the west, and also long range from Rainbow Hill on the north. The St Martin's area and the Friar's Gate 'blockhouse' were major targets, but nowhere was safe. A man and a woman in the nearby Trinity almshouses were killed in their bed by cannon fire. Damage would have been more severe but for the fact that the city had banned the use of thatch in roofs in 1467.

On 14 June the besiegers completed a bridge of boats, with a plank floor allowing passage of eight men abreast, to cross the river to the north of the city at the upper end of Pitchcroft (opposite Henwick). This completed the encirclement of the city. The bridge was defended by a half-moon emplacement on Pitchcroft which would give two points of attack from the west across the river. The south side of the town was still open and the people continued to graze their cattle at Diglis and make hay. Some citizens tried to leave with their children, but Colonel Whalley is reported (by the partisan Townshend) to have tried to take their money and so they returned.[24]

Townshend's diary tells of both sides trading shots with their artillery and mounting sallies. The city troops bolstered their courage by whatever means available. A somewhat drunken sally was launched by the city on 15 June when Captain William Hodgkins ('Wicked Will') raided St John's with a party of sixteen cavalry. He was 'so drunk that he fell twice by the way' and had to be brought back asleep in a boat. Such stories of raiding parties being fired up with alcohol are common from Civil War sieges.[25]

The Parliamentary strategy was a mixture of shows of force and conciliation, mixed with a little deception. On the evening of 16 June there was a ruse as the besiegers paraded their full army, fired three volleys from around the siegeworks and lit a bonfire in St John's. The intention was to convince the inhabitants that this was a celebration for the fall of Oxford (although it did not occur until four days later) and so destroy their confidence. On 17 June, thirteen guns were fired at St Martin's Church and the Cross Inn, but during the conflict Colonel Whalley also sent in a buck for the governor to eat. It may have been an attempt to create conflict with the hungry citizens; Washington refused entreaties by some women of the city and of the Chamber to surrender, and scavenged the country around as best he could for fresh supplies.

Discipline was rapidly breaking down within the city. Soldiers pulled down outhouses and sold the timber for fuel in order to buy drink. Henry Townshend, who was in the city, offered this advice to insert in one's prayers: 'From the plundering of soldiers, their Insolency, Cruelty, Atheism, Blasphemy and Rule over us, *Libera nos Domine* [God deliver us]'. Many of these soldiers would actually have been Worcestershire men but their first loyalty was now to the army and they were seen as a race distinct.[26]

On 19 June new siegeworks were made in St John's in order to control the west bank of the Severn and the bridge crossing. More people were sent out of the city to preserve the food stocks, but, despite the crisis, the bakers went on strike for more pay. Townshend complains that 'few are so sensible of their present danger, nay hazard of ruin. That the citizens will not send out their servants, or poorer sort to come to work to perfect or amend weak places in the works, nor work at all without money'. Such parsimony exasperated the governor. On 22 June a baker was flogged for not baking and was threatened with being hurled over the walls.[27] The crisis had evidently not united the city in its endeavour and even the governor's footman was thought to have deserted. Fault, however, did not lie entirely with the citizens. Townshend complained that the officers failed to maintain supplies in the magazine, and troops would not go out to raise taxes – or only collected supplies for their personal benefit. Washington remained steadfast and refused to surrender without clear instructions from his king. Desperate for news, he had already sent out four messengers, including a woman sent out on 19 June to try to get further orders from the king – but they had failed to return.

By 22 June, perhaps with their thoughts sharpened by an artillery barrage aimed at the Town Hall the day before, the city had been persuaded to carry out some work on the sconce at St Clement's, and began erecting new defences next to The Butts, between Foregate Street and St Clement's Church on the north side of the city. The implication is that the garrison thought that the line of the medieval fortifications might fall to an assault on that side and needed a second line of defence on which to fall back. It was only by 23 June, and despite the city's attempts to dislodge Parliamentary forces from Barnshall Hill, that the besiegers finally completed their ring of siegeworks on the south side. Again the city was asked, curtly now, to surrender, being 'upon the pit's brink', but again Washington refused.[28] Further siegeworks were therefore made at Battenhall, to tighten the ring still further. Conscious of the need to maintain morale, the impetuous Washington tried to inspire confidence by personally leading further sallies. There was also further demolition of buildings outside the city walls to try to prevent artillery being brought up to close range, under their cover.

On 25 June the citizens finally received confirmation via Prince Maurice's secretary Anthony Kempson (sent down by Fairfax) that Oxford had indeed fallen and that another Parliamentary army of 10,000 foot and 5,000 horse was marching on the city. Whalley wrote to the city that his men 'have nothing to do but to wait upon you'.[29] The next day Washington called a Council of War to discuss possible surrender. Their position was clearly hopeless, and what was worse, they were also galled not to have been mentioned in the Articles of Surrender of Oxford, and only to have heard of the royal surrender order of 10 June via a copy purchased from a bookstall rather than directly from King Charles. It must have appeared that they had been abandoned by their king, but it was still hard to admit defeat.

Some gentry, recusants and reformadoes, including Fitzwilliam Conyngsby, former Governor of Hereford, rejected any talk of surrender until a new command came from the king. This may be the same Mr Coningsby who was later accused of secreting away powder (fifty barrels of which were found in the city on 1 July). Many of these diehards were outsiders, including Irish troops, who had come to Worcester for refuge and were resented by the local establishment. For their part, the Irish troops would have realized that they may be under an automatic death sentence if taken under arms. Tentative approaches were made to sound out possible terms but there was then a heated debate. All of Washington's inclinations were to fight on and he seemed to be won over by the hotheads and asked 'if they would live and die with him upon the walls, and fight it out to the last man'. He then attempted to rush off and fire a gun from the city wall which would break off negotiations for surrender, but he was restrained by the bishop and others. A committee of six soldiers, six gentlemen and six citizens together with the bishop and Dr Warmestry (later Dean of Worcester) was appointed to decide more calmly whether they should negotiate for peace. It was unanimously agreed and a meeting arranged for the Monday at Hindlip House, overlooking the city from the north. As part of their delegation, the city chose Aldermen Thomas Hacket and Richard Heming: both had signed the original refusal to surrender on 26 May but were known to have some Parliamentarian sympathies. On this account they were objected to by some of the soldiers, who wanted to send two further soldiers in their place.[30]

A truce was agreed on 27 June. During it, the governor met outside the city with an old comrade from the continental wars, Colonel William Dingley, now fighting for Parliament (later Governor of Evesham), and drank until 10 p.m. This encouraged a considerable fraternization between the troops of both sides, leading to fears from the citizens that private deals were being made and that their fortunes were to be sacrificed 'to the will and pleasure of soldiers of fortune'. The negotiations dragged on at Hindlip and then Hallow as Worcester tried to win better terms, including one month's pay for the troops and a complete amnesty. In the circumstances this was unrealistic. By 30 June, Whalley was getting impatient with this last outpost of the war. He announced that he wanted a quick decision and therefore the truce was ended.

> The kingdom is at great layings out after you and your city, and much increased by the addition of forces. I intend to be a good husband for you, and not to lose time, which may be improved by the reducing Worcester, therefore give you notice the cessation is at an end.[31]

The battle was to begin again. On receipt of this letter the governor fired the first cannon, which was the prelude to a defiant barrage from the city, aimed at Pitchcroft, St John's and Roger's Hill.

It was a brave gesture. Discipline had continued to break down within the garrison. Washington himself was involved in scuffles with his critics and the guards at the magazine in the cloisters even stole the iron bars from one of the windows. But some determined troops continued to make sallies against the siegeworks and even managed to prevent a new sconce being built on Wall's Furlong. Short of ammunition, they received some fortuitous assistance. On 2 July one of the 18 lb cannon-balls that had hit the bishop's palace was found to fit one of the city's culverins and so was promptly fired back.[32]

Tensions between citizens and soldiers mounted as the latter demanded more pay and provisions. Each threatened mutiny and a proper guard was not mounted. On 4 July four Parliamentary troopers quartered at Barnshall managed to drive off seven head of cattle grazing beneath the city defences because there was no guard, which was particularly unfortunate as food was now scarce in the city – fresh meat was selling at 8*d* per lb. On 1 July the pay of the soldiers had to be cut from 2*s* 6*d* a week to 1*s* a week. Eventually (8 July) the magazine had to be opened to release the last of the stores. This had been resisted as providing a signal to the besiegers that the city was having to make use of its last reserves. Nevertheless, work continued in improving the defences and constructing the inner lines of defence behind both The Butts and Castle Hill in case the main defences were breached. Daring sallies, some led by Washington himself, continued in order to disrupt the efforts of the besiegers and retain some of the initiative, including an attempt to capture Colonel Betsworth at Kempsey. On 11 July, further houses on the east suburb outside Sidbury Gate were also demolished. But on 13 July an exacerbated Townshend again complained that 'Workmen, carpenters, and masons expect money now for their work, as though there were no sieges, nor that their lives and estates were not concerned in it if the City be taken by Storm'.[33] On 14 July the Council had to

The siege saw serious tensions develop between the soldiers of the garrison and the citizens. Both thought that they were about to be betrayed by the other and this hampered the defence of the city, (Copyright: Paul Lewis Isemonger.)

make arrangements for each of the 'Twenty Four' aldermen to pay 4*d*, each of the 'Forty Eight' councillors to pay 3*d* and householders to pay 2*d* per day for that week in order to pay workmen to finish the defences; £35 was levied to pay for gunpowder. The threat to the lives and properties of the citizens was real enough. Having refused an offer to surrender, the convention of the time placed the inhabitants at the complete mercy of the attacking troops if the city had to be stormed.

Parliament had entered a new tactical phase in early July. A new commander was appointed – Colonel Thomas Rainsborough – who based himself at Barbourne House. Whalley had shown little inclination during the siege to mount any direct attack. His orders at the time had been simply to contain the garrison until a large enough army had been assembled, but Rainsborough was thought likely to take a more aggressive stance and it seemed he had been appointed to plan the final assault. A well-known radical, he was later to become one of the leaders of the Levellers. To signal his arrival, he drew up his reinforced army on Rainbow Hill on 9 July. The next day, a new siege line was constructed from the top of Perry Hill towards Red Hill Cross, where they planted two sakers (5¼ lb cannon with a range of up to *c.* 1,000 m). They had an immediate success. One made a direct hit on the protective gabions on the south arm of the 'great sconce'; others hit Castle Hill and Priory Gate. There was also an exchange of prisoners, with the city agreeing to return thirty prisoners in return for seventeen of their own.

The city was not done for yet. By 14 July the citizens had finally managed to complete the lining of the city walls. Two sling pieces were mounted on the cathedral spire to help prevent troops concentrating on Windmill Hill. On 15 July a further small cannon was placed on top of the cathedral to 'gall the besiegers'. The defenders also again managed to prevent the besiegers raising a new work on Wall's Furlong, which was a great boost to morale. 'Our men "wifted" all their light matches over their heads, which made a great show and light, and withal gave a cheerful and courageous shout'.[34] (The 'matches' were the lighted cords used to fire matchlock muskets.)

More pressure on the city was evidently required, although what was maintaining the city was not so much the belief that they could win but a hope to achieve the best possible surrender terms. Following a letter from Washington to Rainsborough on 16 July, in which the former offered that 'in conformity to His Majesties Command, we doe not decline the rendring of this City, upon honourable and equall conditions', a further truce was agreed.[35] The atmosphere relaxed. On the following day troops met 'One or other asking for his father, uncle, kinsman, friend, or fellow or countryman whether they be alive or dead'. This allowed the besiegers the opportunity both to obtain fresh intelligence about the state of the city and also to spread propaganda. They bathed in the River Severn to discover how deep the water was and managed to find out how the food stocks and supplies were lasting. They would undoubtedly have been told that, on the day before, the city had been forced to cut the pay of the troops down to 8*d* a week. The Parliamentary officers also spread propaganda among their Royalist counterparts that they believed the citizens were preparing to make a separate peace and that there was a strong party within the city ready to turn on the garrison if there was a frontal assault. They even tried to ameliorate feeling by putting some blame on the former commander, Whalley, for exceeding his orders and for not passing on earlier messages on terms. Finally, stories were circulated that it was planned to storm the town that night, preceded by a barrage of mortars. Mortars were fearsome weapons employing a high trajectory but low velocity, and capable of hurling explosive shells of 60–150 lb on to the city.

It may therefore have been no coincidence that on 18 July Colonel Rainsborough offered what he insisted were his final terms. The city now only had powder for one day's further fighting: three barrels of powder for cannon, five for muskets and one for pistols. There was food only for a further two weeks. Rainsborough was in no mood to negotiate further. He had clearly put the period of fraternization to good use and claimed that he knew the weakness of the stores to a corn of powder or of grain. Many of the garrison had already deserted; the mayor and corporation therefore finally decided to accept terms. The governor and loyalist gentry feared that, as Rainsborough's men had claimed, if they tried to hold out the city might well withdraw their militia from the guard, refuse to provide provisions or even deliver the city up behind their backs. The citizens had already broken the lock on the postern gate at the Foregate. Townsend describes how 'the city began to grow so mutinous that many gave out, they will throw the soldiers over the wall or club them if they should oppose this treaty, being now as all quiet people are weary of war, desiring their trading may go on'.[36] This is all in marked contrast to the bravado shown in the painting of the slogan *Civitas Fidelis Deo et Rege* ('City Faithful To God and King') on the transom of the drawbridge of Severn Gate.[37]

There was now no choice but to accept the terms, which they did on the next day. The city felt keenly that they had been let down by the king: 'Never poor Gentlemen and City held out more loyal and never any so ill-rewarded as being neither remembered, by the king or the Council at Oxford in the Treaty'.[38] The garrison was to disband and promise never to take up arms against Parliament again (very significant for the events of 1651); and all arms and ammunition were to be surrendered. In return, there was to be no plundering of the city. The clause producing the most consternation was that Sir William Russell, the former governor of the city, was to be excluded from these conditions; Rainsborough personally guaranteed his safety, although this care was somewhat ironic as Russell had been threatened with being beaten up by other Royalist factions during the siege.

For the next few days there was a confused hiatus while waiting for the appointed time of the formal surrender. Parliamentary troops entered the city and had to be sought out and returned by their officers; Royalist troops broke into the magazine and stole the remaining provisions. The garrison finally marched out on the 23 July, following a service in the cathedral, and held a ceremony of surrender on Rainbow Hill. The city was then disarmed and lists were made of Royalist 'delinquents' who would be fined for their role in the Civil War, administered by a Committee of Parliament whose members were drawn locally from Hanley, Kidderminster, Madresfield, Feckenham, Stanford, Alvechurch, Bentley, King's Norton, Evesham, Dodford and Astley. Rainsborough finally marched into the city at 5 p.m.

The city presented Rainsborough with a hogshead of claret, 12 gallons of sack and six sugar loaves, presumably to try to appease him, but the spirit of the surrender terms was not met by all. Fairfax sent a letter to Parliament complaining about the behaviour of Massey's cavalry after the siege 'plundering and violating those that marched out of that city'. Attempts were made to restore the pre-war government by restoring Parliamentarian councillors. Parliamentarians such as Edward Elvins (who was elected sheriff), were brought into the council, and Royalists, such as Edward Solley, were again removed. The new governor was Edward Dineley, former leader of the Clubmen. Although the First Civil War was now over, Parliament was taking no chances on a repeat of such a siege. The city defences were partially levelled, with men pressed into service from the surrounding county. John Lench from Droitwich charged £1 16*s* for going to Worcester 'for throwing down the works'.[39]

CHAPTER NINE

ROYALIST PLOTS: 1647–8

The aftermath of war

Afterthe siege of Worcester was over, Parliament ordered all the garrisons in Worcestershire to be disbanded, with the exception of the garrison at Worcester itself, and the defences to be slighted. The county was largely demilitarized but tensions with the remaining soldiery remained. On 11 August 1646, the parish register of Churchill (near Pershore) records how 'John Bamford of Churchill died at Pershore under the surgion being wounded by a soldier and was buried at Churchill the eleventh of August Ano. 1646'. In November, Doddingtree hundred was assessed for quartering troops of Sir Thomas Fairfax.

As the Parliamentarians extended their influence into Worcestershire they took their revenge on the Royalist 'delinquents', by seizing their estates ('sequestering') or imposing heavy fines ('compounding'). Parishioners were also encouraged to inform on their 'malignant' clergy. The Committee of Sequestrations were vilified as the 'dismemberment of estates and ruin of families'.[1] The rates for compounding ranged from one-tenth to one-half of the pre-war value of the estates in question. In February 1649, Sir William Russell's fine was set at one-third of the value of his estate (£2,071). In all, £28,219 14s 8d was raised from sequestered Royalist estates during 1647–48, but everyone suffered to some degree.[2] A sign of the poverty that such exactions brought can be noted in the absence of evidence of gentry house building in the county until the close of the century. Worcester itself suffered a collective punishment for the long resistance of its garrison. A levy of 25 per cent was made on every man's estate in the city.

The war had been fought at both a heavy personal and economic cost. The quality of the surviving records do not allow detailed estimates to be made of local casualties. Many of the soldiers died anonymously, and far from home. An early casualty was recorded on 27 October 1642 at St Michael Bedwardine in Worcester when one of the Earl of Essex's army, 'Thomas Smyth (a soldier borne in Latimer Lacy in Essex)', was buried. In 1643, on 3 February, the Bushley parish register records the death of 'an old poore souldier yt died att ye constbes' (constables). On the day that the siege of Worcester began, on 21 May 1646, the parish register of St Helen's, Worcester, records how 'A souldier, whose name was not known, was buried'. Again in 1646, the register for Over Aveley records 'An unknowne soldier who was taken up dead as he was swimming downe ye river of Sabine, buried 29 of March'. Likewise, Worcestershire men were also killed away from home; the Dymock parish register records the burial, on 9 April 1644 of 'Richard Evans a souldier of Cropton par. Worcs'. There is a

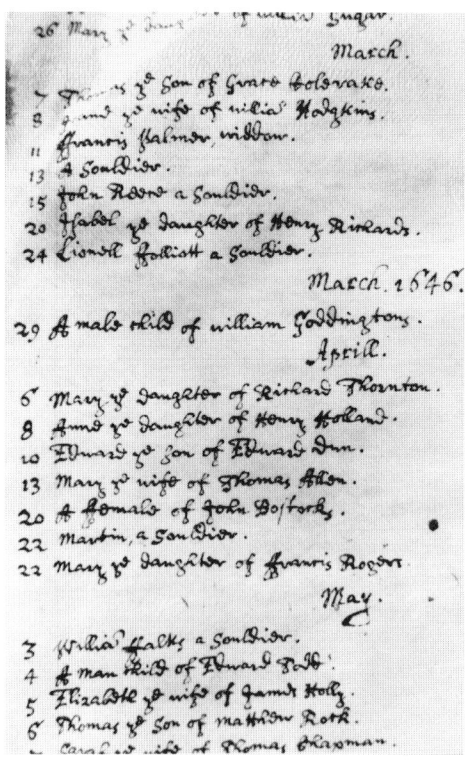

Extract from the parish register of Bewdley for 1645. The deaths of 22 soldiers were recorded in this year, many of them unknown. (Hereford and Worcester Record Office, with permission.)

loneliness too even in the records of the better-off casualties: Captain Francis Alcocke was killed in 1645 while an officer of the Worcester garrison. His inventory records his possessions simply as

His sword and wearing apparell	£5
His two horses	£6
In the hands of captain Humfry Tyrer of the Citty of Worcester in money One hundred & ten pounds	£110

His brothers and deceased sister's orphans were to receive the money while one horse, a chestnut gelding, was to be given to his Lieutenant-Colonel.

The personal consequences were long lasting. Individual examples give a flavour of the difficulties that the county now faced. The county appointed a 'Treasurer of Maimed Soldiers' to award pensions. In April 1644 the overseers of the poor at Stoulton were ordered to pay to H. Hunt 'a maymed soldier, 12d per week untill he hath a pencion'. The Parliamentary Survey of 1649 for Worcester contains an entry under Newnham for 'Humfrey late husband to Mary (who) was slain in the Parliament service, and she left a poor widow in misery'.[3] At Bromsgrove, the Constable's accounts for 1649 records the passage of a number of maimed soldiers through the town who were given overnight accommodation. They included, for 28 March, '3 maymed soldiers Thomas Jones, William Davis and William Laugher quartered over night and sent on with a pass. 1s 4d'.[4] There were other social consequences. The only recently completed St Oswald's almshouses in Worcester were not rebuilt until 1679. What then happened to its inmates? How far were the parishes able to cope with inevitably increased demands from destitute soldiers and other increased claims for poor relief? In the countryside, how far had the continual demands led to a disintegration of local services such as schools?

Inevitably, some individuals and groups profited from the war, such as the iron-master Richard Foley, who had benefited from the increased needs of war production. In Worcester, there are accounts during December 1642–October 1643 for payment of £152 to William Richardson for the making of saltpetre, £55 11s 5d to William and Jane Barber and to James Powell for making powder and to others for casting ammunition, boring cannon and making cartridges.[5] On 7 July 1643, Christopher Gardner applied for payment of £86 9s for three cannon that he had made for the city.[6] The carpenter-turned-builder, Henry Baldwin, made his fortune out of his work on the Worcester fortifications and speculative building, and by the 1660s he was one of the richest men in the city.[7] Some benefited through the discomfort of others. In 1647, the Parliamentarian Sir Walter Devereux petitioned Parliament for four years' losses (1642–6) amounting to £10,000 due to the non-payment of rent from his tenants on his estates at Leigh and Cowleigh.[8] Service did bring other rewards; for instance, on 11 September 1643, it was agreed that Edward Scarlett should be made a freeman of the city for his service as a cannoneer.[9]

Some industries also prospered. The needle industry of the Redditch area benefited in the long term by the migration of skilled workers from Chichester after a battle at the latter.[10] The local clay tobacco pipe-making industry may also have been encouraged by the disruption of trade routes.[11]

In general, however, the war had seriously disrupted the economic life of the county. Vast sums were taken out of the local economy. In five months from December 1642, Sir William Russell received loans of £31,018 0s 9d from local gentry. During 1642–3, John Hornyold's estate of Blackmoor Park in the Malverns paid £12 per month each to the Royalist garrisons of Worcester and Malvern, and also to the Parliamentary garrison of Gloucester.[12] The Dean and Chapter of Worcester agreed to supply King Charles with £1,000 worth of timber from Newnham in February 1643 and in that year the king demanded a loan of £7,000 from the county to defray the costs of the army that he had brought from the unsuccessful siege of Gloucester. The commissioners, quarrelling among themselves, warned that they dare not try to collect such a tax and most of it seems never to have been paid. But tax collectors can have long memories: in February 1649 the constables of Sapey were ordered to appear at Hereford, on the authority of an order of 21 September 1643, to give a full account of all payments made since 1642. On 11 September 1650, John Toms of Longmaston was forced to pay a Parliamentary tax of £2 16s 8d that had been owed since 1642! Toms was a Royalist who helped shelter Charles II on his flight from Worcester in 1651.[13]

The experience of Droitwich provides a good illustration of the crushing effect of the war on a town dominated by a single industry: salt-working. In November 1643, Droitwich had to pay £312 to Lord Byron for clothing regiments as they passed through to Chester. It also had to pay £40 as a bribe 'for saving the town', but this appears not to have worked. In August 1643 Parliamentary troops tried to destroy the saltworks, which were critical not only for the town but for the region as a whole.[14] Although repaired, the Royalists imposed a heavy excise on the saltworks which the salt-masters claimed crippled the industry. In October 1644 the bailiffs and burgesses pleaded that they could not charge more than the existing 2s per bushel as customers could not afford to pay more. This was, however, an oft-used argument. Most of the title deeds to the salt vats had also been destroyed, no

Parish accounts from Pershore detailing the requisitioning of horses for the Parliamentary armies, including those of Essex and Waller. (Public Record Office, with permission.)

doubt causing problems of legal inheritance. The costs were to be long-lasting: as a repayment to those who had contributed to the defence costs of the town, in 1648 it was agreed that one vat of brine was permitted to be drawn from the pit annually for a period of twenty-one years, for each £80 loaned.[15]

The practice of free-quarter was a widespread complaint and appears almost universally in the parish accounts presented after the war and which are now contained within the State Exchequer Papers. Thomas Browne of Powick had to quarter Shropshire troops at the siege of Worcester in 1646 to the sum of 12s; quartering troops at the siege of Hartlebury cost the rector £8; William Saye of Fladbury claimed £120 11s 0d for quartering troops of both sides, together with his monthly contributions.[16]

Apart from such official exactions there were also a host of individual bribes. In 1642, Thomas Pearse of Powick gave 4s to a Parliamentary soldier of Captain Devereux to save his horses. On 28 August 1643, James Hill of Doddingtree was plundered by men of Colonel Sandy's regiment who stole 'certain clothes, woollen and linen to the value of £5'.[17] At Fladbury, George Darby lost two horses worth £6 6s 8d to men of the Earl of Denbigh's forces, then four horses taken by Warwickshire troops worth £40 and a further two seized by Colonel Archer worth £13 6s 8d.[18] In such times, who would invest in, for instance, new buildings? So the building industry was in a severe slump. A good sense of the way in which the populace was exploited by both sides comes from the surviving parish accounts of Hartlebury. The local Royalist garrison was hardly there to protect the surrounding countryside. Thomas Brooke's house, among others, was plundered by the garrison in July 1645, seizing his 'linens, apparell, bedding, pewter and other necessaries' at a cost of £10. He was plundered again by the Scottish army allied to Parliament in the same year, who took exactly the same range of (replacement?) goods to a value of £4 and a further £4 of provisions. He was then plundered a third time by Parliament during the siege of Hartlebury in 1646 when his 'linen, bedding, pewter and brasse, beere and provision and other things' were again taken to a value of £8. The rector, Emmanuel Smith, suffered a similar fate. He lost £4 in provisions to the Earl of Essex in 1642; the Scots seized six oxen worth £27 and goods to the value of £60. He also had to spend £8 in quartering troops during the 1646 siege of Hartlebury. The village also lost corn 'spoyled in the fields by the Scots' as they fanned out across the countryside, while Lynall Wood was stripped of timber for the defences.[19]

Travel in the county became increasingly difficult as roads deteriorated and raiding parties from both sides plundered indiscriminately. Passes were also required and there was the risk of being taken as a spy. There were bans on trade; horses and carts were seized, and it is not clear to what degree non-military traffic survived at all. No one could feel secure in their homes. The diary of Mistress Joyce Jeffreys of Ham Castle at Clifton upon Teme records fees for the burying and digging up of trunks and other property as the armies came and went.[20] In 1849, a hoard of 500 silver coins dating to the time of Charles I was found behind a seventeenth-century inn in Tenbury Wells; they may have been hidden at the time

In 1662 the churchwardens of Little Malvern reported the poor state of repair of the church 'in regard of the late warrs which did so impoverish the people that they were not able to repayre it, being known to be a very small and poore place'.

that the Scottish army occupied the town in 1645. In 1983, a hoard of eighteen silver coins dating to 1646 was found hidden in a timber from an old house in south Worcestershire, an area which had been continually at the mercy of raiding parties from Gloucester.

There was also considerable physical damage. The trade routes were also those routes used by the armies, and the essential bridges had repeatedly been destroyed and roads ruined. At Bewdley, 6*s* 10*d* was paid to repair the paving 'which the reformadoes broke up' during the time of Molyneux's garrison in 1645. It was claimed that £50,000 damage had been done to the county's roads and bridges in the war, meaning that it was increasingly difficult for villages to get their goods to market, if they dared risk the attention of troops on the roads. The fair at Evesham was cancelled in 1643 for this reason. The most systematic damage took place in the suburbs around Worcester as the defenders made a clear field of fire. The account book for Thomas Moore's Bluecoat School for properties in St Martin's suburb states that 'all the houses without St Martyns Gate were Burnt Down and

Destroyed in the late Unhappy warr'.[21] Nevertheless, at least one building – the Plough Inn – did survive in this suburb until the early 1970s. Houses in Ginger Alley were 'fired and pulled downe and the gardens spoyled'. In all around 400 houses in Worcester, one-fifth of the housing stock, may have been destroyed in the Civil War.[22] Some landowners, including the governors of St Oswald's hospital, tried to pass on the cost of the damage to their poor tenants, while attempting to ensure that the new buildings were at least as good as what had been there previously by requiring detailed specifications for the work. Robert James held three tenements in the city that had to be rebuilt by their tenants 'at their own charge'.[23] The best use might be made of any surviving building: a stable on Church Street had been converted to two single-room dwellings by 1649.[24] Not all of the demolition was negative. The 70 yd high lead-roofed bell-tower (then used as a wood shed) next to the cathedral was demolished in 1647 and part of the proceeds of the sale to Colonel Birch (£113 3s 1d) was used to rebuild Inglethorpe's almshouse; a further £180 was used to repair churches in the county,

A plundering soldier. In this contemporary cartoon, the soldier's normal equipment has been replaced by plundered items. It would have been a very familiar image in Worcestershire. (After R. Sherwood.)

including St John Bedwardine (Worcester), St Augustine's Dodderhill and Castlemorton.[25]

Damage extended throughout the whole county. By 1644, Kidderminster was reduced to a 'an empty farm'. At Shurnock we find the farmhouse belonging to John Egioke 'somewhat spoiled by the enemy'.[26] At Great Malvern, an entry in the parish register suggests that the churchwardens had difficulty maintaining the register until 'the rebellion ceased'. In 1662 the churchwardens of Little Malvern reported the poor state of repair of the church 'in regard of the late warrs which did so impoverish the people that they were not able to repayre it, being known to be a very small and poore place'.[27] St Mary Witton in Droitwich was never replaced. In

1674 it was reported that at St Augustine's, Dodderhill, overlooking Droitwich and its important saltworks: 'the body of the church . . . was fired and destroyed by the soldiers in the time of the late distractions and is not rebylt yet'.[28] The vicarage may also have been destroyed at this time (rebuilt 1660–85), perhaps a consequence of the two buildings having formed the core of a defended garrison. Other vicarages were destroyed at Madresfield, Dudley, Evesham and Middle Littleton. The Sheldon family of Beoley described their experiences after their house was burnt down and goods and cattle stolen.[29] William Sheldon and his wife tried to take refuge in Worcester for a time but then moved to Clifton on Teme. After eight months there they were again visited by troops who took their goods and horses and threatened to burn down the farmhouse in which they were staying; they then returned to Worcester and were trapped there during the siege of 1646.

Although the monthly assessments were reduced substantially, the post-war assessment of £749 13s $\frac{1}{2}d$ was still heavy for peacetime. There is, however, some evidence of an economic recovery to some degree up to 1647, stabilizing thereafter. In Worcester, the Chamberlain's Accounts of 1645 show a deficit of £606 14s 6d, but by 1647 this had been translated into a credit of £20 0s 6d. Receipts from Worcester City Council rents rose from £57 11s 2d to £96 12s 0d during 1646–7. This betokens a restoration of order which has been claimed as a rare example during the seventeenth century of a planned direction in local government policy.[30] There was even a rise in the number of apprentices coming into the clothing industry – a process beginning in the latter stages of the war.[31] The quay was

Eighteenth-century engraving of the ruins of Dodderhill Church, Droitwich (1780). The church was used to house a garrison, with a defended enclosure around it, and was partially burnt down during the Civil War.

repaired to facilitate a return of river trade. Property was repaired, in part using material recovered from the slighting of the defences.[32] Even during the war, the city was granting leases on open land that was being developed for building (possibly to accommodate the losses from the suburbs and alleviate the consequent overcrowding within the city).[33] The city did not accept the new political situation easily. In 1647, perhaps with a new-found confidence that came from the signs of recovery, and following its earlier line of perverseness in electing officials against the trend, Worcester tried to elect a noted 'delinquent', George Heming, as mayor (although this was quashed). In the same year, St Michael's in Bedwardine defiantly rang its bells on the anniversary of Charles's coronation.[34]

1648: Royalist plots

Astley's prophecy to his captors after the Battle of Stow that the Parliamentary unity would disintegrate into factional disputes did indeed come true and the Parliamentary party was wracked with divisions. Opinion polarized into monarchists (including those who had fought as Parliamentarians) on one side and republicans (tired with the plotting of Charles II with the Scots) on the other.

The divisions provided the opportunity for a series of risings by Royalists and discontented Parliamentarians that together formed the Second Civil War of 1648. The involvement of Worcestershire in this was somewhat peripheral. Around eighty discontented officers met at Broadway, at the foot of the Cotswolds, in January 1648. Their main targets were said to be Gloucester and Hartlebury and they hoped for the support of 2,000 'capmen' from Bewdley (the manufacturers of the famous 'Monmouth' caps). One of their leaders was Colonel Dud Dudley. Interestingly, however, Worcester is not mentioned as a possible target, although the militia had been mobilized in the city against 'any tumult or uproare that shall arise' (through economic as much as political grievances). Parliament got to hear of the plot and took swift action. Colonel Morgan was sent with his men from Gloucester to block the road to London in case there was an actual rising in the county. Nothing actually came of the plot, but in June the Worcestershire Committee was authorized to raise fresh troops to quell any insurrection. In July, Colonel Turton at Hartlebury appears to have heard of further plotting in Shropshire, probably through information from the noted Worcestershire industrialist and Parliamentarian Captain Andrew Yarranton (whom Parliament rewarded with £500 and sequestrations from a number of Royalist estates in the county and surrounds). Gunpowder was found behind the house of the parson of Wolverley, who was implicated in the plot. One of the leaders, Major Harcot, was arrested and taken to Hartlebury where he was tortured by having lighted musket matches placed on the soles of his feet in order to make him confess and identify his confederates.[35]

Harcot's information allowed Colonel Dud Dudley to be captured while drilling 200 Staffordshire men near Madeley. Dudley subsequently escaped from prison in Worcester. Recaptured, he was taken to London and was ordered to be executed.

Engraving of Worcester Cathedral, 1672. The cathedral was used to store arms by the Royalists in 1642 and the cloisters were subsequently used to stable horses by the Parliamentary army. In 1651 the building was used to contain Scottish prisoners taken after the battle. Although this engraving is dated 1672, it actually shows the building as it was in 1646, prior to the demolition of the bell-tower. The proceeds from the sale of the latter were partially used to help repair other churches in the diocese. (Worcester City Museum, with permission.)

Amazingly, he escaped the night before he was due to be shot and managed to finally escape to Bristol. He died in 1684 and is buried in St Helen's Church, Worcester.

There was a further rising in Herefordshire in August 1648. Some of the arms were supplied from Worcestershire: a Kidderminster joiner, John Brancill, had apparently been employed by Edward Broade of Dunclent (two miles from Kidderminster) to make stocks for muskets to be used in the rebellion. Broade had raised a troop of Royalist horse for his son Edmund during the war.[36] Nothing came of these threats because Parliament managed to keep a tight military hold on the county; as a result, Worcester and Hartlebury were re-garrisoned and further troops raised from the county. This phase of the conflict ended with the fall of Pembroke in July and the defeat of the Scottish army in August at Preston.

The various plots were a significant factor in Parliament's and the army's loss of

Copy of the death warrant of Charles I. Few could have imagined this turn of events at the start of the Civil War. There was a rumour that 'Tinker' Fox was one of the executioners, but there is no other evidence to support this. (Worcester City Library.)

patience with Charles I. He was brought to trial and, in January 1649, was executed. 'Tinker' Fox is said by legend to have been one of the executioners. The monarchy and House of Lords was abolished in 1649, and power was concentrated in a Council of State.

Few in Worcestershire could have been happy with this turn of events. One of Worcestershire's most notable Parliamentarians, the MP Sergeant John Wilde, refused to serve as a judge at the trial of Charles I and consequently fell out of favour with Oliver Cromwell, although he was restored to the Council of State by Oliver's son, Richard. Yet the only popular uprising was not about politics directly but rather the continuing burden of taxation. In January 1649 there was a riot of 2,000 people in Worcester against the Excise Tax. It may, however, have been no coincidence that this took place at the time of the king's trial.

The Wilde family was one local family split by the Civil War. This fine carved bedhead, showing their coat of arms, is still in their former house at the Commandery, Worcester. (Commandery Museum, Worcester, with permission.)

CHAPTER TEN

THE BATTLE OF WORCESTER: 1651

The Lord gave our men to gaine ground of the enemy, till we had beaten them out of the ground: the charges was very hot for a while, but the Lord owned us in this contest, and the enemy fled before us.

(Robert Stapleton at the Battle of Worcester, 1651)[1]

The Third Civil War

In June 1650 Charles II landed in Scotland and took the Covenant. This marked the start of the Third Civil War. In September he was defeated by Cromwell at the Battle of Dunbar. Spies looked for any signs of plotting in England to support Charles but interestingly there is no surviving evidence of plots in Worcestershire at this time. There was, however, some disturbance and bloodshed caused by overzealous tax collectors from the Excise Commission and they were replaced to lessen tensions that Parliament could ill afford.[2] Madresfield House was also ordered to be demolished for fear that it might be fortified in any Royalist rising (although Parliament was still querying in March 1651 as to whether this had actually been carried out).

In January 1651 Charles was crowned at Scone in Scotland. Parliament was still worried about the loyalties of Worcestershire and the Council of State ordered 'special care' for its security including the removal of 'all dangerous and suspicious persons'. Foremost among these was the former Governor of Worcester, Colonel Samuel Sandys, who was refused permission to enter the county in May. By a fortunate chance, his brother Martin Sandys already lay under arrest. He had been accused of a murder in Worcester and had been arrested by accident while in hiding in Essex.[3] In March Parliament had ordered Worcester to be made untenable by slighting the defences (netting a profit of £23 from the sale of materials) and the militia to be raised. Parliament did, however, still feel able to send troops from the county to Ireland in May. So it appears that these were merely precautions rather than the result of clear evidence that the county would rise, or that Charles might march on the county.

At the end of July, Charles marched into England with that part of the Scottish army that would follow him: around 12,000 men and sixteen leather cannon. This

Charles II (1630–85). He chose Worcester as his final stand in his attempt to regain his crown by force in 1651, but was disappointed by the scale of the English support. (Worcester City Library.)

was a foreign army and few English Royalists joined on the march: their leaders had largely been neutralized by exile, prison or were under close watch. The army was also marching through areas that had bad memories of the earlier Scottish army (though then supporting Parliament), under the same leadership, that had marched through in 1645. Rather than march directly on London, Charles followed his earlier strategy in wanting to open up a supply line again from Wales and so headed for Worcester, confident that he would receive support there. The army marched through Lancashire, defeating a Parliamentary army at Warrington, and then continued on south. Shrewsbury refused to surrender and had to be bypassed. The Scottish army therefore marched on to Lichfield, Wolverhampton and then into Worcestershire, stripping the land of crops and livestock as they went. They moved through Kidderminster, Hartlebury and Ombersley to Worcester, arriving there on 23 August after a three-week-long march of around 300 miles.

Although outnumbered, there was some resistance from the 500-strong local Parliamentary garrison of Worcester under Colonel John James (later rewarded with the governorship of Worcester) and the 'country forces' including the men of Captain Andrew Yarranton who had rallied on Pitchcroft. Yarranton tried to demolish the bridge at Bewdley to hinder the march and then skirmished with the Scottish advance guard at Ombersley. These vastly outnumbered troops were reinforced by 500 troopers sent by General Harrison, but the latter arrived too late to have a significant impact.[4] Initially, it appeared that the citizens of Worcester had been prepared to try to defend the city against the approaching Scottish horde. A letter to the Lord President of the Council on 23 August claimed that the garrison had done their best to strengthen the so-recently levelled defences, assisted by the citizens. But the resolve of the latter seems to have quickly crumbled when it became apparent that no great reinforcements were to be expected. In a heated debate of the City Chamber, Edward Elvin (former sheriff and later the governor), Major Estopp and Captain Alie argued to resist the approaching army, but they were outvoted in favour of allowing a peaceful entry. The city therefore laid down its arms and even began shooting at the 'forlorn hope' of Parliamentary troops as the latter finally withdrew from the city (taking the precaution of removing the contents of the ammunition magazine with them).[5] It is not clear whether this was due to a small Royalist faction, a gesture of frustration against soldiers in general or simply an attempt to gain favour with the approaching Scottish army.

So Worcester was occupied with barely a fight. There had clearly been some realization within the City Council as to what the future might bring if the king lost the struggle, but doubts were put aside temporarily as the king was received on 23 August. Charles was formally proclaimed king of England in a show of great pomp and ceremony, 'with all the demonstration of affection and duty that could be expressed' according to Clarendon, writing after the Restoration. Thomas Lysons, the mayor, presented the king with the keys of the city and the mace, and was knighted in return. Retribution soon followed to prominent Parliamentary sympathizers. Symon Moore, a minister at the College 'being a very faithfull precher of God's word and of singular good affection to the Government of this Commonwealth . . . suffered greate losses by the Scotch Army at Worcester' and was later compensated.[6] The Scottish troops were exhausted by their 300 mile march and by now were very poorly equipped. The burden of resupplying the army 'that it wanted nothing that it could desire' fell heavily on the city.[7] New shoes and stockings had to be found; £453 1s 5d worth of cloth was delivered for making up into uniforms. The citizens also had to provide food: £183 14s 4d was spent on veal, mutton, lamb, chicken, rabbit, pigeon, duck, eggs, butter, hams, bread, fruit, candles and wine. On the night before the battle, the city had to spend £7 5s 4d on wine for the troops. On the day of the battle itself, they spent a further £6 6s 0d on sack and claret as the hard-pressed Scots fortified themselves. It was an uncomfortable alliance though between the old Royalists, reformed Parliamentarian and Scottish officers (the latter were divided between 'covenanters' and former 'engagers'). There were more personal disputes, as between Leslie and Buckingham as to who should be Lieutenant-General under the Duke of Hamilton. Leslie was also jealous of another general, Middleton, and was described by Clarendon as being 'disappointed and confused' during the later battle. This fragile unity was threatened by the preacher (Mr Crosby) at the service in the cathedral who offended the covenantor Scots by his praise of the idea of royal supremacy, 'in all causes and over all persons, next under God, Supreme Head and Governor'.[8]

It was immediately clear that this was to be no passing visit. There were feverish orders to refortify the city 'beyond imagination' according to Nicholas Lechmere of Hanley.[9] On Sunday 24 August Charles II ordered the citizens of Salwarpe parish, next to Droitwich: 'You are hereby required to send out of your parish 30 able men to work at the fortifications of this city, and in regard of the necessity to begin tomorrow morning (Monday) at five o'clock, whereof you and they are not to fail, as you tender our displeasure'.[10] City gates were blocked, new earthworks were constructed across the London Road and a large star-shaped sconce, Fort Royal, was built (or restored) to command the high ground to the east (Red Hill) and also the lower ground alongside the rest of the east defences. Colonel Robert Stapleton, based at Spetchley, admired the work: 'They have raised a very fair and large fort on this side of the town, which they possess and man very strongly'. However, Blount

Oliver Cromwell (1599–1658). The victor in the battle of 1651, although his enemies claimed that this was only by the assistance of the Devil.

claimed it was still unfinished at the time of the battle.[11] Cannon-balls and clay pipes were found there in the nineteenth century and the east ditch was excavated in 1969. It was connected to the city walls by earth ramparts on to the St Martin's blockhouse and also to the river below Castle Mound. Eighteenth- and nineteenth-century plans also show a protected 'covered way' leading directly back to the Commandery, and an outer defence to the Fort on the east side. The final resistance in the forthcoming battle came from the castle mound, on the south side of the city. The Vaughan Plan of 1660 shows the castle mound with a four-armed sconce on the top and with the sides of the mound protected with storm poles.

It is unlikely that the defences were properly completed, or that the Royalists had sufficient guns to defend them properly. Stapleton also adds, 'They have burnt many outhouses', reflecting a renewed clearance of the suburbs.[12] As an outer defence, the bridges across the Severn, at Upton and Bewdley, were broken down on the Monday to try to stop the Parliamentary forces massing on both east and west sides of the city. If this did not work then the River Teme would provide an outer line of defence on the south side. Bransford and Powick Bridges were also, therefore, partially demolished. The subsequent rebuilding of the two northernmost piers of Powick Bridge is still visible.

The king was housed within the city beside the Old Cornmarket, and the Duke of Hamilton at the Commandery just outside Sidbury Gate on the east side. It is likely that the army was encamped as far out of the city as Upton and up towards the Malverns, as well as on Pitchcroft. The troops were divided into three segments: the main force lay within the new defences of the city; Leslie's cavalry protected the left flank on Pitchcroft; and on the right flank was a large body of infantry on the floodplain to the south of the city, between the Teme and the Severn.

The significance of this activity is that the king had obviously decided that it would be here, at Worcester, that he made his stand to determine the fate of the nation. Either he hoped to outmanoeuvre the attempts to encircle him and bring Cromwell's approaching army to open battle (with the security of the town behind him), or else he hoped that any ensuing siege would be a focus for his loyal subjects to flock to him. It was a dangerous gamble with little opportunity for a second chance.

Even at this stage the odds seemed firmly against the king. The king's generals were at loggerheads with each other; expected reinforcements from the Earl of Derby were intercepted, and destroyed, by Lilburne at Wigan. Most of the local gentry were therefore not prepared to support openly what already seemed like a lost cause, and some may also have remembered their oath at the surrender of the city in 1646 not to take up arms against Parliament again. They might remember that Major William Pitcher, a member of the Worcester garrison in 1646, had been executed in 1648 for breaking this oath and for taking part in the Second Civil War. For whatever reason, few of the Worcestershire gentry turned up in answer to the king's summons to meet on the Pitchcroft on 26 August. In all, twenty-four of the local gentry were listed as being present, including Sir John Pakington of Westwood (who later claimed duress but still faced a massive fine), Sir Ralph Clare, the Blount family and Ralph Sheldon of Beoley – they had all been members of the Committee of Safety during the First Civil War. Two others who joined were the Worcester clothiers Walter Heming and William Clarke, who deserted Yarranton's militia for the Scots. Sir Rowland Berkeley, for one, resolved 'not to meddle' and remained at home. Others were said to have joined only 'out of fear and terror.'[13] Two further manifestos to gain support failed equally dismally, despite attempts to win over the Parliamentary army by promising to pay their arrears of pay.[14] Some hope had been made of the possibility that old friends might join the local hero Edward Massey, who had now joined the Royalist cause. He too was ignored. King Charles had been deserted by the English and now had to fall back almost entirely on his detested Scottish army, with a total force of around 12,000–16,000 men.

Meanwhile Parliament was gathering troops from all across the country. The Royalist Blount, writing in the *Boscobel Tracts*, called them 'generally the scum and froth of the whole kingdom'.[15] Militia marched at the double from Essex, Norfolk, Suffolk, Cambridgeshire, Cheshire, Staffordshire, Surrey, Somerset, Leicestershire and Warwickshire. They were rejoined by Worcestershire troops as well, returning from their flight to Gloucester. Cromwell was eventually able to bring an army of 28,000 men to the city. On 27 August the Parliamentary forces rendezvoused at Evesham, sixteen miles from Worcester. Feeding such a body of men must have been a logistical nightmare. Gloucester sent 40 barrels of strong beer to the army, with a cask of 'better quality' for Cromwell himself on 30 August. The city also provided ammunition, hides (to cover the ammunition) and hay.

Cromwell's plan was to cut the Scottish army off from either an advance to London or a retreat to Wales, and then destroy it. The Parliamentary army had succeeded in the first part of the plan by occupying Evesham. Now the task was to try to close off any escape route to Wales. Massey had occupied Upton-upon-Severn for the king with around 200–300 Scottish troops in order to defend the Severn river-crossing and prevent Cromwell attacking the city from both east and south sides. He still perhaps thought that he would be reinforced from old allies across the border in Gloucestershire. To prevent the Parliamentary army from crossing the river, the two western arches of the bridge had been destroyed; however, following normal practice in these situations, one plank had been laid across it for

The tower of Upton-upon-Severn Church. The Parliamentary advance party took shelter here while waiting for reinforcements to cross the river. The Scottish troops tried, unsuccessfully, to burn them out.

convenience. He had also dug in upstream of the bridge to cover the Worcester Road; part of a rectangular emplacement survives in the field adjacent to Pool Brook, on the left side of the road leading to Hanley Castle, and now cut by the modern road.[16] Massey himself was quartered at Nicholas Lechmere's house at Hanley Castle, one mile behind the bridge.

On 29 August Major-General Lambert's men, including the Worcestershire militia, led a desperate assault on the bridge at Upton to allow forces to occupy the west bank and so turn the Royalist's right flank. No sentry had been placed on the bridge and so, at dawn, an advance party of eighteen dragoons shuffled silently across the remaining plank laid across the demolished bridge. Although eventually spotted, they managed to reach the nearby church which they barricaded and defended, despite it being set on fire by the Scots. Fortunately, they were then relieved by Lambert's dragoons who had subsequently managed to ford the low river at Fisher's Row. It was now possible to throw more planks across the bridge and, as more and more troops poured across, Lambert was able to storm Massey's positions across the Worcester Road. Massey himself was seriously wounded in the fight: as reported, at 'least forty carbines were shot at him within half pistol shot'.[17] General Fleetwood, Cromwell's second-in-command, made all speed to send reinforcements to the bridgehead. As a first step, he sent on 300 horse, with a musketeer riding behind each trooper. The Scottish army now faced encirclement with troops pouring across the Severn at an alarming rate. During the next day 12,000 troops are reported to have crossed over the Severn, a force almost equal to the total strength of the poorly equipped and tired Scots. Dragoons (mounted infantry) under Colonels Twistleton and Kendrick raced ahead and westwards to set up outposts across the Teme valley, crossing by ford to the east of the demolished Bransford Bridge. This was to cut off communication with any possible reinforcements from Wales. Other troops occupied Madresfield House. The second stage of the trap was therefore laid.

Remains of a rectangular earthwork dug by the Scottish army to block the main road from Upton to Worcester. Its bank and ditch would have provided shelter for musketeers but proved little obstacle to the advancing Parliamentarians.

With forces now in position on both sides of the Severn, and the route to Wales blocked, Cromwell sought to block any line of retreat northwards. Again, local troops played a significant role. Worcestershire cavalry under Major Mercer and Colonel Blundell were sent to Bewdley to block any line of retreat across its bridge. Letters were also sent to the commanders of the northern militias to warn them to deal with any stragglers that might manage to escape the battle that was clearly soon to come.

The ring had now closed on the desperate Scottish army, with Parliamentary troops massing on the high ground overlooking the city from the north and east, and now also on the floodplain to the south. The front was eight miles long in all. This was not to be the long, cautious attempt to win the city by starving the garrison out or by negotiation, as seen in 1646. Cromwell had enough men to bring the Scottish army out to open battle, and then to take the city by storm if needs be. First came the softening-up. The new artillery positions on Red Hill and Perry Wood opened up a heavy barrage into the city from the east. The Scots had somehow to relieve the pressure. They returned fire from Fort Royal and attempted a night attack on two Parliamentary gun positions. One was on Red Hill to the east (where Cromwell may have had a forward command post – hence the place-name

'Oliver's Mount' beside the old London Road) and the other on either Battenhall Mount or Bund's Hill, further to the south. To identify themselves in the darkness they wore their white shirts over their armour – a 'camisado' or 'shirt-tail fight' – but the Scots, led by Lieutenant-General Middleton and Sir William Keith, were betrayed by an informer from the town, a tailor named William Guyes, and were themselves ambushed with considerable loss of life. Guyes himself was arrested and hanged outside the Golden Cross on Broad Street. After the siege, Parliament granted his widow £200 and £200 p.a. as compensation. There were evidently other spies who were passing on information to Cromwell. After the battle a payment of £40 was divided among 'such persons as gave intelligence to our forces of the transactions in Worcester' and a mysterious further £100 'to the little maid'.

But the Parliamentary barrage was, in reality, only a diversion to Cromwell's main plan. On the morning of 3 September, Cromwell launched the final element of the strategy: the crushing of the Scottish army itself. The first stage was to try to defeat the Scots in open battle on the plain west of the Severn. General Fleetwood, with 12,000 men, advanced from Upton soon after dawn in two columns, accompanied by a small fleet of boats that were rowed up in preparation to make bridges in order to cross the Severn and Teme. Civil War battles could be confused affairs. According to Robert Stapleton, the Parliamentary army identified itself by showing nothing white, to distinguish itself from the white colours carried by the Scots. Their watchword was 'The Lord of Hosts' (Appendix 2).

Fleetwood's army was in position to attack between 2 p.m. and 3 p.m. The westernmost column under Dean tried to drive out the Scottish outpost at Powick and seize the bridge there. The Scots, under General Keith, doggedly fought their way back through the village – the marks of bullets are still visible on the tower of the church – and down on to the floodplain of the Teme, fighting from hedge to hedge back to Powick Bridge. It proved impossible to use cavalry in the enclosed fields and so the battle was one of furious hand-to-hand fighting. Robert Stapleton described how the contest 'was very hot, but the Lord gave our men to gaine ground of the enemy, till we had beaten them out of the ground' (Appendix 2).[18] Reinforcements had been hurriedly sent down from St John's and the Scots still managed to hold on to the bridge.[19] There was a battery on the high ground behind the bridge at Manor Farm and a cannon-ball was found when the Electricity Generating Station was built in 1894.

The eastern column initially had somewhat better fortune. The boats were towed into position to form one bridge across the 35 m wide Teme and a second bridge 'within pistol shot' (*c*. 45 m) to the north just beyond the confluence of the Teme and the much wider Severn (over 70 m wide). A 'forlorn hope' was put across to defend the far bank, with the Scots massed on the fields beyond, taking advantage of the slightly higher ground. Fighting developed all along the river bank. All this was visible from King Charles's vantage point at the top of the cathedral tower. He rode out to encourage his hard-pressed troops at Powick, urging them to hold the bridge to the last man, but he failed to reach Pitscottie's Highlanders fighting it out at the junction of the Teme and Severn. Much of the area of the battle on the

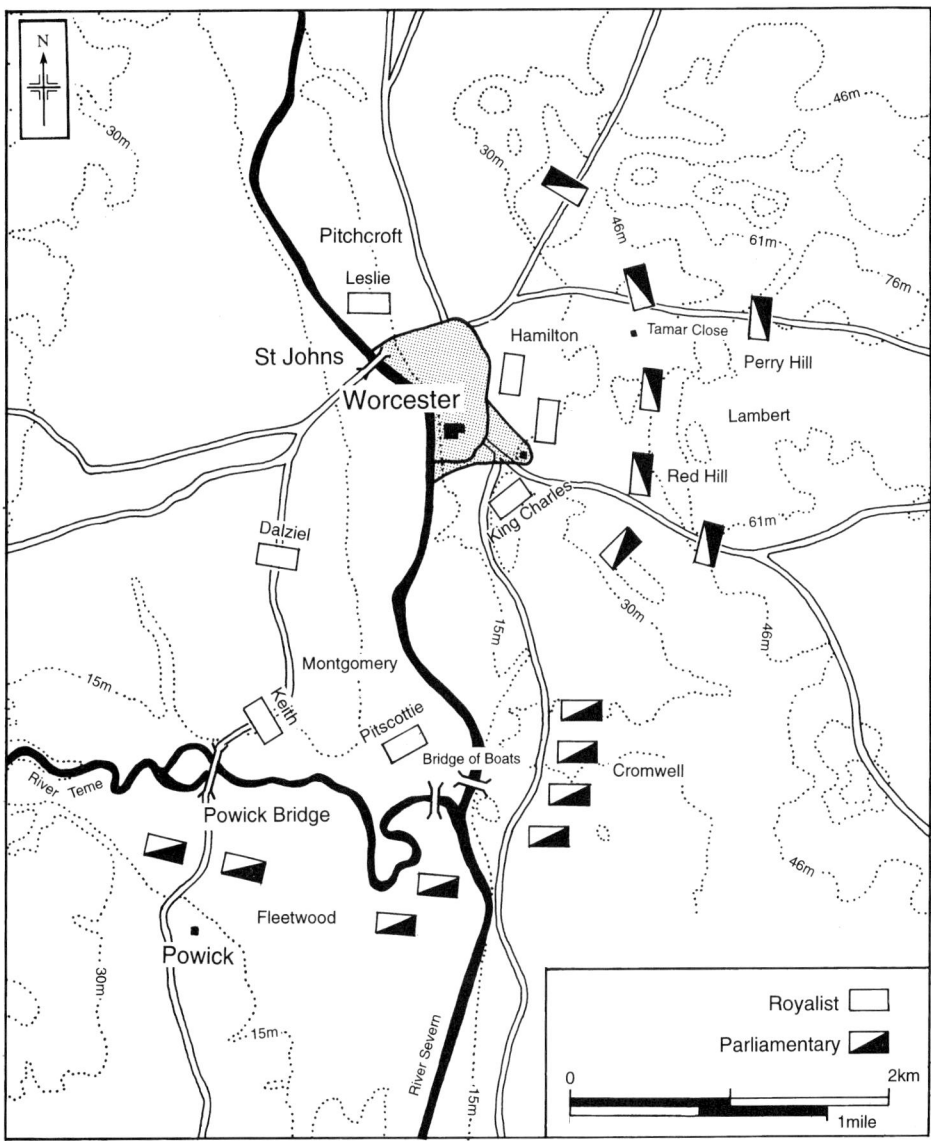

Plan of the initial disposition of troops at the Battle of Worcester.

open pasture land south of the bridge looks much the same today as it did then. With the battle bogged down on the banks of the Teme, Cromwell now brought up three brigades of reinforcements from the east side of the Severn to attack the Highlanders in the flank. The regiments of Ingolsby, Fairfax, Hacker, the Lifeguard and part of Cromwell's regiment itself came off the shoulder overlooking the east bank in Timberdine and crossed over the bridge of boats built across the Severn. The Scots fought furiously against the expanding bridgehead, fighting now on two fronts and held to the west by Twistleton's dragoons. The latter now managed to repair Bransford Bridge and send further troops across.[20] The Scots were now under assault from east, south and west. They were eventually worn back by sheer weight of numbers, hedge by hedge and often by push of pike. Colonel Haines managed to ford the Teme at Powick with his regiment and the bridge finally fell into Parliamentary hands. Fleetwood and Dean were now able to bring their full forces across the Teme at three bridging points. After half an hour to one hour the Scots, with no sign of reinforcements coming to support them, began to retreat, and the retreat then turned into a rout as the survivors escaped as best they could. Some of Keith's men escaped to Cotheridge and then Bewdley, hotly pursued by the Parliamentary cavalry, but the rest were forced through St John's and eventually into what became the death trap of Worcester itself. Cromwell describes in a letter how 'We beat the enemy from hedge to hedge, till we beat him into Worcester', which included forcing the passage over the River Severn itself.[21]

Part of the blame for this disaster must lie with the bickering and jealousies of the Royalist and Scottish generals. For some reason, Leslie refused to send out his cavalry from Pitchcroft to cover the retreat. Meanwhile, however, Charles thought that Cromwell may have over-weakened his forces on the east side of the river by his reinforcement of Fleetwood. This was his chance to seize the initiative. Around 4 p.m. he therefore launched a diversion in order to relieve the pressure on his hard-pressed Highlanders by a pincer movement on the Parliamentary centre on the adjacent Red Hill and Perry Hill. Inexperienced militia troops from Cheshire and Essex bore the brunt of the attack. Charging out of Sidbury Gate through the cleared suburb, Charles himself led the assault to the right, with Hamilton on the left. At first they seemed victorious and Hamilton captured the guns on Perry Hill while Charles reached the crest of Red Hill. It is still possible to visualize the attack on Perry Hill from the ground: the face of Perry Hill was too steep for a frontal assault so Hamilton swung up the flank, via a lane leading to a former watercourse (this is the feature popularly described as 'Cromwell's Trenches'). The sides of the lane were lined with musketeers and in the field at the end (still containing the earthworks of medieval ridge and furrow) was a troop of cavalry.[22] Hamilton's troops managed to break their way through and then attack the guns on the top of Perry Hill from the flank. Under the ferocity of this onslaught, the Parliamentary forces began to retreat, but Charles and Hamilton had neither the reserves nor the ammunition to follow up their success. After they ran out of ammunition, the Scots desperately fought on as long as they could with the butt-ends of their muskets.[23] Again, the Scottish cavalry reserve would not come out to fight, and so press home

Powick again played an important role in the ensuing battle. Parliamentary troops fought the desperate Scots back through the village 'hedge by hedge' until they reached the bridge. (Copyright: Paul Lewis Isemonger.)

the advantage. The Parliamentary troops rallied and held their ground, giving Cromwell time to bring back his three regular brigades and force back the Scots. Hamilton, shot in the leg with a 'slug shot', was mortally wounded and was carried back to the Commandery. The Scots then began a general retreat and Cromwell pressed on after them. Fort Royal was stormed by the Essex militia; the 1,500 strong garrison under Sir Alexander Forbes was cut down and its guns turned on the city. Stapleton describes how they 'followed them boldly to the very mouth of their cannon, which was planted on their mountain-works [Fort Royal]; at length we gained their works, (and planted their great guns against them in the town)'.[24] The fort is a mere 200 m above the south gate and dominates the whole city. From being a key part of Worcester's defences, Fort Royal now became a terrifying weapon in its destruction as its cannon pounded retreating Scots and the city.

With this shift in focus of the battle, part of the Parliamentary army on the west bank of the Severn now re-crossed on the bridge of boats and marched up through Diglis to attack the city on the south side, below the castle. They broke through the defence lines between Fort Royal and Sidbury Gate, thus taking the Scots in their flank. As night fell, the Scots tried to escape into the city through Sidbury Gate but were cut down or crushed in the rush as the Parliamentary army pushed

The marks of musket fire can still be seen on the walls of Powick Church tower.

through the gate behind them. King Charles was unable to prevent Cromwell's forces from entering the city as they pressed home their attacks on the very heels of the retreating Scots, and thereby preventing the access points from being blocked. Charles tried desperately to rally his men outside the Commandery. A later story tells how he was only saved from capture or death by a Worcester man, William Bagnell, driving his ox team between the king and advancing Parliamentary cavalry. To the west, Fleetwood had been able to take advantage of the battle on the east side and continued his advance to take St John's Bridge and cross into the city. This might have been expected to be more difficult, but here, according to Blount, the Scots laid down their arms and surrendered 'without any great resistance'.[25] The bridgehead defence as shown on the plan of 1660 obviously proved little hindrance. This success was critical. Fleetwood's cavalry now poured down Broad Street into the heart of the city.

Attacked on three sides, according to Clarendon, the Royalist cavalry now fled in panic – with Charles vainly trying to rally the officers by calling to them by name. Indeed Clarendon says that Charles was almost knocked down by his own men as they retreated past him. 'There were few to command and none to obey'. Charles only just managed to escape the city from his quarters off the Cornmarket on the north-east side via St Martin's Gate and galloped out to Barbourne Bridge, where there was a hurried conference to plan the escape route – this was at about 6 p.m. As he fled he was encumbered by other escaping horsemen and later complained 'We had such a number of beaten men with us, of the horse, that I strove . . . to get from them; and though I could not get them to stand by me against the enemy, I could not get rid of them now I had a mind to it'. Major-General Harrison's brigade of cavalry was sent in hot pursuit.

The final resistance in the city came from Castle Mound where eventually the 1,300 exhausted troops under the Earl of Rothes and Colonel Drummond were forced to surrender. By 10 p.m. the battle was over. Of the Scots, 3,000 had been killed, another 10,000 taken prisoner and driven into the cathedral. Almost all the

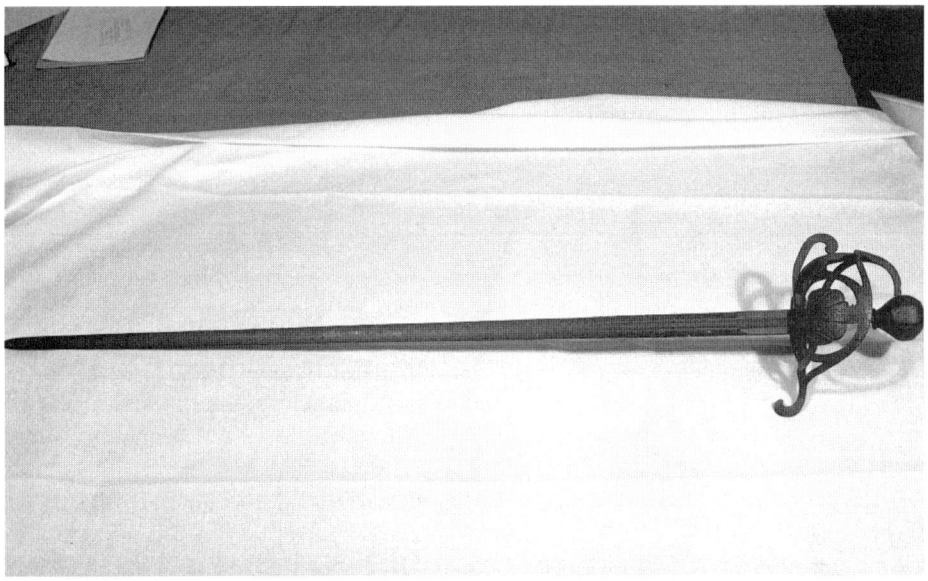

Civil War sword found at Powick (Commandery Museum, Worcester, with permission).

Model of Fort Royal at the Commandery Museum, Worcester, showing the earthen rampart and ditches. Note the storm poles providing an additional obstacle on the ramparts.

officers had been wounded. Only around 2,000 escaped and, since they were so widely scattered, they were no longer any serious threat. The victors showed little mercy as 'Lords, knights and gentlemen were there plucked out of holes by the soldiers'. The Scots had been used as a threat to both sides on too many occasions and as the survivors fled, Cromwell reported 'the country riseth upon them everywhere'. Now eager to show their loyalty, and with the memories of years of torment inflicted on them by the soldiery, Clarendon wrote, 'very many of those who ran away were every day knocked in the head by the country people, and used with barbarity'. Others were shot down as they were ambushed by the outlying garrisons at Bewdley, Kidderminster and elsewhere. A shallow grave of a man with a purse of Scottish and French coins was found in 1902 at Himbleton, south-east of Droitwich; he may well have been one of the casualties as he fled homewards. South of Broome is the place name 'Scots Graves' which may mark a point where fleeing Scots were cut down.[26] Cromwell claimed only to have lost 200 men. In all, the battle had lasted ten hours.

All contemporary writers agree on the terrible fate that was now to befall Worcester. Nicholas Lechmere of Hanley wrote in his diary, 'The city of Worcester

View of the Civil War artillery emplacement in Tamar Close, Worcester. The Parliamentary army occupied the high ground to the east of the city. They lined the crest of the hills with their artillery and sited other guns in emplacements on the lower slopes. Although possibly built in 1646, it is also likely that this is one of the emplacements overrun by the Duke of Hamilton's men in the early stages of the battle of 1651.

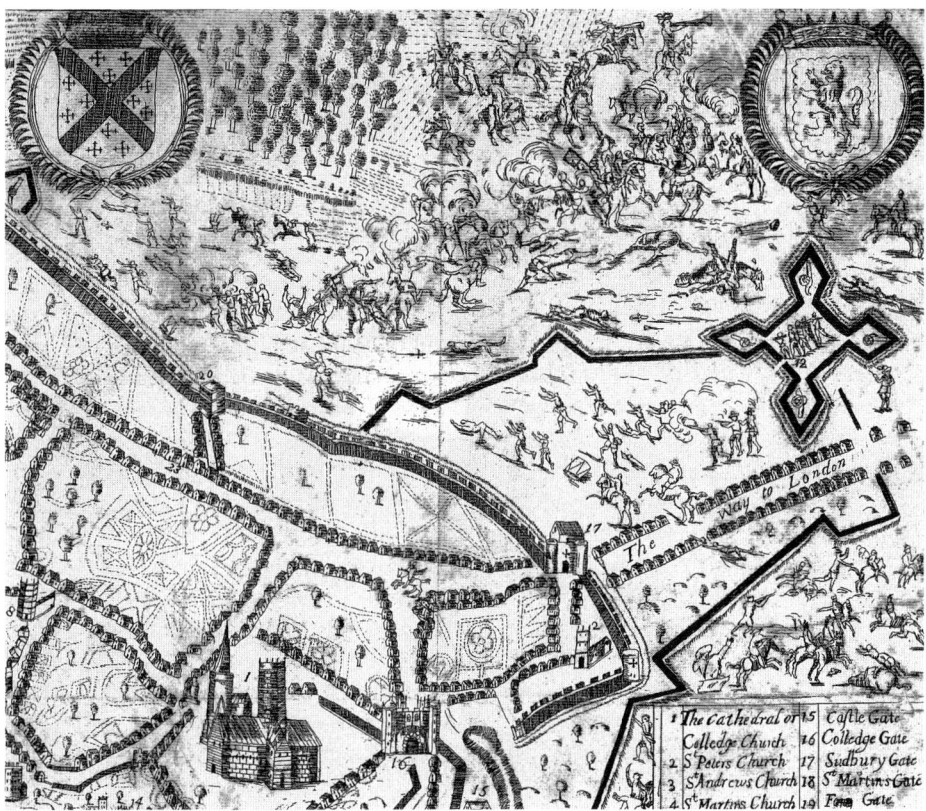

1	The Cathedral or	15	Castle Gate
	Colledge Church	16	Colledge Gate
2	S.ᵗ Peters Church	17	Sudbury Gate
3	S.ᵗ Andrews Church	18	S.ᵗ Martins Gate
4	S.ᵗ Martins Church	19	Fryor Gate

An extract from an early version of the Vaughan map of 1660 showing the battle of 3 September 1651. King Charles tried to divert attention away from the fighting to the west of the River Severn by launching an attack on the Parliamentary centre around Red Hill, to the east of the city. (Worcester City Museum, with permission.)

was taken by storm and all the wealth in it became booty to the soldiers'. Sir Rowland Berkeley of Cotheridge wrote about 'all houses being ransacked from top to bottom, the very persons of men and women not excepted'. Richard Baxter wrote how the city 'was much plundered by Cromwell's Souldiers'.[27] Even Cromwell was forced to write to Parliament that supporters in the town suffered alongside the Royalists, 'The town being entered by storm, some honest men, promiscuously and without distinction, suffered by your Soldier; – which could not at that time possibly be prevented, in the fury and heat of the battle'.[28] He therefore asked that they might be compensated from the sequestrations of Royalist estates. The losses of 266 citizens described as 'well-affected' to Parliament but whose property had been destroyed none the less was put at £18,708 19s 7d.[29] The city later estimated the total cost of the battle at £80,000. Even some of the city records were stolen by

Cromwell's men. The bodies of men and horses were left in the street so that 'there was such a nastiness that a man could hardly abide the town'.[30] The Guildhall had to be disinfected at a cost of 2*s* 'Paid for pitch and rosen to perfume the hall after the Scots'. The official figures list as captured 3 English earls, 7 Scottish lords, 640 officers and 10,000 men. They included Massey, Pitscottie and Keith; Hamilton was dead. The mayor and sheriff were also arrested and taken to London. Many of the lesser prisoners were taken to Bristol and transported to the West Indies tobacco plantations for seven years or more. Charles II himself witnessed the fate of his common soldiers as he hid from view 'all of them stript, many of them cutt, some without stockings or shoes and scarce so much left upon them as to cover their nakedness, eating peas and handfuls of straw in their hands which they had pulled upon the fields as they passed'.[31] Those local gentry who had supported the Crown faced a heavy financial penalty. Sir John Pakington of Westwood was fined £5,000, his estates seized and house in Buckinghamshire levelled. His total losses were estimated as £20,348. There was then a search for other collaborators. On 11 September a warrant was issued to Salwarpe to apprehend people assisting in the 'Scottish invasion'.[32] But this produced few results as local society closed ranks to put this last phase of the Civil War behind them.

The disparity in casualty figures between the two sides suggests that many had been slaughtered out of hand. Sir Rowland Berkeley wrote how the dead bodies lay from Powick Bridge to the town and in almost every street of the city. Many of the dead were buried in the churchyards of the cathedral, St Michael's and other city churches, and others were buried in two large pits on Powick Ham. £2 9*s* 4*d* was paid to St Michael's parish (which contained the cathedral),

> for the burial of the Scots that were slain and died in our parish, the Palace, the College, College Green, Castle Hill, and the precincts of the said several places, and of divers others that were brought out of the City of Worcester and laid in the churchyard.

The agony was shared by those who waited at home for news. Lady Anne Fanshawe's husband, Richard, fought in the battle. She later wrote 'for three days I neither ate, nor slept, but trembled at every motion I heard, expecting the fatal news'.[33] Sir Richard was, in fact, captured and imprisoned in the Tower of London. At Bewdley, the Mayor paid £1 10*s* 0*d* to the bell ringers 'at the news of the good success at Worcester'. Whether this was a statement of popular opinion or not is difficult to say as a force of Parliamentary horse and dragoons had been stationed in the town to cut off stragglers from the Royalist army.

The Civil War was finally over, although the romance was just beginning. Charles II rode to Hartlebury then to Kidderminster, via Chaddesley Corbett to Stourbridge and then into Staffordshire. He then doubled back, through the Cotswolds and finally to Shoreham and from there to the continent. Legends now abound of his famous six-week-long escape, including the famous incident of hiding in the Boscobel oak. Samuel Pepys records how Charles II told him of some

As part of the Royalist counter attack, the Duke of Hamilton tried to storm Perry Hill, probably using the line of this former watercourse as an easy access (now known as 'Cromwell's Trenches').

of his adventures following the battle as they travelled back to England for the Restoration.

> Where it made me ready to weep to hear the stories that he told of his difficulties that he had passed through. As his travelling four days and three nights on foot, every step up to the knees in dirt, with nothing but a green coat and a pair of country breeches on and a pair of country shoes, that made him so sore all over his feet that he could scarce stir. His sitting at table at one place, where the master of the house, that had not seen him in eight years, did know him but kept it private; when at the same table there was one that had been of his own Regiment at Worcester, could not know him but made him drink the Kings health and said that the King was at least four fingers higher than he.

If all the tales as to the inns in the country where Charles stopped off to refresh himself are true, it is a miracle that he was able to ride at all! One local legend has the fleeing king stopping at the Black Cross Inn at Bromsgrove to have his horse

The Commandery lay just outside the Sidbury Gate. The Scottish troops desperately tried to retreat past here into the relative safety of the city walls. The crush was intense and King Charles himself was almost captured.

re-shod, but this story, in danger of now being taken up as established fact, is based on a number of unproven assumptions based on an anecdote of Charles II.[34] It demands first of all the equation of Bromsgrove with a 'scattering village' two hours ride from Bentley, near Wolverhampton, 'whose name began with something like "Long —"'. All other contemporary documents clearly refer to Bromsgrove by name. No inn is mentioned in the original account and the Black Cross has been chosen to accommodate the legend simply because it is the only surviving seventeenth-century inn within Bromsgrove and did have a smithy. King Charles was not to return until 1660.

Immediate orders were given to demolish the city walls of Worcester and fill in the city ditches, and workers were drafted in from the countryside with spades, mattocks and shovels.[35] Demolition included the tower of St Clement's Church, which lay too close to the city walls. The city walls now rarely survive to a height of more than 1.5 m. The gates were, however, rebuilt at the Restoration.

The city must have been stunned by this last, furious stage in the conflict – all the more so because of its still continuing efforts to rebuild the damage of the First Civil War. Nevertheless, there were soon some attempts to restore the damage, assisted no doubt by a failure of the witch-hunt against those suspected of supporting the Scottish army and which therefore helped retain local society fairly intact. This is an aspect of urban recovery that may have been underestimated in the past.[36] New building work on the Tything had begun by 1654 and the rebuilding of the street was complete by 1664. New buildings had been completed just inside the line of the 1651 southern defences (on Frog Lane) by 1657, but other efforts took much longer.[37] The damage to the cathedral was estimated in November 1660 to amount to £16,354.[38] St Nicholas's parish only recovered its pre-war population figure in 1670. The task of rebuilding the housing stock was enormous. Some former building plots, especially in the suburbs, remained as waste ground into the 1680s; squatter cottages were eventually built over the demolished cottages in the Sidbury suburb.[39] Excavations in 1976 on what is now part of City Walls Road, Worcester (the site of nos 23, 25 and 29 Sidbury), suggested that the site, formerly used for bronze-working, may have been cleared around 1680 of debris from the destruction of

The Scots could do nothing to stop Cromwell's army from breaking into the city. King Charles managed to reach his quarters next to the Cornmarket and slipped out to safety through the back of what is now known as 'King Charles's House'.

buildings just within the defences during the Civil War. The site was then levelled and rebuilt. There was a similar pattern from within the medieval city walls on Friar Street, where the levelling layers contained extensive traces of charcoal left by burnt timbers.[40] Such destruction created a rare dislocation of medieval property boundaries in some areas. The steward of the Bishop of Worcester had to report that he was unable to collect rents because he did not know 'the very ground where each house stood'.[41]

The rest of the dispossessed were probably housed in a new building campaign within the city walls. The plan of 1660, although schematic in internal detail, still shows a city with large open spaces and with no evident sign of increased building pressure following the First Civil War from that of the Speed map of 1610. Existing properties were probably subdivided, although this has left little trace.

In 1653 Cromwell became Lord Protector but was never able to create a stable government. He turned down the title of king in 1657 and died the following year.

Worcester suffered badly through being occupied as a garrison town, being besieged in 1643 and 1646 and being chosen as the last stand of Charles II in 1651. Most of its suburbs were destroyed and there was considerable loss of property following the battle of 1651. The city has remained proud of its role as a Royalist base. The door of the Guildhall is flanked by statues of Charles I and Charles II, with the head of Cromwell pinned by his ears above the door! Yet the city received scant thanks for its sacrifices at the Restoration.

Local legend held that the devil claimed his own: the result of a pact made to ensure him victory in the Battle of Worcester. Jane Gallett of Tarrington (Herefordshire), who died in 1749 aged over 105 years old, remembered 'Oliver's Wind' passing over on the day of his death, 3 September 1658 (when she was fourteen or fifteen).

In 1660 Parliament opened negotiations with the exiled Charles II. He finally landed at Dover on 25 May and arrived in London in time for his thirtieth birthday. As they had rung the bells in celebration of his defeat in 1651, so at the Restoration Bewdley paid £6 3s for 'wine and beare at the p(ro)clayminge the King'. But Charles II returned to a very different kingship, with the concept of the 'divine right' of the monarch gone forever and Parliament an unchallengeable part of the constitution.

The Duke of Hamilton was mortally wounded in the battle and died at the Commandery. He is buried inside Worcester Cathedral. (Worcester City Library, with permission.)

CONCLUSION

Nothing appears to our sight but ruin. Families ruined; congregations ruined; sumptuous structures ruined; cities ruined; court ruined; kingdoms ruined. Who weeps not when all these bleed?

(Richard Baxter)[1]

The overwhelming impression from this study is not of a fanatically Royalist city or county, although some families were fiercely Royalist, but rather of a moderate and conservative part of England loyal to the status quo and fearful of change brought about by either extreme. It was also a county worn out by the continual exactions of a war that few sought or wished to participate in. In 1666, Worcester estimated its losses at around £200,000, amounting to £7,885 13s 7d in disbursements, £80,000 in loss of goods through plunder, £100,000 in burning of property in the suburbs and £8,640 in the cost of maintaining defences plus the costs of free-quarter, etc.[2] The cathedral estimated its losses at £16,354 (November 1660), half consisting of the cost of lead stripped from the roofs.[3] Some parts of the city were left desolate into the 1680s. Damage extended throughout the whole county, disturbing not only the economic life of those communities directly affected but also the delicate balance of support to the towns. In 1662 the churchwardens of Little Malvern reported the poor state of repair of the church 'in regard of the late warrs which did so impoverish the people that they were not able to repayre it, being known to be a very small and poore place'.[4] As if repairing the damage within the county was not a burden enough in itself, some parishes were called upon to provide help for further afield. In 1658, the parish of Lindridge was obliged to collect 2s 1d for the repair of Oswestry church by order of 'his late highness Oliver Lord Protector'.

It is more difficult to estimate the cost in human terms. Perhaps one-quarter of the male population of the county had been recruited or conscripted into the forces during the course of the wars. Most of these were raised for the Royalist cause, with 7,000 men recruited in the first year, but Parliament also managed to raise regiments from the county, particularly in the later stages of the war.[5] Most soldiers were recruited from the towns such as Worcester and Kidderminster but large numbers were also taken out of the agricultural workforce. In 1646, nineteen men were recruited (for Parliament) from the south Worcestershire parish of Longdon, probably after three and a half years of other, undocumented attempts to recruit their menfolk. Not all of the troops were willing volunteers. In 1644, the Royalist Edward Broade threatened the countrymen around Kidderminster with hanging if they did not join his regiment.

Military estimates of casualties at the time are biased and unreliable. Richard

Baxter gleefully reported how most of the volunteers for the Royalist army recruited from the mob in Kidderminster had been killed. Many of the parish registers do not survive for the period and, although some do record the deaths of 'souldiers', this probably underestimates the deaths of local men whose names were known and incidental civilian casualties. A good many of the Worcestershire men would, in any case, have been killed in campaigns outside the county and therefore be impossible to detect. Many of the casualties were not buried within the churchyards and so do not appear on the registers. The occurrence of 'Scots Graves' on the 1831 Ordnance Survey map (as at Broome) is probably a reminder of the dead of 1651. For years afterwards paupers claimed that they had been wounded at the Battle of Worcester and the county appointed a 'Treasurer of the Maimed Soldiers'. During 1653–5, £229 15s 5d was collected for disbursement as pensions.[6] Even less easy to establish is the effect of the Civil War on the fabric of society itself as individual families and whole communities were turned against each other. This aspect of 'a nation divided' is most clearly focused in military terms as family, friends and neighbours were recruited into different sides. But there was also an effect in the way in which people were encouraged to inform on neighbouring 'papists' or 'roundheads', clergy of opposing sides were hounded out of their livings, and the leadership of local society was disrupted by the seizing or fining of the estates of the gentry.

The motto 'faithful city' was coined in Worcester as a piece of graffiti during the siege of 1646 when it was occupied only by a rump of its former population (elements of both rich and poor having fled). At the start of the First Civil War, Worcester very much had its own agenda in trying to protect its privilege and assert its independence from the rest of the county, and this shaped its negative reaction to the initial demands of the Royalist Commissioners. At the end of the First Civil War, the city was being defended not so much for itself but to ensure the best possible surrender deal for the broken Royalist garrison, especially the professional soldiers and the Irish troops – who could otherwise expect a cruel reception from the Parliamentary forces. The rest of the county spent the war under the control of Royalist garrisons and then by the rising influence of Parliamentary raiders. The population wearily paid dues to whichever party had control at the time, and sometimes to both.

In the Third Civil War of 1651, Worcester did not invite Charles to its gates – he chose to march in its direction for strategic reasons. Unlike Shrewsbury, the citizens did not resist his entry, but in practicalities the king and his Scottish army received very little local support from his 'faithful' city beyond acceding to the demand to resupply the Scottish army – a request which in the circumstances it would have been difficult to oppose. There was only limited military support from the local gentry and, indeed, the Worcestershire militia fought on the side of Cromwell. Ironically, it was actually Worcester's arch-antagonist – the scourge of Worcestershire's southern borders from 1643 to 1645, the now-Royalist Edward Massey – who was supposed to act as the main catalyst for raising local sympathizers. Even worse, whatever personal loyalty people might have felt to the

Fragment of tin-glazed earthenware plate from Worcester, showing Charles II, with a complete example from collections at Manchester for comparison. (Manchester City Art Galleries.)

idea of kingship, Charles now appeared at the head of the same foreign army that had wasted the county on behalf of Parliament during 1645.

The concept of 'faithful' city was essentially a marketing exercise promoted at the Restoration to try to ensure rewards for anyone who could claim to have helped the Royalist cause, and popularized by partisan historians such as Clarendon. Some did benefit, but it is interesting that few in the county (from either side) received any outstanding reward for their services. King Charles himself never returned to the city (despite an attempt to invite him on the anniversary of the Battle of Worcester in 1661) and the city itself displayed little love of the later Stuarts.[7] The tradition of 'Oak Apple Day' was an eighteenth-century revival to try to inspire loyalty and dissuade those tendencies that abroad had led to the French Revolution. This was the context for the eighteenth-century historian, Valentine Green, to write of the 'truly Roman firmness of support' of Worcester for the Royalists during the war.[8]

Faced with army after army raging through the countryside and local garrisons who could only support themselves by plundering surrounding villages, there were few who would risk the consequences of antagonizing whichever army held the upper hand at that particular time. Bewdley cheerfully rang its bells to celebrate the triumph of whichever army was in the neighbourhood and Worcester provided all visiting generals with barrels of drink. The main exception in taking a stand on principle was Evesham which, in 1644, risked the royal wrath by assisting the Parliamentary army over the bridge that Charles had so recently ordered to be demolished.

There was a steady fall in morale in the county, brought about by military action on a small, but relentless, scale, combined with economic pressures and a degree of administrative muddle and bickering between the Royalist military and civilian governments, and this greatly affected local loyalties. Although a high proportion of the initial Royalist garrisons were probably composed of local men under local commanders such as Russell or Sandys, desertions became ever more common and volunteers were replaced by conscripts. The interests of the soldiers, whether local or not, came to be seen as something very distinct from the interests of the civilian population. The citizens of Worcester certainly distanced themselves from the garrison during the siege of 1646, even to the point of going on strike. There is, therefore, an important distinction to be made between a Royalist county and a county under Royalist control. The truest expression of local moderate feeling probably came with the Clubmen, who sought a restoration of law and order and the chance to get on with their lives. Both Royalists and Parliamentarians sought to exploit these concerns, while still viewing the movement with considerable distrust. The Clubmen first tried to support the stated aims of the Royalist occupying forces and local government but then, disillusioned, they finally gave military support to the rising tide of Parliamentary activity on the fringes of the county. Thus it was that Clubmen and locally raised troops eventually combined with the Parliamentary army to defeat the Royalist garrisons of the First Civil War. Worcestershire took no real part in the Second Civil War and, it can be argued, sided with Cromwell's army against the Scots in the Third Civil War.

To a very great extent the romance of the 'faithful' city has, therefore, overshadowed the true role and conditions of Worcestershire during the Civil War. The history of wars tend to concentrate on the focal point of the battles and sieges. Increasingly in this conflict, such events had little to do with the ordinary people of Worcestershire. What emerges is the sheer resilience of local communities in the county as their everyday lives were ruthlessly, and repeatedly, disrupted in the name of greater causes, whose high ideals had slipped in the need to maintain and supply the war effort. The dogged determination to survive repeated plundering from both sides, and in 1645–6 to make a stand for impartial law and order, is surely something in which the county can take a lasting pride.

Trade token from Bewdley following the Restoration, 'War Bring Pece [Peace]'.

CHRONOLOGY OF THE CIVIL WAR IN WORCESTERSHIRE

First Civil War

1642

4 January	Attempted arrest of the five MPs
9 January	King leaves London
5 March	Parliament issues the Militia Ordinance to claim control of the army
22 August	King Charles raises his Royal Standard at Nottingham to start the war
16 September	Byron occupies Worcester for the king
23 September	Skirmish at Powick
24 September	Essex takes Worcester for Parliament
30 September	Earl of Stamford occupies Hereford for Parliament
23 October	Battle of Edgehill
10 November	Sir William Russell garrisons Worcester for the king
3 December	Earl of Stamford withdraws from Hereford

1643

2 February	Cirencester falls to Royalists
3 April	Prince Rupert wins Battle of Camp Hill and slaughters inhabitants of Birmingham
13 April	Battle at Ripple. Prince Maurice defeats Waller
24–5 April	Siege of Hereford. Waller takes city for Parliament but later withdraws
18 May	Waller withdraws from Hereford
29 May	Siege of Worcester. Waller unsuccessful and forced to withdraw
5 July	Battle of Lansdowne. Royalist victory
13 July	Battle of Roundway Down. Royalist victory
27 July	Fall of Bristol to Royalists
10 August– 5 September	Siege of Gloucester. Held by Parliament
20 September	Battle of Newbury. Parliamentary victory

1644

April	'Tinker' Fox takes Bewdley
4 June	Massey takes Tewkesbury
5 June	Pershore and Evesham bridges demolished by Royalists
10 June	Siege of Dudley lifted by Royalists
11 June	Evesham Bridge repaired by citizens to assist Waller
16 June	Royalists try again to demolish Evesham Bridge
18 June	Pershore Bridge demolished by Parliament
	Evesham defences and bridge demolished by Parliament
29 June	Battle of Cropredy Bridge. Royalist victory
2 July	Battle of Marston Moor. Parliamentary victory
?13 July	Battle of Corse Lawn, Eldersfield
September	Parliamentary Militia Committee for Worcestershire authorized to raise new army from the county
December	Royalist Association formed to raise local troops from Worcestershire and surrounding counties

1645

5 March	Meeting of Woodbury Clubmen
March	Clubmen rising in Herefordshire
22 April	Battle of Ledbury
May	Charles marches through Inkberrow, Droitwich, Bromsgrove
26 May	Battle of Evesham. Seized by Parliament
14 June	Battle of Naseby. Parliamentary victory
31 July	Scottish army besieges Hereford (relieved 4 September)
24 September	Battle of Rowton Heath
8 November	Battle at Trimpley, Kidderminster
11 November	Clubmen meet on Bredon Hill
December	Clubmen of Worcestershire attack Prince Rupert and Prince Maurice
18 December	Hereford falls to Parliament

1646

5 February	Chester falls to Parliament
21 March	Battle of Stow-on-the-Wold. The last Royalist field army is defeated
25 March	Parliamentary army arrives before Worcester but departs for Droitwich
30 March	Garrison at Worcester clears the suburbs in preparation for siege
19 April	Skirmish at Worcester
5 May	King Charles surrenders to Scots
13 May	Dudley surrenders to Parliament
16 May	Hartlebury surrenders to Parliament
20 May	Siege of Worcester begins
10 June	Charles commands Worcester to surrender (but garrison does not receive message)
21 June	Madresfield surrenders to Parliament

| 24 June | Oxford surrenders to Parliament |
| 23 July | Worcester surrenders to Parliament |

1647

3 February	King Charles handed over to English parliament by the Scots
	Broadway Plot by disgruntled Parliamentary officers
11 November	King Charles escapes to the Isle of Wight but is captured

Second Civil War

1648

23 March	Revolt in Wales
26 May	Kentish revolt fails
8 June	Revolt in Essex
July	Col. Dudley's rising in Worcestershire
5 July	Battle of Willoughby, Notts.
26 August	Rising at Colchester is defeated
	Rising in Herefordshire
17 August	Battle of Preston
6 December	Pride's Purge of the House of Commons

1649

January	Riot in Worcester against the Excise
20 January	Trial of King Charles begins
30 January	King Charles executed
22 March	Surrender of Pontefract Castle
17 March	Monarchy abolished by Act of Parliament
19 March	House of Lords abolished
19 May	England proclaimed a Commonwealth
15 August	Cromwell begins campaign in Ireland

Third Civil War

1650

| 26 June | Cromwell replaces Fairfax as Lord-General of the Parliamentary army |
| 3 September | Battle of Dunbar. Scottish army defeated by Cromwell |

1651

1 January	Charles II crowned at Scone
1 August	Charles II marches on England with Scottish army
23 August	Scottish army occupies Worcester
3 September	Battle of Worcester. Scottish army defeated
16 October	Charles flees England (Charles II was finally restored to the throne in 1660)

PLACES TO VISIT

Broadway (SP 09 37)

Lygon Arms

Tradition holds that Cromwell stayed here during the campaign of 1651. Civil War period armour is mounted on the walls of the dining room.

Evesham (SO 03 43)

Langstone House, 13 Bridge Street

This is reputedly where Charles I stayed during July 1644.

Abbey bell-tower

Has marks on the south face, reputedly the result of damage from gunfire during the Civil War.

Defences

The line of the Civil War defences of the town survives on the north side as a watercourse and sunken way leading towards the railway station.

Hartlebury (SO 836 712)

Hartlebury Castle

The present 'castle' is the result of late seventeenth- and eighteenth-century rebuilding. The original castle was fortified in the Civil War and served as a mint from 1644. Part of the possible Civil War ditches survive.

The *County Museum* on the site houses some material from the period.

Pershore (SO 94 46)

Pershore Bridge

Like Twyford Bridge at Evesham, this bridge was also ordered by the king to be destroyed in June 1644. Unfortunately, the job was rushed so that around forty of the soldiers and eighty workmen fell into the river with the collapsing masonry and were killed. Some reports say that Waller had a similar experience a short while later when 'The great stone bridge being pulled down by the inhabitants, after they had demolished the arches the rest suddenly tumbled down, whereby about sixty of the workmen were knocked on the head or drowned.' This may, however, be a confused report of the earlier incident. The post-Civil War red sandstone replacement of the central arch is still visible.

Powick (SO 835 524)

Powick Church

Marks on the church tower are reputed to be the result of gun shot from the fierce battle of 1651 when the Parliamentary troops tried to dislodge the Scots.

Powick Bridge

The fifteenth-century bridge was the centre of the first major action in the Civil War. The two northern spans, across the mill race, have clearly been repaired and were possibly those demolished during the battle of 1651.

Powick Ham

The open land to the south of the bridge, with its narrow lane and hedged fields, is where the Parliamentary troops drew up their forces in 1642 and the site of fierce close-quarter combat during the battle of 1651. Despite the close proximity of new roadworks, it still preserves much of its character.

Strensham (SO 91 40)

Strensham Castle

The overgrown earthworks of the fortified moated manor house (belonging to Sir William Russell, Governor of Worcester) still survive, on the slope below the church. The protrusions at the corners of the medieval moated site, to provide artillery platforms, are typical of works of this period.

Upton-upon-Severn (SO 85 40)

Church of St Peter and St Paul

The church was occupied by a Parliamentary advance guard in 1651, and held until the main force could cross the river. Only the fourteenth-century tower of the church still survives.

Upton Heritage Centre

Contains a display on Upton in the Civil War.

Pool Brook

Part of a rectangular emplacement dug by Colonel Massey to protect the road to Worcester in 1651 is still visible from the road, adjacent to the stream.

Worcester (SO 85 55)

Fort Royal

Fort Royal Park contains the remains of the 1651 sconce. As viewed today, this now dominates the city, but the fort was really intended to face eastwards and defend Worcester against attack from the high ground to the east. The outline of the rectangular fort, with three of its four corner bastions, can still easily be made out on the ground, although the outlines have been softened by landscaping. The fort was built to help defend the city, but its capture during the battle of 1651 allowed Cromwell's army to pound the city with cannon from close range.

The Commandery, Sidbury Street

The Royalist HQ during the battle of 1651. It lies outside Sidbury Gate, but within the defences probably constructed in 1644. The Royalist general, the Duke of Hamilton, died here of his wounds. Now a Civil War museum.

Worcester Cathedral

Suffered from both Parliamentary and Royalist armies. It was used as a Royalist ammunition magazine and was then desecrated by Essex's army in 1642. Subsequently, Royalist troops stripped the lead off the roof to make into musket-balls. Then the bell-tower, with its 50 yd high lead-covered steeple was demolished in 1647. The Royalist general, the Duke of Hamilton (killed in the battle of 1651), is buried in front of the High Altar.

St Helen's Church and Records Office

Collections of original documents of the period. Memorial to Colonel Dud Dudley (d. 1684) on the south side of the chancel. He was an iron-master by trade and served as Royalist general of artillery during the siege of 1646. On the north side is the memorial to Alderman John Nash, a Parliamentary captain.

Guildhall, High Street

The Georgian building has statues of Charles I and Charles II in front, and a carving of Cromwell's head above the doorway – nailed to the wall by his ears. Cromwell is shown as a horned devil. On the morning of the Battle of Worcester in 1651 he is said to have met with the devil in Nunnery Wood and sold his soul to him in return for victory and seven more years good fortune – he died on 3 September 1658.

King Charles's House, New Street

Built in 1577, and owned during the Civil War by Edward Durrant. King Charles took refuge here before escaping the Battle of Worcester in 1651.

Nos 4–5 New Street

Built in 1605, it was occupied by Alderman John Nash. He was a captain in the Parliamentary army, local MP and JP, and is buried in St Helen's Church.

City Walls, City Walls Road

Remains of the medieval city walls and footings of St Martin's Gate are still visible. King Charles escaped through St Martin's Gate after the battle of 1651.

The Viewpoint, A38 Tewkesbury Road (off the Malvern/Worcester roundabout)

Overlooks the site of the bridge of boats built by Cromwell's men to cross the Severn and attack the flank of the Scots during the battle of 1651. Despite the presence of modern roadworks, it is still possible to appreciate the character of the open countryside beside the Teme and Severn over which the battle was fought. Includes a panoramic display of the battlefield.

City Library, Foregate Street

Collections of original documents of the period in the Stuart Collection.

Perry Wood

Part of Worcester Woods Country Park, Spetchley. This was the scene of bitter fighting in 1651 as the gun positions on top of Perry Hill were stormed by the Earl of Hamilton. What are popularly described as 'Cromwell's Trenches' off Peterborough Close are actually part of a former natural watercourse but the feature was important in allowing an access on to the hill from the city. The view from the top of Perry Hill gives a good impression of the commanding position that Cromwell's artillery had over the city.

Tamar Close, off Ronkswood Crescent

Rectangular earthwork, 73 × 82 m, probably an artillery emplacement of 1646 or of Cromwell's army at the battle of 1651. The surrounding ditch is clearly visible on three sides. That on the city side has probably been ploughed flat.

EXTRACTS FROM THE LETTERS OF NEHEMIAH WHARTON, 1642[1]

Nehemiah Wharton was a volunteer in the London regiment of Denzil Holles. He had been an employee of the St Swithin's merchant, George Willingham, and was probably a journeyman which meant that he was a qualified apprentice and therefore of some status. His rank in this regiment of foot was that of a sergeant. There would have been around twenty such men in a regiment of 1,200. He marched into Worcester with the Earl of Essex's army in September 1642 and took part in the occupation of Worcester, following the skirmish at Powick (in which he took no direct part). His letters cease abruptly after the battle of Edgehill and it is likely that he was killed there, fulfilling the premonition that he felt in the second of the two letters published here.

The two letters paint a vivid portrait of Worcestershire, and the character of the inhabitants, as seen from the eyes of a Londoner after a long and difficult march, with the soldiers tired, cold and hungry – and plagued by lice (the 'backbiters' of Letter 7). Wharton was a puritan idealist. He disliked his commanding officer as being a 'godamme blade' and 'ungodly'. He found the Worcestershire countryside attractive, but clearly believed the population to be a foreign and hostile race – 'papisticall' and 'atheisticall', with Worcester itself compared to Sodom and Gomorrah. In his mind, he was clearly coming as part of an invading army and this is important both for the way that the Earl of Essex's army behaved in Worcester and the reaction of the local population against the military.

The letters are also interesting as they show how quickly rumours could circulate. In his first letter of 26 September he tells stories of atrocities committed on the Parliamentary prisoners after what he believed to be the ambush at Powick. But his second letter, written four days later, refutes this, although still portraying an accurate picture of events. The damage caused by the circulation of such stories among the advancing troops had probably already been done, but he still maintains that the citizens took part in an ambush of his comrades. He also still believes that Prince Maurice had been fatally wounded.

Letter 7   Worcester, 26 September, 1642

Noble Sir

September the 13th was my last unto you; this even wee had tidings that Killingworth Castle, in Warwickshire, six miles from Coventry, was taken, with store of ammunition and money, and some prisoners, their number uncertain; the rest fled, and the country persued them, and wanted but the assistance of Coventry to destroy them all. Wednesday, Sept. 14th, our forces, both foot and horse, marched into the field, and the lord General viewed us, both front, rear and flank, when the drums beating and the trumpets sounding made a harmony delectable to our friends, but terrible to our enemies. This even, contrary to expectation, our regiment marched five miles north-east unto Stratton, where we, and as many as could billited in the town; the rest quartered thro' the country. Thursday our regiment met again, when those famous lawes for our army were read and expounded. This day we received and accepted Serjt. Major Neale. Friday our regiment were commanded to meet here again to be mustered, where we exercised in the field the whole day, and the muster master came not, whereat we were all much displeased. This night our company by lot watched the town. Saterday our regiment met again and were mustered. This even Captain Francis, returning from London, informed me of the couragiousness and constancy of the City of London, and also of their constant supply of money and plate; and also told me that the whole city were now either real or constrained Roundheads. Sabbath day wee peaceably injoyed with Mr Obadiah Sedgwick, who gave us two heavenly sermons. Munday morninge our regiment began to march towards Warwickshire and passed through West-Haddon, Creeke, and Hill Morton, where we had a supply of drink, which upon a march is very rare and extraordinary welcome, and at the end of ten miles we came to Rugby, in Warwickshire, where we had good quarter. At this town Mr. Norton formerly preached. This town also was lately disarmed by the Cavaliers on the Sabbath day, the inhabitants being at church. Tuesday morning our regiment marched two miles unto Dunsmore Heath where the Lord General and his regiment, met us, as also the Lord of Stanford, Colonel Chomley, and Colonel Hampden, with many troops of horse and eighteen field pieces, where we kept our rendezvous until even, when we had tidings that all the malignants in Worcestershire, with the Cavaliers, were got into Worcester and fortified themselves, whereupon we marched six miles unto Baggington, within two miles of Coventry. This night the rest of our regiments quartered about the country. Wednesday morning we marched towards Warwick, leaving Killingworth Castle upon the right, and after we had marched six miles our forces met again and quartered before Warwick, until forty pieces of ordnance, with other carriages, passed by, in which time I viewed the antiquities on this side Warwick, as Sr Guy's Cave, his chapel, and his picture in it; his stables all hewed out of the main rock, as also his garden and the two springing wells whereat he drank, as is reported. From hence our regiment marched through Warwick in such haste that I could not view the town, but had only a site of the castle, which is very strong, built upon a mighty rock, whereof there are a store in this country. This night we marched two miles further unto Burford, where our quarter was as constantly since his Excellency's coming. It is very poor, for many of our soldiers can get neither beds, bread, nor water, which makes them grow very strong, for backbiters have been seen to march upon some of them six on breast and eight deep at their open order, and I fear I shall be in the same condition e'er long, for we can get no carriage for officers, so that my trunk is more slighted than any other, which is occasioned, as I conceive, partly by the false informations of Lieut.-Col. Biddeman and our late Sergeant Major General Ballard, profane wretches; but cheifly for want of our Colonel, who should be one of the Council of War, at which Council we have none to pleade for us or remove false aspersions cast upon us, in so much that I have heard some of our captains repent their coming forth, and all for want of a Colonel. Thursday morning we marched in the front four miles towards Worcester, where we met one riding post from Worcester, informing us that our troops and the cavaliers were there in fight; but it was false, only to hast the captains from Warwick. Upon this report our whole regiment ran shouting for two miles together, and crying 'To Worcester, to Worcester,' and desired to march all night: but after we had marched two miles further unto Assincantlo, where we could get no quarter, neither bread nor drink, by reason of the Lord Compton's late being there. Friday we marched unto oster where our forces met and from there 8 miles and in rain 4 miles on this side of Worcester, but our soldiers cried out for one hour together to go foreward to set upon the enemy, but could get no commission. This day we had such foul weather that before I marched one mile I was wet to the skin. This day our horse forces, namely, Sir William Belford, Col. Sands, Col. Vines, Col. Clarke, Major Duglas, kept all the passages over the Severne, and by that means kept in the Cavaliers, who often assayed to fly, but were repelled. Those commanders sent to his Excellency for three field pieces, and offered with them to keep them in on that side untill we had surrounded them: but they were denied this day. Towards even Prince Robert [Rupert] entered the city at a bye passage with eighteen troops of horse, most of the city crying 'Welcome, welcome,' but principally the mayor, who desired to entertain him; but he answered, 'God damn him, he would not stay, but would go wash his hands in the blood of the Roundheads,' and immediately set some to lye in ambush, and with the rest sallied out upon our forces; and immediately Col. Sands came on bravely, even unto the breast of their chief commander, and discharged. The rest undauntedly followed, but their forces immediately fled, and ours followed them, and by the ambushment were beset before and behind, so that the battle was very hot, and many fell on both sides. Some of our chief commanders, as Col. Sands and Duglas, was wounded, and are since both dead. The chief among the Cavaliers were Prince Robert, who, I hear, was wounded, the Lord Craven, and the Lord Northampton. Our wounded men they brought into the city, and stripped, stabbed, and slashed their dead bodies in a most barbarous manner, and imbued their hands in their blood. They also at their return met a young gentleman, a Parliament man, as I am informed – his name I cannot learn – and stabbed him on horseback with many wounds, and trampled upon him, and also most maliciously shot his horse. This even, our general's troop of gentlemen, going to quarter themselves about the country, were betrayed and beset by the enemy, and, overmuch timerous, immediately fled so confusedly that some broke their horse's necks, others their own; some were taken, others slain; and scarcely half of them escaped; which is such a blot upon them as nothing but some desperate exploit will wipe off. Hearing this news, we immediately cried out to march unto them, and forthwith drew out a forlorne hope – some out of every company – and sent them before, intending to march after them; but about eleven of the clock, the enemies fled, and our hope returned. Here we abode all night, where we had small comfort, for it rained hard. Our food was fruit, for those that could get it; our drink, water; our beds, the earth; our canopy, the clouds, but we pulled up the hedges, pales, and gates, and made good fires; his Excellency promising us that, if the country relieved us not the day following, he would fire their towns. Thus we continued singing of psalms until the morning. Saturday morning we marched into Worcester – our regiment in the rear of the waggons – the rain continuing the whole day, and the way so base that we went up to the ancles in thick clay; and, about four of the clock after noon, entred the city, where we found twenty-eight dead men, which we buried – some of them Cavaliers – and these were all that we can find slain on our side. This even, by lot, our company watched one of the gates, and also the day following until even. This even his Excellency's gaurd entred the mayor's house, and took him prisoner, who is now more gaurded that regarded. Sabbath day morning our soldiers entered a vault of the Colledge, where his Excellency was to hear a sermon, and found eleven barrels of gunpowder and a pot of bullets. This day Mr. Marshall Sedgewick, &c. preached about the city, but I, being upon the court of gaurd, could not heare them. This even his Excellency proclaimed that no soldier should plunder either church or private house, upon pain of death. We shortly expect a pitched battle, which, if the Cavaliers will but stand, will be very hot; for we are all much enraged against them for their barbarisms, and shall shew them little mercy. But I want time to enlarge myself. To conclude, I humbly entreat you to present my humble service to my Mrs., as also to Mr. Edgerton's, our quartermaster, and mine to Mr. Molloyne and his wife; my service also to my aunt, Mr. Priaux, Mr. Simpson and his wife, Mr. Hawkins, Mr. Sarkey; and I humbly intreate, let me hear from you of your welfare, my mistress, and your family. Sir it is extreme hast that makes me compose so confusedly; and, therefore, with my service to Mrs. Elizabeth, Anna, John, and little Samuel, and my love to all my fellow servants, I rest yours in all good services, until death,

NEHEMIAH WHARTON

My captain presents you with his best respects, and drinks to you every day we sit at table together. I have recieved your feather, for which I give you humble thanks.

Letter 8   Worcester, 30 September, 1642

My much honored Mr. I humbly greete you. My last unto you was Sept. 26th, in which there were some errors, occasioned partly by my over hastinesse in wrightinge, for the bearer promised me to deliver it on Wednesday, Sept. the 28th, partly by the various relations dyspersed, but cheifly by reason I was upon the gaurd, and upon paine of death durst not stir from it to se or heare any occurences; but I had as good intelligence as the city then afforded, for the truth of thinges was not then knowne. The errors are these. First, I wrote that the Earle of Northampton and the Lord Craven were with the Prince, but they were not; but upon sufficient information they were these, Prince Robert, Duke Mawrice, the Lord Digby, Commissary Wilmot, Sir Lewes Dives, Sir William Russell, and Mr. Hastings. A second was, that most of the curoseers, his Exellencies trope, were cut off, but they are since returned and but few lost, but doe still beare the aspersion of cowards. The third was that Colonell Sands was dead; but both he and Captain Sands, though both wounded yet are still livinge. But that I may not trouble you with common relations which commonly are fictions, I have confered with commaunders, the best intelligencers, and have also viewed the place where the bataile was fought, but breifly. Worcestershire is a pleasaunt, fruitfull, and rich countrey, aboundinge in corne, woods, pastures, hills, and valleyes, every hedge and heigh way beset with fruits, but especially with peares, whereof they make that pleasant drinke called perry, wch they sell for a penny a quart, though better than ever you tasted at London. Touchinge the city, it is more large than any I have seene since I left London, and like London it abounds in outward thinges of all kinds, but for want of the Word the people perrish. It is pleasantly seated, exceedingly populous, and doubtles very rich. It is situate on the east bank of that famous river Severne. The wall in the form of a triangle, the gates seaven, the bulwarkes five, but much decayed: no castle, only a mount of earth. In this citty there is a very stately cathederal, called St. Maries, in which there are many stately monuments; but among the rest, in the middle of the quire, is the monument of Kinge John, all of white marble, with his picture thereon to the life. On the south side, Kinge Arthur's tombe, of jette, but no picture thereon. This citty hath also a stronge stone bridge over the Severne, consistinge of six arches, with a gate in the middle of the bridge, as stronge as that on London Bridge, with a percullis. Five miles upon the left of this is Maluern Hills, which, for height and length and breadth, doe many degrees exceede all that ever I see. I nominate them because they are famous, for on the top of them there is a very brave chase for many miles together, a large ditch, and springs also, all on the very top. Between these hills and the river was the late skirmish, about one mile from the city, which was in this manner:– Our troopes on that side were devided to keepe the severall passages, and Colonell Sands, Colonell Vines, and Serjant-Major Duglas, with their troopes, were set to keep this passage, which was at the end of a narrow lane, which the treacherous inhabitants neare them discovered to the Prince, and he forthwith set some troopes to lye in ambush, who brake downe a hedge and lay in the feild on the right of them; the treacherous citizens attending them in multitudes with muskets, who lay on each side the hedge. This done, the Prince with other forces went to meete them, but first sent a false alarum, informinge them that the Cavalleeres weere all fled and had left the citty, and also that his Excellency was come even to the gates, and immediately these three troopes poasted away to meet his Excellency, for Sir William Balfore, Colonell Clarke, and our other commaunders, heard not of it, but hastinge downe a narrow lane the Prince met them. Colonell Sands beinge in the front, the Prince asked him whom he was for, he answered 'For Kinge and Parliament.' He replyed, 'Not for the Kinge alone?' He answered, 'No.' Then said the Prince, 'For the King have at you.' The Colonell answered, 'For the Parliament have at you.' And so they discharged each at other. The rest followed them, and presently those in ambush fired upon them, as also the musquetteers behind the hedges. The horsemen charged not the second time, but immediately fell to their swords, so that for the space of almost an hour the skirmishe was exceedinge hot. This relation I had from an gentleman that was in the front of the battel, and was wounded with the sword and bullets in seaven severall places, was stripped naked, and yet liveth. He affermeth that, though there were ten for one, yet there were more slaine an wounded of them then of us and I spoke with one that heard the Prince, at his returne, say, that our men fought more like lions then men. Our wounded commaunders he brought into the city, and gave commaund that they should be carefully looked unto, and with all speed gathered his forces together and fled, leavinge all their reconinge to pay; in some places twenty pounde, in others ten, in some more, some lesse, pretendinge and also promising to returne. Since their departure we heare that the Prince is wounded, but it is certaine Duke Maurice is mortally wounded. They report unto the Kinge that they have slaine eight hundred of our men, when there were but twenty-eight slaine in all, and some of them were Cavalleeres; of this I am certaine, for I told all their gunnes, and searched the register of St. Jones parrish, where they were all buried. They boast wonderfully, and sweare most hellishly, that the next time they meete us they will make but a mouthfull of us; but I am persuaded the Lord hath given them this small victory, that they may, in the day of battell, come on more presumptuously to thir own destruction, in which battell, though I and many more may be cut off, yet I am confident the Lord of Hoasts will in the end triumph gloriously over these horses and all their cursed riders. They left, at their flight, in the city, some horses, truncks, and other thinges, all which his Excellency hath seized on. Colonell Essex is made governor of this citty, and his regiment shall be garrisons here.

Sir, our army did little think to have seene Worcester, but the providence of God hath brought us heither, and had it not, the city is so vile, and the country so base, papisticall and atheisticall and abominable, that it resembles

Sodom, and is the very embleme of Gomorrah, and doubtlesse it would have ben worse than either Algiers or Malta, a very den of thieves, and refuge for all the hel-hounds in the countrey; I should have said in the land; but we have handsomely handled some of them, and doe cull out the rest as fast as we can, who verbally cry peccavi, but cordially iterum faciam, and indeed they do as they are taught by Dr. Prediux, late made Byshop, and other popish priests, who are all run awaye. To conclude, Monday, Sept. 26th one of Prince Robert's trumpeters came to our gates and sounded a point of warre, who was presently taken and led blindfold through the city unto his Excellency. This night Sargeant Major Duglas was nobly buried. Tuesday our soildiers, by commission from his Excellency, marched seven miles to Sir William Russell's house, and pillaged it unto the bare walls. Wensday we fasted, and Mr. Obadiah Sedgewick preached unto us, whom the Lord extraordinarily assisted, so that his doctrine wrought wonderfully upon many of us, and doubtless hath fitted many of us for death, which we all shortly expect. Thursday his Excellency proclaimed that whosoever had any goods of the Cavalleers in custody should forthwith surrender them this day. I met with your servant Davy who is in good health, with his horse. He was on the west of Severne, near the battell, but untill it was ended heard not of it. Wee joyntly present you and my Mrs. with our humble service, as also Mr Willingham, your brother, with his family. Mr. Chappel's man and I do present our service to Mr. Chappell and his wife, Mr. Felton and his wife, and desire to heare of their welfare. Fryday morninge our drummes beat for our regiment to march away, but wither I know not. Wee should be very glad to see our colonell. Sir, I humbly intreate to excuse my late errours, and to accept these my pore indevours, beinge the last I suppose that ever I shall present unto you. Thus with my dearest love to all your children and my fellow servants wheither with you or from you, beinge to march away in hast, I must conclude your everlovinge, humble, thankfull, and antient servant,

NEHEMIAH WHARTON

LETTER OF ROBERT STAPLETON, 1651

This account of the Battle of Worcester by Robert Stapleton was published in the news-sheet *Perfect Diurnall* for 1–8 September 1651.[1]

Robert Stapleton was a colonel in Cromwell's army and was stationed at Spetchley during the Battle of Worcester in 1651. The letter was written in the very closing stages of the battle (at 10 p.m.). Stapleton has no doubts as to the reasons for the Parliamentary victory – 'the Lord owned us in this contest'.

Sir, This day hath been a very glorious day, this day twelve-moneth was glorious at Dunbar, this day hath been glorious before Worcester, the word then was 'The Lord of Hosts', and so it was now, and indeed the Lord of Hosts was wonderfully with us; the same signall we had now as then, which was to have no white about us, and indeed the Lord hath cloathed us with white garments, though to the enemy they have been bloody, only this hath been the difference, that at Dunbar, our worke was at breake of day, and done ere the morning was over; but now it was towards the shutting of the evening, and not past till the night came so on us, that we could not see far before us; that this was the beginning of their fall before the appearance of the Lord Jesus, this seems to be the setting of the young King's glory. In the morning Lieut. Gen. Fleetwood, had order to advance with his brigade, on the other side Severne, and all things being prepared for the making of a bridge, and having cleared our passages with a forlorn, we laid a bridge over Severne, in that place where the River Tame runs into it, so that by this means we had an advantage to lay another bridge over the River Tame, which accordingly was done; our foot disputed the hedges with much courage and resolution; the fight began on the other side of Severn, and our foot from this side began it, they clearing the way for the rest to come over after them; the right wing of Lieut. Generall Fleetwood's forces came over the bridge that was made over Tame, while the left wing disputed the bridge at Poyke, a quarter of a mile beyond the River, which dispute lasted a long time, and was very hot, but the Lord gave our men to gaine ground of the enemy, till we had beaten them out of the ground: the charges was very hot for a while, but the Lord owned us in this contest, and the enemy fled before us. While this was doing, the enemy rallying, made a very bold sally out on this side of the towne, and came with great bodyes of horse and foot, supposing most of our army had been drawne out on the other side, they gave our men a very hot salute, and put them to a little retreat, and disorder; but in a short while the Lord gave us victory on this side also. Our foot did very noble and gallant service, and they disputed with them not onely the hedges, but followed them boldly to the very mouth of their cannon, which was planted on their mountain works, at length we gained their works (and planted their great guns against them in the town) and wee heare that some of our horse and foot are in the north and east end of the town; the night came on so fast that we could not pursue further. Most of their horse are escaped, but my Lord Generall hath dispatched Major Generall Harrison's brigade after them, to follow them which way soever they are gone: we cannot yet give an account who are taken or slaine, but we conceive the number of their slain farre exceeds the number of the prisoners (but I guesse the number of the kild and taken to be about 8 or 10000) tomorrow we shall be able to give you a fuller relation, the Lord hath done great things for England. Our Quartermaster-Generall, and Capt. Jones are slain, and Mr Howard, Captain of the life-guard, is wounded; Major-Generall Lambert's horse was shot under him, but through the goodnesse of God we have not lost many. A prisoner that we have taken tels us, that he beleeves their King is either slain or taken. The countrey would do well to rise upon the fugitives, that they may not rally again, or imbody to do any more mischief. You know now what you have to doe; bless the Lord with us, and for us. The next shall be more punctual. I am,

Your's to serve you,
Robert Stapylton

From our quarters on the east side of Severne, neer the River, 10 at night, Septemb. 3. 1651

NOTES

Abbreviations

BCA	Birmingham City Archives.
BL	British Library.
Bond 1974	S. Bond (ed.), *The Chamber Order Book of Worcester 1602–1650*, new ser., vol. viii (Worcs. Hist. Soc., 1974).
CJ	W.D. Hamilton (ed.), *Commons Journal* (London, 1887).
CSPD	Calendar of State Papers Domestic.
Dore 1984	R.N. Dore (ed.), *The Letter Books of Sir William Brereton* (Lancs. and Cheshire Record Soc., 1984), vol. I.
Dore 1990	R.N. Dore (ed.), *The Letter Books of Sir William Brereton* (Lancs. and Cheshire Record Soc., 1990), vol. II.
HMC	Historical Manuscripts Commission.
HWRO	Hereford and Worcester Record Office.
Luke's Journal	I.G. Philip (ed.), *The Journal of Sir Samuel Luke* (Oxford Record Soc., 1950–3).
PRO	Public Record Office.
Quarter Sessions	J.W. Bund (ed.), *Worcestershire County Records, 1591–1643* (Worcs. Hist. Soc., 1899–1900).
Symonds Diary	C.E. Long (ed.), *Diary of the Marche of the Royal Army During the great Civil War by Richard Symonds* (Camden Soc., 1859).
Townshend i	J.W. Willis-Bund (ed.), *Diary of Henry Townshend of Elmley Lovett, 1640–1663* (Worcs. Hist. Soc., 1915), vol. i.
Townshend ii	J.W. Willis-Bund (ed.), *Diary of Henry Townshend of Elmley Lovett, 1640–1663* (Worcs. Hist. Soc., 1920), vol. ii.
TWAS	*Transactions of the Worcestershire Archaeological Society.*
VCH	Victoria County History of Worcestershire.
Webb I and II	Rev. J. Webb and Rev. T.W. Webb, *Memorials of the Civil War . . . as it affected Herefordshire and the adjacent counties* (2 vols, London, 1879).
Wharton Letters	H. Ellis, 'Letters from a Subaltern Officer in the Earl of Essex's Army', *Archaeologia*, xxxv (1853).
Willis-Bund 1905	J.W. Willis-Bund, *The Civil War in Worcestershire, 1642–1646 and the Scotch Invasion of 1651* (Birmingham, 1905).

Introduction

1. *A Perfect Diurnall* cited by S.R. Gardiner, *History of the Commonwealth and Protectorate* (1894), i, 445. Hugh Peters (1598–1660) had been a minister in Salem, Mass. but returned to England in 1641. In 1651 he was chaplain to Oliver Cromwell and was executed as a regicide after the Restoration.

2. C. Carlton, 'The Impact of the Fighting' in J. Morrill (ed.), *The Impact of the English Civil War* (London, 1991), p. 20.

3. See also R.H. Silcock, 'County Government in Worcestershire 1603–1660' (Ph.D. thesis, University of London, 1974); P. Styles, 'The Royalist Government of Worcestershire during the Civil War 1642–6', *TWAS*, 3rd ser., 5 (1976).

4. W. Bowen, *A Perfect and True Relation of the Great and Bloody Skirmish, Fought Before the City of Worcester, upon Friday, Septemb 23 1642* (1642); N. Fiennes, *A Letter Purporting the True Relation of the Skirmish at Worcester* (1642). These accounts differ greatly from the account of the Earl of Essex contained in: Earl of Essex, *True and Happy News from Worcester read in the Honourable House of Commons Septem 24 1642*.

5. Townshend i and ii.

6. Although, curiously, there is no Royalist account of this atrocity, as one might have expected: P. Tennant, *Edgehill and Beyond: The People's War in the South Midlands 1642–1645* (Stroud, 1992), pp. 210–12.

7. C.J. Bond, 'Anglo-Saxon and Medieval Defences' in J. Schofield and R. Leech (eds), *Urban Archaeology in Britain* (CBA Res. Report 61, 1987), p. 100; Victoria Buteux, personal communication, with thanks.

8. Ceramic grenades made in moulds may also have been made by ironfounders, as operating in the north of the county: P. Courtney and Y. Courtney, 'A Siege Examined: the Civil War Archaeology of Leicester', *Post-Medieval Archaeol.*, 26 (1992), 70.

9. J. Corbet, *The Historical Relation of the Military Government of Gloucester* (Gloucester, 1645), reprinted in J. Washbourn, *Bibliotheca Gloucestrensis* (Gloucester, 1825), p. 68.

1 Life in Seventeenth-century Worcestershire

1. Wharton Letters, pp. 310–34.

2. Andrew Yarranton, 1616–*c.* 1684. Originally an iron-master.

3. Silcock, op. cit., p. 20.

4. Quarter Sessions for 1633, p. 525.

5. Quarter Sessions for 1662–3, pp. 526, 528, 557; Napthan, M. *Watching Brief on the North of City Foul Water Sewer, Worcester* (County Archaeological Service, Internal Report 164, 1993), p. 3.

6. Quarter Sessions, pp. xxxvi–xxxix.

7. W.G. Hoskins, 'Harvest fluctuation', *Agricultural History Review*, 16 (1968), 20, 29.

8. Quarter Sessions, p. xxxvi.

9. C. Currie, draft text of 'Historical Survey', Deansway Excavation, (County Archaeological Service).

10. Personal communication, Charles Mundy, with thanks.

11. G. Hughes and S. Litherland, 'Excavations to the Rear of 37 High Street, Pershore 1992', *TWAS*, 3rd ser., 14 (1994), 153–4.

12. I am grateful to Jenny Townshend for this information.

13. S. Woodiwiss (ed.), *Iron Age and Roman Salt Production and the medieval town of Droitwich* (CBA Research Report 81, 1992).

14. E. Morris, 'A Seventeenth Century Pit Deposit from Worcester', *TWAS*, 3rd ser., 6 (1978), 83–7.

15. Will of 17 July 1676 and Inventory of 6 September 1676: HWRO 008.7, BA 3585.

16. D.A. Higgins, 'The Interpretation and Regional Study of Clay Tobacco Pipes: A Case Study of the Brosely District' (Ph.D. Thesis, University of Liverpool, 1987), pp. 320–1, 362.

17. Higgins, op. cit., fig. 81; P. Boland (ed.), *Dudley Castle Archaeological Project – An Introduction and Summary of Excavations 1983–5* (Manpower services Commission, 1985), p. 10.

18. HWRO X496.5, BA9360, packet 96, doc. 15–21: Quarter Sessions for 1659.

19. Discussed in detail in Silcock, op. cit., pp. 70–97.

20. Quarter Sessions, p. 497.

21. Quarter Sessions, p. 703.

22. Quarter Sessions, p. 561.

23. Quarter Sessions, p. 638.

24. Quarter Sessions, p. 639.

25. P.M. Hughes, 'Buildings and the Building Trade in Worcester 1540–1650' (Ph.D. Thesis, University of Birmingham, 1990), p. 46.

26. D. Lloyd, *A History of Worcestershire* (Chichester, 1993), pp. 92–3.

27. Silcock, op. cit., p. 172.

28. Corbet, op. cit., p. 11.

2 Taking Sides

1. Richard Baxter, *Reliquae Baxtrianae* part I (London, 1696), p. 44.
2. Sir Arthur Haselrig, quoted in M. Ashley, *The English Civil War* (Stroud, 1990), p. 2.
3. Corbet, op. cit.
4. Baxter, op. cit., pp. 40, 42.
5. Ibid., pp. 30, 41.
6. Willis-Bund 1905, p. 56.
7. SP 28/253 B/13, quoted in Tennant, op. cit., p. 97.
8. Baxter, op. cit., p. 16.
9. Baxter, op. cit., p. 17.
10. Silcock, op. cit., p. 42.
11. HMC 14th Report, App. 8, p. 203.
12. Baxter, op. cit., p. 20.
13. CSPD 1644–5, p. 355.
14. BL E239 (22) *Special Passages*, 6–13 September 1642.
15. W.R. Buchanan-Dunlop, 'Seventeenth Century Puritans in Worcester', *TWAS*, XXIII (1946), 33–7.
16. Worcester Chamberlain's Accounts, 1640.
17. Parliamentary Survey 1649, published in T. Cave and R.A. Wilson (eds), *The Parliamentary Survey of the Lands of the Dean and Chapter of Worcester* (Worcs. Hist. Soc., 1924), p. 181.
18. HMC 14th Report, App. 8, p. 203.
19. VCH II, p. 68.
20. Baxter, op. cit., p. 89.
21. Ibid., pp. 30, 86.
22. Dore 1984, letter of 28.3.45, no. 130.
23. PRO SP28/187.
24. CSPD 1645–7, p. 4. He continued to make munitions for the Commonwealth navy.
25. HWRO 850 (Salwarpe), p. 1054 (A53).
26. Letter of Sergeant Wilde and Humphrey Salway to the Speaker of the House of Commons: HWRO 899: 31, BA 3669/1.
27. HWRO 3669/1 (iv); Townshend ii, p. 68.
28. CJ II, p. 710.
29. Townshend ii, p. 73.
30. HMC 13th Report Portland MSS, App. 1, p. 52.
31. Townshend ii, p. 69.
32. Styles, op. cit., p. 25.
33. Townshend ii, pp. 81, 84: Commission of Array to the Council at Whitchurch.

34. Townshend ii, pp. 79, 81.
35. Townshend ii, pp. 87–9.
36. BL E118(27): *A True Character of Worster's Late Hurly-burley*, 22 Sep. 1642.
37. Townshend ii, pp. 66–7, 81.
38. CJ II, pp. 761, 763–4.
39. PRO SP28/188.
40. Symonds Diary, p. 14.
41. HMC 4th Report (1874), Denbigh MSS, p. 265.
42. 'Letter from Prince Rupert to all Commanders, Officers, Souldiers in the King's Army, 2 Jan. 1644' in R. Warner (ed.), *Epistolary Curiosities* (London, 1818), pp. 32–4: quoted in R.E. Sherwood, *Civil War in the Midlands 1642–1651* (Stroud, 1992), p. 29.
43. CSPD 1645–6, pp. 332.
44. Townshend ii, pp. 102–5; Tennant, op. cit., pp. 106–7.
45. BCA 398331 (HCC 587).

3 The County Occupied: 1642

1. Bond 1974, pp. 353, 355.
2. HMC 14th Report, App. 8, p. 203.
3. Tennant, op. cit., p. 437.
4. P. Young, R. Holmes, *The English Civil War* (London, 1974), pp. 69–70.
5. Earl of Clarendon, *The History of the Rebellion*, vol. III (Oxford, 1807), p. 37.
6. *A letter purporting the true relation of the skirmish at Worcester* written by a soldier in Nathaniel Fiennes troop, undated. HWRO 899: 31, BA 3669.
7. *True and Happy News from Worcester 24 September 1642*. HWRO 899: 31, BA 3669.
8. Clarendon, op. cit., III, pp. 37–8.
9. *A Perfect and True Relation of the great and bloudy Skirmish, fought before the City of Worcester, upon Friday, September 23, 1642* (October 1642) by William Bowen, Ensign to the Earl of Essex; Worcester City Library W 942.4406.
10. Wharton Letters, p. 326.
11. Ibid., pp. 326, 330.
12. Bond 1974, p. 364.
13. Wharton Letters, p. 325.
14. Bond 1974, p. 359.
15. HWRO b.857.06, BA 2335/16, f. 45d.
16. BL E.123(6): *Weekly Intelligence* 10–18

October 1642. The 'horse' was a sharp-edged box that the soldier was forced to sit astride.

17.   Bond 1974, p. 359.

18.   BL E.123 (5): *Special Passages* for 11–18 October; BL E.123(6): *Weekly Intelligence* for 10–18 October.

19.   HMC 7th Report, App. (1879), p. 530.

20.   Baxter, op. cit., p. 43.

21.   Information from Granville Calder, with thanks.

22.   *A true relation of a great and cruel battle fought by the Lord Willoughby . . . October 17th*, dated 20 October.

23.   PRO SP28/187, ff. 477–89.

24.   Bond 1974, p. 363.

25.   BCA 398274 (HCC 572), quoted in E.A.B. Barnard, 'Some Original Documents Concerning Worcestershire and the Great Rebellion', TWAS, (1928), 78.

26.   BCA 398276 (HCC 574), quoted in Barnard, op. cit., p. 79.

27.   Townshend ii, p. 141.

28.   Commission of 20 January, 1643: private papers of the Sandys family.

4   The Battle of Ripple and the First Siege of Worcester: 1643

1.   BM Harl. Mss 6851, ff. 129–30; Townshend ii, pp. 108–10; Styles, op. cit., pp. 26–7.

2.   Bond 1974, p. 364.

3.   Townshend ii, pp. 106–7.

4.   Bond 1974, p. 364; the major, Edward Solley, was appointed Lt.-Col. of the regiment with Francis Sharman as Lieutenant and Francis Hughes as Ensign.

5.   BCA 398281 (HCC 579); BCA 398282 (HCC 580).

6.   Bond 1974, pp. 373, 383.

7.   Styles, op. cit., p. 25.

8.   Townshend i, p. xxxii.

9.   He allowed a cavalry trooper £1 5s 0d per week, a dragoon 10s 6d per week and a foot soldier 6s per week. In June the king ordered this to be cut to 12s per week for a trooper and 4s per week for a foot soldier.

10.   HWRO BA 1714, 899: 192, f. 346; HWRO BA 3762: 8, f. 185.

11.   Corbet, op. cit., p. 33.

12.   HWRO 899: 31, BA 3669 no. 122: *Mercurius Aulicus*, transcribed by E.J. Gray.

13.   CBA 398282 (HCC 580).

14.   CBA 398325 (HCC 581); CBA 398326 (HCC 582).

15.   Townshend ii, p. 125.

16.   Silcock, op. cit., p. 256.

17.   PRO SP28/187, ff. 387–9.

18.   HMC XII, App. 1, p. 703; HWRO 1714/899/192, ff. 313–16.

19.   Luke's Journal, p. 87; CBA 398330 (HCC 586).

20.   Townshend ii, p. 122.

21.   M. Atkin and W. Laughlin, *Gloucester and the Civil War: A City Under Siege* (Stroud, 1992).

22.   Luke's Journal, p. 151; Bod. Lib. MS Eng. Hist. c 53, f.71.

23.   Burghall's Diary, quoted in VCH II, p. 260.

24.   Luke's Journal, p. 151; Townshend ii, p. 129.

25.   Luke's Journal, p. 146.

26.   Tennant, op. cit., p. 211. It was also plundered in September of the following year according to *Mercurius Aulicus*, personal communication Philip Tennant.

5   The Civil War Defences of Worcester

1.   Wharton Letters, p. 328.

2.   P. Styles, *Studies in Seventeenth Century West Midlands History* (Kineton, 1978), p. 218.

3.   Wharton Letters, p. 333.

4.   BL E.123(6): *Weekly Intelligence* for 10–18 October.

5.   Wharton letters, p. 333.

6.   HWRO B899: 31, BA 3762/8B, f. 185.

7.   R. Jackson, *Evaluation at the Butts, Worcester* (County Archaeological Service, Internal Report 106, 1992), pp. 6–7; HWRO Worcester Chamber Orders II, 1605.

8.   P. Barker, 'The Origins of Worcester', TWAS, 3rd ser., 2 (1968–69), pp. 102–3; Bond 1974, p. 371.

9.   C.H. Dalwood, V.A. Buteux and J. Darlington, *Excavations at Farrier St. and other sites north of the city wall, Worcester 1988–1992*, TWAS 3rd ser., 14 (1994), p. 82; cf. Atkin and Laughlin, op. cit., pp. 58, 122.

10.   Ibid., p. 82.

11.   P. Hughes and N. Molyneux, *Worcester Streets: Friar Street* (1984).
12.   Bond 1974, p. 374.
13.   Bond 1974, p. 396.
14.   Parliamentary Survey 1649, published in Cave and Wilson, op. cit., pp. 185, 187, 199, 200, 203, 208, 210.
15.   Ibid., p. 70.
16.   HWRO 261.1, BA 36174, f. 3.
17.   Bond 1974, p. 395.
18.   Bond 1974, p. 377.
19.   Bond 1974, pp. 382, 399.
20.   Townshend ii, p. 191.
21.   Barker, op. cit., p. 99 and fig. 35; R. Jackson, *Salvage Recording at King's School, Worcester* (County Archaeological Service, Internal Report 97, 1991), pp. 3–4.
22.   P.J. Reynolds, 'Talbot Street, Worcester', *Worcestershire Archaeological Newsletter*, no. 10 (June 1972), 6.
23.   Townshend ii, p. 174; BCA 398329 (HCC 585).
24.   Townshend ii, p. 123.
25.   Symonds Diary, pp. 231–2.
26.   Townshend ii, p. 158.
27.   Townshend ii, p. 133.
28.   C.F. Mundy, *Trial Excavation in Worcester 1985* (County Archaeological Service, 1985), pp. 6–7. With thanks to Charles Mundy for discussion of this site in advance of final publication.
29.   Atkin and Laughlin, op. cit., p. 86.
30.   C. Beardsmore, 'Documentary Evidence for the History of Worcester City Defences' in M.O.H. Carver, *Medieval Worcester: An Archaeological Framework*, *TWAS*, 3rd ser., 7 (1980), p. 61.
31.   Bond 1974, p. 392.
32.   Jackson, op. cit., p. 9 and App. 2.

6   Under Attack: 1644

1.   Webb I, p. 362.
2.   BL E.18 (16).
3.   BL Harl. 6852, f. 199; Silcock, op. cit., p. 257.
4.   BL Add. MS. 18980, f. 165.
5.   J.R. Burton, *History of Bewdley* (1883), appendix p. xxxii.
6.   VCH II, p. 165.

7.   HWRO BA 110: 85/54.
8.   The opposing armies of this period were not distinguished by uniforms as such. Each regiment would wear a coat of a particular colour but blue-, red- and green-coated regiments could be found on either side.
9.   BL E.53(11): *The Weekly Account*, 26 June–3 July 1644.
10.   BL E.53(11): *The Weekly Account*, 26 June–3 July 1644.
11.   Symonds Diary, p. 8.
12.   Clarendon, op. cit., IV, p. 735.
13.   Minutes of Council of War held at Worcester 10 June, 1644: private papers of the Sandys family.
14.   E. Besby, *Coins and Medals of the English Civil War* (London, 1990), p. 66.
15.   CPSD 1644, pp. 235–7.
16.   Clarendon IV, p. 737; PRO SP28/187, ff. 387–9.
17.   CSPD 1644, p. 238.
18.   Webb II, p. 45.
19.   Order of J. Wemys, Commander of the Train of Artillery. HWRO BA 1006, f. 629.
20.   Symonds Diary, p. 27.
21.   HMC 4th Report, pp. 269–70.
22.   HWRO 1714/899/192, ff. 387–9; CSPD 1644, pp. 512–13.
23.   Townshend ii, pp. 171–5.
24.   HMC 4th Report, p. 270.
25.   P. Styles, op. cit., p. 31.
26.   HMC XI, App. VII, p. 217.
27.   Lords Journal VI, p. 698.
28.   Townshend ii, pp. 191–2.
29.   Townshend ii, p. 205.

7   The Battle of Evesham and Civilian Revolt: 1645

1.   Townshend ii, p. 9.
2.   *London Post* no. 29, 25 March–1 April 1645; B. Gwilliam, *Old Worcester: People and Places* (Bromsgrove, 1993), p. 61.
3.   BL E.279 (1): *Mercurius Verdicus* for 19 April–26 April; E.281 (3): *A Diary or exact journal for 24 April–1 May*.
4.   Besby, op. cit., pp. 68–9.
5.   Strensham was garrisoned by Col. Massey in January 1645. CSPD 1644–5, pp. 269, 271, 393.

6. F. McAvoy, *Dodderhill, Droitwich. Excavations between 1977–85*, (Draft report, English Heritage).

7. HWRO B899: 31, BA 3762/8B, f. 186; Symonds Diary, p. 167.

8. Townshend i, p. 225; Dore 1984, 123, no. 177.

9. Townshend ii, p. 229.

10. Dore 1984, 123, no. 423.

11. Dore 1984, 123, no. 543.

12. Symonds Diary, pp. 166–7.

13. Corbet, op. cit., p. 148.

14. PRO SP 28/187, ff. 161–4.

15. Tennant, op. cit., p. 267.

16. Journal of Sir Samuel Luke, p. 87.

17. HWRO B899: 31, BA 3762/8B, f. 185.

18. Symonds Diary, p. 273.

19. PRO SP 28/188.

20. HWRO 850, BA 8371/1: Parish Register of Ribbesford with Bewdley.

21. BL E.313(31): *The Weekly Account*, 16–30 December 1645.

22. Dore 1990, 128, no. 1120.

23. CSPD 1645–7, p. 157.

24. PRO SP16/510 quoted in P. Styles, *Studies in Seventeenth Century West Midlands History* (Kineton, 1978), p. 229.

25. CSPD 1645–7, p. 157.

26. Townshend ii, pp. 236–9.

27. Dore 1990, 128, no. 1093 and note 2, p. 424.

28. Trimpley parish register.

29. Dore 1990, 128, no. 839.

30. Dore 1990, 128, no. 888.

31. CSPD 1645–7, pp. 249, 258.

32. Dore 1990, 128, no. 976.

33. Dore 1990, 128, no. 977.

34. Dore 1984, 123, no. 974.

35. Dore 1990, nos. 992, 1041 and 1153.

36. Dore 1990, 128, no. 1121.

37. Dore 1990, 128, nos. 897 and 983.

38. BL E.258 (26): *Perfect Occurrences*, 14–21 February, 1645.

39. E. Warburton, *Memoirs of Prince Rupert, and the Cavaliers*, III (1849), p. 60.

40. BL E.279 (1): *Mercurius Verdicus*, 19–26 April 1645.

41. Townshend ii, pp. 230–3.

42. Letter of 30 September 1645: private papers of the Sandys family.

43. Letter of 7 November 1645: private papers of the Sandys family.

44. Letter of King Charles to Samuel Sandys, 26 February 1646: private papers of the Sandys family.

45. There is a general survey of the Clubmen in G.J. Lynch, 'The Risings of the Clubmen in the English Civil War' (MA thesis, University of Manchester, 1973).

46. R. Hutton, 'The Worcestershire Clubmen in the English Civil War', *Midland History*, 5 (1979–80), 44–5.

47. Lynch, op. cit., pp. 65–66.

48. Townshend ii, p. 222.

49. BL E.279 (11): *Kingdom's Weekly Intelligencer*, 22–29 April 1645.

50. Letter of Sir Edward Massey to Sir Samuel Luke, quoted in Webb II, p. 154.

51. Letter of 22 March 1645 to Sir Samuel Luke published in J. Webb and T.W. Webb (eds) 'A Military Memoir of Colonel John Birch', *Camden Society*, 7 (1873), 216–17.

52. Dore 1984, 123, no. 225.

53. BL E.266 (24): *Perfect Occurrences*, 21 November 1645.

54. HWRO 899: 31, BA 3669 1(xxiii): *The Humble Desires of Prince Rupert, Prince Maurice . . . to be tryed at a Council of War . . . Together with His Majesties Letter to Colonel Samuel Sandys 30 December 1645*.

55. Dore 1990, 128, no. 1003.

56. D. Gilbert, 'Two Royalist Garrisons in Worcestershire, part I', *Worcester Archaeology Newsletter*, no. 39 (1987), 4–5.

57. Townshend ii, p. 241.

58. Townshend ii, pp. 240–3, 243–8.

59. Styles, op. cit., p. 35.

8 The County Falls: 1646

1. CSPD 1645–47, pp. 323–4.

2. PRO SP28/187, f. 482; PRO SP28/188.

3. *Trans Ass. Architect. Socs* XVII (1883–4), 290, no.39, 5.

4. Gilbert, op. cit., p. 5.

5. HWRO B899: 31, BA 3762/8B, f. 186.

6. Ibid.

7. Letter of Governor of Dudley to the Lichfield garrison, 6 April 1646: Letterbook of

Sir William Brereton 4 April–19 May 1646, BCA 595611, transcribed by J. Hemingway.

8. Townshend i, p. 102.

9. HWRO B899: 31, BA 3762/8B, f. 186.

10. Townshend i, p. 102.

11. D.A. Johnson and D.G. Vaisey, *Staffordshire and the Great Rebellion* (Staffordshire County Records Committee, 1965), p. 69.

12. Townshend i, p. 106.

13. Townshend i, p. 135; Townshend ii, p. 247.

14. CSPD 1645–7, p. 444.

15. J. Nash, *Collections for the History of Worcestershire* (1782), vol. II, p. XCIX.

16. Townshend i, p. 132.

17. Townshend ii, p. 266; Townshend i, p. 105.

18. *Perfect Diurnal* quoted in V. Green, *History and Antiquities of the City and Suburbs of Worcester* (1796), vol. I, p. 277.

19. Townshend ii, p. 257.

20. PRO SP28/187, f. 131.

21. PRO SP28/187, ff. 44–9.

22. Gwilliam, op. cit., p. 154; PRO SP28/187, f. 170.

23. R. Baxter, *Plain Scripture Proof of Infants' Church-Membership and Baptisms* (1651), ci.

24. Townshend i, p. 127.

25. Townshend i, p. 126.

26. Townshend i, p. 129.

27. Townshend i, p. 133.

28. Townshend i, p. 136.

29. Townshend i, p. 140.

30. Symonds Diary, p. 144.

31. Townshend i, p. 155.

32. Townshend i, p. 159.

33. Townshend i, pp. 172, 174.

34. Townshend i, p. 171.

35. HWRO 899: 31, BA 3669.

36. Townshend i, p. 190.

37. Townshend i, p. 156.

38. Townshend i, p. 142.

39. HWRO B899: 31, BA 3762/8B, f. 186.

9 Royalist Plots: 1647–8

1. BCA 398334 (HCC 590). Webb II, App. XXXI.

2. Silcock, op. cit., p. 275.

3. Parliamentary Survey 1649, in Cave and Wilson, op. cit., p. 108.

4. I am grateful to Jenny Townshend for this information.

5. Townshend ii, pp. 140–1.

6. Bond 1974, p. 367.

7. Hughes, op. cit., p. 45.

8. Gilbert, op. cit., p. 3.

9. Bond 1974, p. 369.

10. J.G. Rollins, *A History of Redditch* (Chichester, 1984), p. 46.

11. With local industries also developing elsewhere (such as south Lancashire) in the 1640s: personal communication David Higgins.

12. PRO SP1. lxxxv, f. 251.

13. BCA 398335 (HCC 591).

14. HWRO 261.4, BA 1006, f. 638; Burghall's Diary quoted in VCH II, p. 260.

15. HWRO 261.4, BA 1006, f. 630; E.K. Berry, 'The Borough of Droitwich and its Salt Industry, 1215–1700', *Historical Journal*, VI, no.1 (1957), 47, 52.

16. PRO SP28/187, ff. 52–69, f. 161.

17. Barnard, op. cit., p. 89.

18. PRO SP28/187, f. 161.

19. PRO SP28/187, ff. 52–69.

20. *Archaeologia* XXXVII (1851), 189–223.

21. HWRO 261.1, BA 3617/4.

22. J. Nash, *Collections for the History of Worcestershire*, II (1782), appendix p. cvi.

23. HWRO 705.753, BA 9951/31; Cave and Wilson, op. cit., p. 217.

24. Hughes, op. cit., p. 249.

25. HWRO X496.5, BA 9360, Worcester Corporation Records, Charities: Inglethorpe's Charity, 1632–1717, unfol. D247 (accounts approved at Quarter Sessions 1652).

26. Cave and Wilson, op. cit., p. 104.

27. Quoted in P. Hurle, *The Malverns* (Chichester, 1992), p. 51.

28. Morgan (ed.), *Inspections . . . in the Diocese of Worcester*, p. 36; VCH Worcestershire III, (1913), pp. 65–6.

29. PRO SP28/253B.

30. Styles 1978, op. cit., p. 247.

31. Hughes, op. cit., p. 47.

32. Bond 1974, p. 430; Styles 1978, op. cit., p. 243.

33. Bond 1974, pp. 399–400, 403, 407; Hughes, op. cit., p. 47.

34. Churchwarden's Accounts 1640–99, f. 79; Townshend i, p. 156.

35. Willis-Bund 1905, pp. 201–5.

36. HWRO Quarter Sessions 1651, packet 85 doc. 54.

10 The Battle of Worcester: 1651

1. Letter of Robert Stapleton, 3 September 1651 in *Perfect Diurnall*, 1–8 Sept.

2. CSPD 1649–50, f. 515.

3. CSPD 1649–50, f. 278.

4. J.W. Willis-Bund, *The Battle of Worcester* (Worcester, 1913), pp. 50–3.

5. B. Whitlocke, *Memorials of the English Affairs ...*, III (1853), 335.

6. HMC 14th Report, App. 8, p. 188.

7. Clarendon, op. cit., XIII, p. 78.

8. H. Blount, *Boscobel Tracts* (1660), p. 7.

9. Nicholas Lechmere's diary.

10. HWRO 850 Salwarpe, BA 1054/1.

11. Blount, op. cit., p. 11.

12. Letter of Stapleton to Captain George Bishop, 29 August 1651, in H. Cary, *Memorials of the Great Civil War in England*, II (1842), p. 348.

13. Letter of Sir Rowland Berkeley to Sir Thomas Cave, 12 September 1651, published in Willis-Bund 1905, p. 259; HWRO 989.9.91, BA 10509/1.

14. Valentine Green claimed that these gentry had brought with them 2000 supporters, but this is likely to have been an exaggeration.

15. Blount, op. cit., p. 8.

16. This emplacement was mistakenly described in J. Noake, *Guide to Worcestershire* (1868), p. 347 as being on the right-hand side of the road, in a confusion with the earthworks of former brickworks.

17. According to reports, he was hit in the hand, head, arm and thigh. He still managed to escape Worcester with King Charles after the battle, surrendered and then escaped from the Tower of London. He was involved in plotting in Gloucestershire in 1654, was back again in 1656 and, ending his remarkable career during the Civil War, was elected as Gloucester's MP just before the Restoration.

18. Letter of Robert Stapleton, 3 September 1651 in *Perfect Diurnall*, 1–8 Sept.

19. HWRO 899: 31, BA 3669 2(v): *An Exact Relation of Every Particular of the Fight at Worcester*, 5 September 1651.

20. Ibid.

21. Letter of Oliver Cromwell, 10 p.m. 3 September, in T. Carlyle, *Oliver Cromwell's Letters and Speeches* (1890), vol. 3, pp. 155–6.

22. Willis-Bund 1905, p. 244.

23. Blount, op. cit., p. 10.

24. Letter of Robert Stapleton, 3 September 1651 in *Perfect Diurnall*, 1–8 Sept.

25. Blount, op. cit., p. 12.

26. Ordnance Survey map, Sheet 54, 1st edn.

27. Letter of Sir Rowland Berkeley to Sir Thomas Cave, 8 September 1651, published in Willis-Bund 1905, p. 258; *Reliquiae Baxterianae*, Lib. I, part I, p. 69.

28. Carlyle op. cit., vol. 5, p. 212, Appendix No.22.

29. *CJ* VII, 1651–9, pp. 103.

30. Whitelock, op. cit., III, p. 348.

31. BM Add. Mss 31955, transcript of Pepys Mss 2141: copy in HWRO 899.31.

32. HWRO 850 (Salwarpe), BA 10541, A34; Calendar of the Committee for the Advance of Money, Domestic 1642–1656, p. 108.

33. *Memoirs of Lady Fanshawe* (Colburn and Bentley, London, 1830), p. 113.

34. *Boscobel Tracts*, p. 145.

35. HWRO 850 (Salwarpe), BA 10541, A34.

36. Cf. a comparable picture in Gloucester in Atkin and Laughlin, op. cit., pp. 142–5.

37. Hughes, op. cit., pp. 49, 239: a lease had been granted in 1645 to the mayor, Thomas Hackett, for a tenement and garden at the east end of the former millpool. He was supposed to build on the property within three years but, coming one year before the siege of 1646, it is not clear whether he achieved this. The area was also in a part of the city that saw heavy fighting in 1651. It therefore seems likely that the work was carried out between 1651 and 1657.

38. J.M. Wilson, 'Some notes from the Cathedral records as to Barnabas Oley and the restoration of Worcester Cathedral 1660–66', *TWAS*, 1 (1924), 35.

39.   HWRO, BA 7811/14(i); Carver 1980, p. 181.

40.   J. Darlington, *Evaluation at Friar Street, Worcester* (County Archaeological Service Internal Report 16, 1989), p. 9.

41.   HWRO, BA 2636/161.

Conclusion

1.   I. R. Baxter, *Saints Everlasting Rest* II (1650), p. 259.

2.   Webb II, p. 276.

3.   HMC 14th Report, App. 8, p. 189.

4.   Quoted in Hurle, op. cit., p. 51.

5.   Styles 1976, op. cit., p. 25.

6.   HWRO Quarter Sessions 1655, packet 90 no. 23.

7.   HMC 14th Report, App. 8, p. 190.

8.   V. Green, *History and Antiquities of the City and Suburbs of Worcester*, i (1796), p. 277.

Appendix 1

1.   The letters were first published in 1853. They have been recently reprinted in S. Peachey, *The Edgehill Campaign and the Letters of Nehemiah Wharton* (Leigh-on-Sea, Partizan Press, 1989).

Appendix 2

1.   Reprinted in *Cromwelliana* (London, 1810), pp. 112–13.

FURTHER READING

General

A good general account of the Civil War is:
Ashley, M. *The English Civil War*, Stroud, 1990.
A collection of essays on the impact of the war is:
Morrill, J. *The Impact of the English Civil War*, London, 1991.
The period is vividly brought to life in:
Isemonger, P.L. *The English Civil War: A Living History*, Stroud, 1994.

Regional

Regional studies that broaden the scope of the present work are:
Sherwood, R.E. *Civil War in the Midlands 1642–1651*, Stroud, 1992.
Tennant, P. *Edgehill and Beyond: The People's War in the South Midlands 1642–1645*, Stroud, 1992.
The context of Worcestershire within the wider Royalist war effort is dealt with in some detail by:
Hutton, R. *The Royalist War Effort 1642–46*, London, 1982.

Local

The basis for any study of the war in Worcestershire remains:
Willis-Bund, J.W. *The Civil War in Worcestershire 1642–1646 and the Scotch Invasion of 1651*, Birmingham, 1905.
The administrative basis of the war in the county is discussed in:
Silcock, R.H. 'County Government in Worcestershire 1603–1660', Ph.D. thesis, University of London, 1974.
Styles, P. 'The Royalist government of Worcestershire during the Civil War, 1642–6', *TWAS*, 3rd ser., v (1976), 23–39.
Styles, P. *Studies in Seventeenth Century West Midlands History*, Kineton, 1978, 213–57.
For those wishing to get a flavour of the fighting on the ground, The Commandery Museum, Worcester publish a useful *Civil War Trail for Worcester*.

Accessible documentary sources

A flavour of original documents of the period is most easily accessible in the publication of the Worcester Chamber Orders, in:
Bond, S. *The Chamber Order Book of Worcester 1602–1650*, Worcs. Hist. Soc., new ser., vol. viii, 1974; and the Diary of Henry Townshend in:
Willis-Bund, J.W. (ed.) *Diaries of Henry Townshend of Elmley Lovett, 1640–1663*, Worcestershire, History Society, 1915–20.

ACKNOWLEDGEMENTS

Any study of the Civil War in the county must acknowledge J.W. Willis-Bund (1864–1928), a chairman of Worcestershire County Council and Editor-in-chief of the Victoria County History. His synthesis of the evidence in 1905 and publication of the Townshend Diaries in 1920 remain a backbone of any modern study. A further landmark was the publication in 1974 of further source material in the Worcester Chamber Books, by Shelagh Bond. While early accounts of the war concentrated on the military aspects, Philip Styles introduced new elements in his 1976 publication of aspects of local government during the war in the county.

Thanks are owed to the Rt. Hon. The Lord Sandys for access to some of the private papers of the family. Thanks are also owed to the staff of Worcester City Library, the Hereford and Worcester County Records Office (County Hall and St Helen's, Worcester) and to Birmingham City Archives for their patient assistance, to David Guyatt and Jenny Townshend for their assistance with the documentary evidence, and to the Worcester City Archaeologist, Charles Mundy and Tim Bridges of Worcester City Museum for their help. Special thanks must go to my colleagues in the County Archaeological Service, especially Duncan Brown, Victoria Buteux, Hal Dalwood, Carolyn Hunt, Derek Hurst, Stephanie Ratkai, Stephen Rigby, Laura Templeton and Simon Woodiwiss for their discussion of the archaeological evidence and general support. I am also grateful to Philip Tennant and Alan Turton for their comments on an earlier draft. Thanks are also due to those individuals and bodies who have given permission for illustrative material to be used in the book, including Peter Boland and Steve Linnane (Dudley Metropolitan Borough), Paul Lewis Isemonger, Andrew Noakes, Rev. Cross of Inkberrow, Grenville Calder, Robin Hill (County Museum, Hartlebury), Manchester City Art Galleries and the Public Record Office. All other illustrations are copyright of the County Archaeological Service, Hereford and Worcester County Council. The illustrations are acknowledged individually. I am also very appreciative of the collective efforts of Susanne Atkin, Rachel Edwards and Deborah Overton for trying to improve my grammar. The index was prepared by Susanne Atkin.

The production of this book has only been made possible through the continued support and encouragement of the County Archaeological Service by the Hereford and Worcester Libraries and Arts Department, under the County Librarian and Arts Officer, Mr Michael Messenger, and of the County Council Libraries, Recreation and Environment Committee, under the chairmanship of Cllr Diane Rayner.

Photographs of re-enactments are by Paul Lewis Isemonger/Living History Photo Library. Tel. 01453 886140.

The royalties from this book have been assigned to the County Archaeological Service to further archaeological work in Herefordshire and Worcestershire.

Finally, special thanks to Susanne and Kate for their forbearance!

INDEX

Page numbers in italics refer to illustrations.